BEHIND THE STEAM

Bill Morgan
and
Bette Meyrick

KRB Publications

Behind the Steam

ISBN 0954485904

© Bette V. Meyrick

First Published by Hutchinson & Co (Publishers) Ltd.
3 Fitzroy Square, London W1, in 1973
under ISBN 0091176700

Republished without illustrations and in smaller page size
by Firecrest, Chivers Press, Bath, in 1988
under ISBN 0859979644

Revised edition 2003 by arrangement with Bette Meyrick

KRB Publications
2 Denewulf Close
BISHOPS WALTHAM
Hants
SO32 1GZ

KevinRobertsonBooks.co.uk

Rescanned and printed by
The Amadeus Press

To the Railwaymen of the G.W.R.

Introduction to the 2003 edition.

It is now 30 years since my father and I affectionately collaborated in writing BEHIND THE STEAM.

Bill Morgan was a railwayman all his life, from his first signing-on as a firebox-cleaner during the First World War to his retirement as an express-driver in 1965. A born raconteur, he has told his story to his daughter, Bette Meyrick, who has made it ready for publication.

Bill Morgan died in 1976, but we now have another William in the family - his Danish great-grandson, William Meyrick, born 2002, brother of Holly, born 2000. Sometime in the future I hope they will both visit Neyland!

I know this new printing will delight the many steam enthusiasts and social historians who have contacted me over the years so desperate to obtain a copy. This edition, with its additional photographs of the Neyland area, will not disappoint them.

Bette Meyrick

Broadstairs 2003.

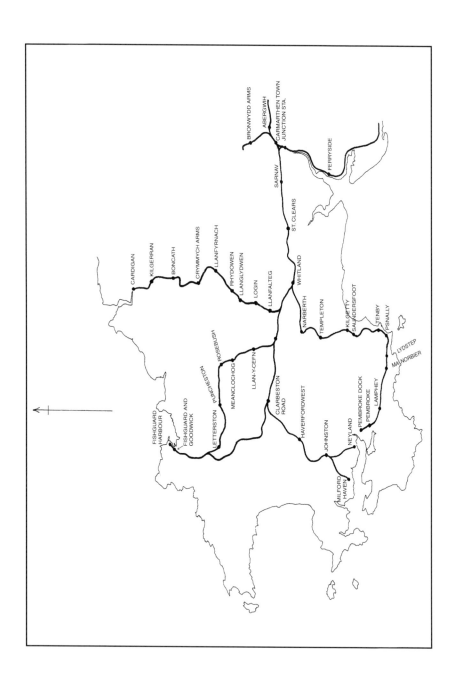

ILLUSTRATIONS

Driver Bill Morgan at Gloucester Shed, May 1952. (By kind permission of R. Cobbin)

Relief crews at Severn Tunnel Junction, waiting to travel 'on the cushions' back to Gloucester.

Driver Bill Morgan with Fireman Ivor Smith on the stopping passengers at Newport.

Express Driver – Bill Morgan in his retirement. 'By, hedges, it was a grand life!' (By kind permission of P. Kemp)

Acknowledgements for research: Margaret James, John E. Hooper, John L. Crawley, Richard Neale, Hilliard James and Richard Parker.

Preface

I knew, with certainty, that it would find its way into my boots. It always did. I looked down at the polished toe-caps flashing in front of me with every step and at the tightly laced leather which reached half-way up my calves. The Ash Path . . . it had defeated all the footwear I had ever possessed. There it was, that first, small, splintery sharp irritation. Minute pieces of volcanic-like ash finding their way into my grey woollen socks. I cursed under my breath as I thought of the time I would have to spend, carefully searching out every gritty particle from the thickened, felted wool. These were the third set of feet Mam had knit onto the original tops, and I felt glad that no-one could see the join of the different coloured wools.

The Ash Path led me past Railway Terrace and the Company Houses, each house with its scrubbed steps leading up to the Front Door (which no-one ever used except strangers who knew no better). Each door no more than a few feet from its neighbour, but between each, a heavily laced curtain guarding a family's respectability.

The ashes finally petered out, and turning off the path I scrambled down the steep hill through the gorse and brambles which overgrew my own personal short cut to the railway below.

Harry James, a Great Western driver who sometimes found himself way up the line on double-home working on payday, had chosen me, Bill Morgan, to fetch his wages from the railway shed. I was full of pride at having been chosen as his wage carrier, although, on reflection, the fact that he lived next door might have had something to do with it!

It was the highlight of my schooldays, actually to have legal access to the railway yard, and my good fortune seemed unbelievable. Just let anyone challenge me, I thought as I made my final jump down onto railway property.

I walked onto Neyland platform. It was May 1913 and I was eleven years old, my heart and soul already given to the Great Western Railway and to the ambition of being an express driver. I fretted with impatience at the thought of the three years I still had to wait before I could take my first step on the ladder of a railway career.

As I walked along the echoing platform, my eye fell on the names on the tops of the passenger coaches standing in the siding: PADDING-TON—NEWPORT—CARDIFF—and that final, most important name of all—NEYLAND.

Neyland was one of the most Westerly points of the Great Western Railway in Wales. A sister terminus to Paddington, and to my mind, a terminus of equal standing. What did it matter that Neyland had a population of only a few thousand? It was obvious to me, by the equal billing we shared with Paddington on the coaches, that the G.W.R. company considered us to be in the top bracket of the railway towns' hierarchy.

I was very proud of Neyland. I tried to forget that Fishguard had stolen some of our glory when they had taken the terminus of the Irish Packet Boats from us. Although it had happened over six years before, the townspeople were only just getting over the shock of it, and the South Wales Railway Hotel, which had largely catered for the Irish passenger traffic was beginning to look a little neglected. It was a shame, I thought, as it was by far the grandest building in Neyland, discount-ing, of course, the numerous chapels and churches which punctuated the High Street with what I considered to be depressing regularity.

My eyes raked the platforms for one single G.W.R. official, but the station remained uncooperatively quiet and empty in the early after-noon sunshine. I was not going to give up the hope of being challenged so that I could reply, with studied nonchalance, 'O.C.S.', and walk on feeling ten feet tall, leaving an open-mouthed official behind me! But no-one contended my right to be there and I continued on my way unable to use my knowledge of Company procedure, which had been passed on to me, in great secrecy, by Harry James. I was 'On Company Service' and no-one wanted to know!

The platform was incredibly long for such a small town, the pavings gradually becoming more and more interspersed with tufts of grass and yellow-topped groundsel, until the final slope was reached culminating in the forbidding notice, warning the Public of the Penalty of £5 if they took a step further and trespassed on G.W.R. property.

I experienced that special inner glow of the initiated in an exclusive club. I was, no longer, merely one of the Public or a common or garden passenger, I was on official business, and I strode defiantly down the ramp which would divide 'us' from 'them'.

I was on real railway territory now, boots crunching on ashes again, ashes bounded on either side by gleaming sinuous rails. A small shiver of excitement and fear went through me as the first locomotive came steaming relentlessly towards me, causing me to make a quick check to see that I was, in actual fact, walking outside the tracks and not by some hideous mistake between those compelling, parallel lines. The 32 roared throbbingly past me, appearing far more formidable when viewed from equal level instead of from the raised, safe expanse of platform, its connecting rod thrusting remorselessly back and forth at the two huge driving wheels. I felt frail and vulnerable.

A friendly wave and a nod from the driver as he passed by, heartened me and I waved back, experiencing a cameraderie with the ruddy cheeked, mellowed figure leaning over the cabside, wiping his hands on the inevitable cotton waste. How I longed for the day when I, too, would look down on the rest of the world from my olympus, accepting the awe and wonder from the young and the gratitude, and perhaps the occasional tip, from the passenger. But I was not merely going to shunt wagons around the yard, I was going to get to the very top—The Express Driver . . . Me.

Apart from the prestige and glamour of being an express driver, there were many other lesser reasons, at that impressionable age of eleven, for my eagerness to be a Great Western man. From my observations of railway families in the town, and especially of our neighbours on either side—Harry James the driver above us and Ernie Perry the fireman below us—I had long come to the conclusion that they were extremely privileged members of the community.

Railway People always had an abundance of firewood from creosoted pine sleepers, chopped fine for firelighting or into blocks for building up a glowing, spark-spitting fire on the beds of their reduced price coal. Railway People always had crisp, crackly lavatory paper rolls with G.W.R. stamped across the sheets, instead of neatly knife-cut newspaper, threaded with string in one corner to hang from the nail behind the door of the privy at the top of the garden. I had to admit, however, that perhaps there was a slight drawback in this privilege as it was a little monotonous reading G.W.R. for the hundredth time instead of perusing odd snippets of old news, as that knife always managed to cut through the most crucial line of newsprint. Many boy-hours, not to mention man-hours, had been lost in the fruitless search for the remainder of an article.

Railway People always had lovely thick tea-cloths, beautifully embroidered with artistically entwined G.W.R. letters in one corner. I knew this from bitter wiping-up experience as Mam insisted that we boys did our share of household chores. She had borrowed one from somebody, and it was the best wiping-up cloth we had ever had.

Railway People always had, in their homes, an abundance of magazines and newspapers from far-away places like Cardiff, Swansea, Gloucester and Llanelly, gleaned from the empty carriages as they arrived at our terminus station. I had once read, in Harry James' kitchen, a newspaper which had actually come from London, Late Edition it was called—now that was what I considered real privilege.

Railway People could travel at reduced fares all over the world (I thought at that time), and what an exciting prospect of far-away travel that could open up.

Railway People were always practising First Aid and this would satisfy my secondary ambition which was to be a doctor! I spent endless hours with Ernie Perry, especially just before the annual St. John's Ambulance Examination, when medical activities in the Neyland Railway populace reached fever pitch. The black First Aid manual with its silver starred cover was in constant use, and I found myself conscripted into being a passenger patient who had either unfortunately collapsed between the seats of a First Class compartment, or who had inadvertently slipped and broken a collar bone whilst descending from a Third Class carriage. I bled to order from various contusions, lay unconscious from mysterious diseases or sat patiently whilst my limbs were bandaged and re-bandaged, splinted and re-splinted, until perfection was reached. I could recite, at a moment's notice, the symptoms of small-pox or heart failure, appendicitis or an imminent birth, and when the great Testing Day arrived, great apprehension was felt until Ernie returned, once more declared competent to treat any unfortunate traveller who might suffer from illness or accident whilst journeying on the G.W.R.

How I loved visiting those next-door kitchens with their evocative acrid-smelling, sulphurous overalls and coats hanging behind the back door and the huge double-home box standing in the corner.

Harry James' double-homer was a beauty, dome-topped like an old sea chest and weighing a good five pounds even when empty. To me it was a box of intriguing delights.

'Can I look in your box, Mr. James?' Opened, it revealed mysterious hollow glass tubes, corks, timetables and lists of emergency workings, lengths of lampwick, buff-paged notebooks with knicker elastic bands securing indelible purple pencils which I watched grow shorter week by week until, at last, the prized puce lead was bequeathed to me. Wonderfully realistic tattoos they made, provided you gave them a good licking first. An occasional curl-edged, stale sandwich sometimes lay awaiting my exploring fingers. And always, the cotton waste.

'You'll never have a dirty hand, Willy boy, so long as you've got some waste,' was Harry James' maxim.

The huge, black shape of the Shed loomed in front of me, grimy, noisy and full of life. No sun ever shone inside this tar black, sulphur-laden enclosure, but, to me, it was the zenith of my aspirations. I entered its dark, smutty embrace with a deep breath of appreciation. Skirting the pits where overalled figures were blackly oiling and cleaning a gorgeous loco, gleaming with polished blue steel it was, I approached the pay window and rapped authoritatively on the blackened sill of grain-proud wood. In spite of my imperious rap the little window remained blankly shuttered, so hands in pockets I strolled back to the pits to watch the whistling, ribald calling, gang of cleaners who were attending to—I spelt out the name curved over the top of the front driving wheel—SKYLARK—a 4-4-0, 33 class loco. No. 3454 was on her cabside and I thought she was the most beautiful thing I had ever seen.

The pay window scraped behind me and an enquiring face peered at me from the gloomy interior of the little pay office.

'I've come for Harry James' wages, mister,' I proclaimed, giving Harry's G.W.R. number, and handing over the necessary voucher.

'Is it Willie Morgan, you are?' queried the peering face, examining me from head to toe. I assured him that I was, and he pushed the small cylindrical pay box over the sill into my waiting hands. It was cool and heavy, little bigger than a cotton reel, with Harry's Company number etched into the metal, and as I made my way out of the Shed I wondered what number I would call when I came to collect my own wages. Bill Morgan 75 seemed to roll off the tongue very pleasingly, I thought, or Bill Morgan 28 or 66. I experimented with various numbers, picturing myself, heavily booted and overall clad, lining up with the other men at the dim little pay window. In reality, it was Bill Morgan, number 69, who, three years later, at the age of fourteen years one month, picked up his first wage tin containing thirteen shillings and sixpence on that bright May day of 1916. My life with steam was about to begin.

1

I had slept fitfully throughout the previous night and now I lay listening to the echoing tramp of the call-boy's boots as he passed beneath my window on his way to call up Harry James next door. Harry was taking the first train out of Neyland that early Monday morning in May 1916, the 4.45 Goods, Neyland to Llandeilo, double-home.

I lay in the soft cocoon of the feather bed, the heavy Welsh quilt pressing down on me. The night air was still, a late frost was biting at the bedding plants and I was waiting for five o'clock and the start of my first day as a workman on the Great Western Railway. And I could not normally be raised from bed with the school bell ringing in my ears!

I heard the rap of knuckles on the next door and I knew it was four o'clock. Harry James was known to have a nasty temper if an unfortunate call-boy awakened him a minute too soon. Rather than risk a tongue-lashing they would sit on the slate window-sill, quietly whistling or kicking their heels until they thought it safe to awaken Harry from his slumbers. I could not hear the answering call but I knew there must have been one, as the footsteps started off back down the hill, past our front door and gradually echoed away as Charlie made his way back to the Shed.

I knew it was Charlie Matthias, because he had started on the railway a few months earlier, and it would be his place I would be taking, while he moved the first step up the ladder to Cleaner. I would be the new Box-boy and Call-boy, until another lad started and gave me the chance of taking my first step towards Express Driver!

I lay there, my mind pleasantly savouring the idea of my new status of workman. But I could wait no longer. Sleep was gone for me, and slipping carefully out of the high bed I dressed in my oldest trousers and collarless flannel shirt, then, boots in hand, I crept quietly down the stairs. The embers in the kitchen grate were still warm as I silently lifted the smooth black latch of the side oven door. There, inside was my warm mug of Oxo which Mam had prepared for me the previous night. I took a few sips before bending down to put on my boots, warm and savoury it was and drained to the last drop in a few seconds. The sight of my breakfast sandwiches ready wrapped on the table made me feel the pangs of hunger, but I knew that Mam had intended them for me to take to the Shed, so I quickly decided to make myself some sop before I left for work. After all I had plenty of time, but first, I unbolted the back door to make a quick trip to the privy at the top of the garden.

The morning was fresh and still. A slight mist, hanging over the harbour, promised a warm day ahead while hundreds of snails decorated the stone garden walls with glistening ribbons. I gave a nod and a wave to our next-door-neighbour-but-three, who was on a similar mission as myself, and I thought how good it was to be up and about at this time of the morning. It seemed incredible that I had never thought so before! Carefully re-bolting the back door I had a quick swill in an eyeful of water from the can and wiped my face on the rough towelling which hung behind the kitchen door. Now for my sop.

Sop is a rare South Walean breakfast delicacy which our family considered it to be the best breakfast ever devised, beating even eggs and bacon hollow! Fetching a large white pudding basin from the wicker crockery basket under the stairs, I proceeded to fill it with chunks of bread, finishing with a large dab of butter on the top and a sprinkling of sugar. Hopefully I peeped under the cheese dish lid and was delighted to find a piece left. With great care I sliced it on top of the sugary, buttered chunks of bread. Now for the tea, I thought, knowing that Mam would have left some in the pot on the hob. Meticulously straining every tealeaf through the sieve, I poured it over the contents of my pudding basin. A splash of milk and my sop was ready to eat.

There's lovely it was, the pungent half-melted warmed cheese contrasting with the sugared, tea-soaked bread, the butter floating in fatty globules on the top—beautiful!

I finally decided that it was time for me to set out on my first day's work. The G.W.R. was a serious business and I was determined that I would prove myself to be the most outstanding cleaner they had ever had!

I had already decided that, as it was such a special day, I was going to walk down through the High Street instead of sliding and scrambling down the bank to the station. It was twenty to six, and to my amazement the High Street was as busy as at eight o'clock. Dozens of workmen were making their way down the hill, some morose, some cheery, all seeming to walk with that backward sloping stance, mindful of horses straining back when taking a cart downhill. Nearly all swung a box and a tea-can at their side. The tea-can—I had forgotten my tea-can! It was the first and last time I was ever to do that.

The smell of beer drifted into my nostrils as I approached the Lawrenny Castle. The doors were open and a few workmen disappeared inside for their morning beer, obviously believing in starting the day with their tubes well lubricated! Most of the men were on their way to the Fish Market and Ice Factory or to the Dockyard across the other side of the harbour at Pembroke Dock. But I soon spotted a few of my own mates who were on their way to the Railway Sheds, and returning their greeting with a grin, I joined them as they turned off the road by the Railway Hotel, clattered their way through the kissing gates and made their way past the coal stage and into the Railway Yard.

This was it. I was going to receive my Company Number at last. Happiness was supposed to be felt in the heart, so I had heard, but mine was more like a knot in my stomach! I walked up to the time-clerk's office and gave my name. It seemed an eternity as I waited while he sorted through the brass number tags. He picked one out.

'William John Morgan, number 69,' he announced. 'Go on over to the cabin, boy, the Chargeman will be there, just now.' And he returned to his paper work as if I didn't exist.

I started to make my way in the direction he had pointed, thinking to myself that nobody seemed very impressed that I was starting my first day on the G.W.R. I think I had been expecting a warm welcome or at least, a mention of what a momentous day this was. But nothing.

Everyone was so busy with their own lives that no-one had time to notice mine.

The Cleaners' Cabin was a ramshackle zinc hut, windowless and grimy. Its dark, sooty interior was furnished with a stove and two benches which lined the walls on either side and which were now filled with sprawling cleaners, laughing, chatting, yawning and swearing.

'Here he is!' somebody yelled as I stood at the doorway waiting for my eyes to become accustomed to the gloom. 'The new Box-boy's here, Charlie—Bill Morgan's arrived.'

Charlie Matthias came over to me out of the darkness, slapped me resoundingly on the back and said jubilantly, 'It's all yours, boy, no more fire-boxes for me!' He clasped his hands above his head like a victorious boxer in the ring and danced exultantly round the cabin amidst congratulations from everyone in the place. A slight feeling of apprehension filled me for a moment as I wondered just how hard fire-box work was if it caused Charlie to be so delighted at the thought of leaving it. Then in I went, swaggering slightly to prove that being a box-boy was going to be no hardship to me.

The Cabin gradually thinned out as each cleaner was sent out with his duty sheet by Tom John, the day Chargeman. 'Come on, then, Morgan,' he said finally, 'Charlie'll show you what you've got to do this morning, then you can take over from him. All right then, you two?'

I followed Charlie out of the Cabin into the clean bright air once more. We made our way into the Shed where some of the cleaners were already setting to work on sprucing up a 32 class engine, and climbed up onto the footplate. I had no time to appreciate the feeling of actually standing on a loco at last, before an iron hook and a wire brush were thrust into my hands.

'Here, hold this,' said Charlie, taking a quick look at the pressure gauge.

'It's going to be a bloody hot one this morning,' he added with some relish. I watched as he crouched down with his back to the fire-box opening. The heat radiated over us from the small aperture as, feet first, he backed into the black, hot interior, grinning at me until he finally disappeared into the darkness inside.

'Pass me the flare lamp, by there,' came a far-away voice as Charlie's hand appeared through the hole. I looked round the footplate and spied what looked like a small Aladdin's lamp, its wick flaming quietly and gently, standing in the corner. Tucking the wire brush under one arm, I picked up the lamp and passed it to the outstretched hand. 'Come on in, then,' yelled Charlie, and hesitating for a moment I carefully copied him and backed into the fire-box, taking my wire brush and my iron hook with me. The intensity of the heat hit me as I finally drew my head inside, the air seemed too dry to breathe and the heat tangible enough to touch. By the light of the flare lamp and by the small amount of light which filtered in through the opening, I could make out that I was in a chamber about seven feet long, five feet wide and eight feet high. It was a hell hole all right.

'Jesus Jones!' I muttered. 'You weren't joking, boy, when you said it was going to be bloody hot, were you?' I licked my lips, which were already feeling dried and cracked, the heat radiating from all around seeming to dry up the air before I could breathe it in.

'See these nuts and stays, by 'ere?' asked Charlie, holding the flare up so that its light flickered on the walls of the box. I nodded, feeling too stunned to waste breath talking.

'Well, clean them all off with your wire brush, like this, see, and rake all that old clinker out down by there, with your hook.' It seemed impossible that we were actually expected to work inside this oven. Just existing in it was as much as I could envisage. But I obeyed the instructions and started scraping and brushing, adding dust and flying grit to the already impossible atmosphere.

Charlie worked by my side, his grin was gone and his face streaked with sweat and dust. After ten minutes or so he announced that he thought that I had the right idea.

'I'll leave you to it, now then,' he gasped, 'take care of the flare, mind,' he warned as he climbed out of the box, turning to wish me the best of luck.

'I'll manage!' I shouted back, enviably thinking of the delicious cool air he was now breathing out on the footplate. I heard him clamber down and I was alone.

I was conscious of the other cleaners working on the outside of the loco, but the muffled noises echoed strangely in my ears, serving only to increase my sense of isolation. I worked on steadily, afraid that if I stopped I would never start again. The grit and ash stuck damply to my face and irritated my eyes, my underwear felt clammy with sweat, but gradually, by the flickering light, I could see the nuts, the stays and the brick arch over my head becoming crisper and cleaner. Charlie hadn't told me how long I was supposed to take to clean out the fire-box, would I have to stay in there all the morning, I wondered, and how clean was I supposed to get it?

The heat, made fiercer by my hard work, was becoming unbearable. The choking dust filled my nostrils and I would willingly have given my first week's wages for a drink to ease my rasp-dry throat.

I went doggedly on, scraping and chiselling at the clinker, skinning my knuckles as my sweaty hand slipped off the hooker and cursing as I'd never cursed before. But I was determined not to come out of my hell hole until I was expected, as the derision I would receive from the other cleaners would be a hundred times worse than the physical discomfort of remaining inside. I knew it would take me weeks to live it down, if it was thought that I could not stick my first job for the expected length of time.

I vaguely heard a bell ringing in the far-away outside world, and gradually the sounds of activity died away from around the loco. I strained my ears to hear what was going on, when suddenly a face peered in at me. It was Charlie, the grin once more decorating his face.

'Come on, you,' he winked at me and I stared foolishly back at him, my eyes feeling stiff and large. 'It's time to eat, you stupid ass.' I had been in the fire-box for an hour and a half and it had seemed like an eternity. The cool air hit my face like an icy flow of water as I climbed gratefully out onto the footplate once more, my tongue licking the salt encrusted around my lips and my hand wiping the grime from my forehead.

'Use this, Bill,' suggested Charlie, handing me a handful of cotton waste. I did, and found it ideal for the job.

In the Cabin the breakfast break was well under way. Tea cans decorated the stove and munching cleaners filled the benches. For a brief moment I could not remember where I had put my sandwiches. I could recall picking them up from the kitchen table, hours and hours ago it seemed, then slowly I put my hand into my pocket and withdrew a squashed, misshapen bundle, which emitted a pungent aroma of toasted cheese!

'Phew! What's that smell?' asked a disgusted voice from a dark corner.

'It's Morgy's bait, he took it into the fire-box with him,' someone answered with a chuckle. The bread was curled up at the edges, crispy brittle and the middle was soggy with melted cheese. But they were hot and spicy and I was starving, so down they went. I enjoyed every bite!

Then followed the first part of the initiation ceremony, which was to sing a song. I gave a falsetto version of 'My Darling Clementine' to an accompaniment of boos and cat-calls from everyone present, and was promptly marched off to the Fish Stage where I was ordered to jump in the harbour under threat of being thrown in if I refused. I jumped. It was no hardship to me, on that lovely May morning, to swim naked in the harbour, the cool waters were like heaven after the heat of the fire-box, but, as I was drying myself on more handfuls of cotton waste, I wondered about the poor devils who were unfortunate enough to start on the railway on a freezing cold winter's morning! I didn't imagine that they would be let off, and I was right!

I was accepted. I had passed the initiation with flying colours and was rewarded with a mug of strong tea, as soon as the others realised that I had none of my own.

I returned to my second fire-box, no longer feeling the new boy and a little better prepared this time, with a wet rag tied around my mouth and nose, as suggested by a few old hands of at least a few months standing! Half an hour should do it, they had said, you needn't be too fussy on a Monday, it's only on a Wednesday the Inspector comes round. I took their word for it and was out of the suffocating heat in less than half the time I had taken to clean the first box. I stood on the footplate, breathing in the cool air again, and this time I took the opportunity to survey my surroundings. I traced, with my eye, the maze of pipe and tubes, shining with the warm glow of polished copper and leading to the various gauges and levers. I tapped a pressure gauge experimentally, in the same manner as Pa tapped the barometer at home, and cautiously fondled a few levers. The regulator handle was unmistakable because of its size, but the function of the rest remained a mystery to me. 'Well, I'm blowed!' I suddenly exclaimed to myself as I caught sight of the intriguing hollow glass tube which I had seen so often in Harry James' double-home box. There it was, obviously gauging something, behind a protective sheet of glass, water gauge, I thought to myself, and I was right!

The tender behind me was full of coal, always the first thing which was done when an engine came into the yard, so Harry James had told me. The fireman's long scooped and long handled shovel lay propped in the corner; eight tons, Ernie Perry said he shifted on the run from Neyland to Llandeilo, the last few tons having to be shovelled twice, once from the rear of the tender to the fore, and again from the front of the tender into the fire-box. Firemen had to be fit and strong to stand the pace of a long run, but I had no doubt that I would be able to cope easily when my turn came. If I lacked anything, it certainly was not confidence! Even the fire-boxes held no threat for me now, for after the shock of the first one, no other ever seemed so hot or so arduous.

I cleaned three fire-boxes that first morning and even found that I had a little time to spare to watch the other cleaners who were working on *my* engine. (I was already beginning to think possessively about any loco I was cleaning!) Teddy Morgan was on the framing with Arthur Evans, Billie James was cleaning the tender, Charlie Green was on the motions and Charlie Matthias was down the pit, singing his head off and wiping oil over everything in sight!

Sperm oil was used by every cleaner, irrespective of which part of the engine he was working on. It produced a soft, clean sheen on the metal, keeping it well protected and smoothly efficient. The brasswork, of course, needed extra special treatment, and a tin of brick dust and soot was pushed into my hand as I stood contemplating the others working, with instructions to help out with the brass cleaning. There's no peace for the wicked, as Mam used to say.

Not every loco which came into the Shed had to have its fire-box cleaned out—thank God, only the ones which were due for boiler washing. The remainder merely had their fires tidied up, leaving a small fire burning in the box, free of clinker and ashes. On these locos which were going straight back into service, I helped out with the general scouring and rough cleaning before the fine polishing could be done.

Old Tubey was sitting in the corner of the Shed hammering away at his firelighters. He had finished blowing and cleaning the tubes of his locos and was now working on his other job of making firelighters for engines which had to be newly-lit up. I left the brass polishing for a few minutes and walked over to watch him. He always used eleven sticks and ten nails, building up a criss-cross patterned cube to be placed in the fire-box. I soon realised that he was very proud of the speed in which he could knock up his firelighters and of the symmetrical shape they always took. He appreciated an audience, did old Tubey.

The dinner break came at half past twelve. Everyone downed tools as the bell rang out and the clamour of the Shed gradually died down as we made our way out into the eye-blinding sunlight.

Work had not stopped outside the Shed, however. Yard Pilotmen were busy shunting the coal empties and goods wagons, which never seemed to be where they were needed. This meant complicated shuffling and shunting in order to place them on the correct road and in the correct order. At least, that was how it appeared to me during those first few weeks. Later, patterns emerged, and what had resembled a totally disorganised muddle took on the look of highly efficient handling.

My hunger taking priority over my newly found status as a workman, I scrambled my way home through the brambles and gorse of the bank instead of walking up the High Street. I had never appreciated Mam's cooking as much as I did that first dinner break on the railway. It was salt beef broth. I can still sense the delicious smell which met me as I opened the door.

'Well, Willie, how did it go then?' asked Mam as she ladled the leek-stiff broth into the basins.

'Great,' I answered through the water and bubbles which I was rubbing over my face, hair and neck. 'Just great,' I added and proceeded to relate my adventures in the fire-box to Hughie and Jim.

'Your Pa would love to hear you telling us about your job, Willie,' interrupted Mam with a sigh. 'Never mind though, only another three weeks and he'll be home.' She straightened herself up and smiled round at us all. 'Let's hope the weather stays good, we don't want any more of those old storms keeping him aboard longer than he's due, do we now?'

I looked around the table at Lillian, Anne and young Leonard, until my eyes came level with Hughie's and Jim's, and I knew they were thinking the same as I was. The others had been too young to remember that awful day.

Pa was a Trinity man and kept the light on the lightships studded around the wild, rocky, West Wales coast—the Helwick, the Scarweather, the St. Govan's and the Cardigan Bay. He and six others had been manning the St. Govan's light at the time, their turn of duty being two months aboard ship and one month shore work. But this timing was purely arbitrary and relied entirely on the state of the weather.

I had known rough seas delay the relief reaching Pa's lightship for over a fortnight. Often attempts were made in wild high-running seas but they had to be abandoned, sometimes with only a few yards separating the relief ship from the lightship. Those few yards were the most treacherous in the sea.

When relief was delayed it meant that the men aboard ship missed out on their time on shore. On some occasions Pa was away from home for two and a half months, and he then would have only two weeks shore work before he had to return aboard. Of course, it sometimes worked the other way round and we would have Pa home for six weeks while he waited for favourable weather for *The Vestal, The Irene* or *The Siren* to take the relief men, the water barrels and the oil barrels out to the lighthouses and lightships. But we didn't often find ourselves on the lucky end of a delayed relief.

It had been a particularly stormy season that winter a few years back, which Hughie, Mam and I were each silently recalling as we sat sipping our salt beef broth. The crews of The Smalls Lighthouse, which was one of the most inaccessible during rough seas, had had many long spells of extra duty and the lightships had fared little better.

A lull in the weather had brought hurried preparations for the S.S. *Siren* to get steam up and set sail with her relief men, fresh water and fuel oil, in an endeavour to make a round trip of all the lighthouses and lightships before the weather broke again. Pa was just ten days overdue for relief and Mam was delighted when she saw the *Siren*, with Sam Briggs, Pa's relief, on board, gliding down the harbour to The Heads and the open sea.

It took anything from two to four days to carry out the changeover of men and barrels, and the news would spread round the town like lightning as soon as the Trinity ship was spotted rounding the head-land, on her return. Hughie and I would race down to the pontoon to wait for Pa's arrival.

The weather had closed in again, however, not long after the *Siren* had steamed out, in fact, there had been times when we had thought that she might have had to cut short her trip and abandon, once more, any attempts to get the men on and off the lightships. The winds had been high and the seas, even inside the harbour, had been wicked, but the *Siren* had not returned early and we had all hoped for a successful trip.

Days later she same round the headland in a late afternoon drizzle, but as soon as I saw her a cold hand clutched at my insides. Hughie and I gazed at the flags flying at half mast, and listened with fearful apprehension to the *Siren*'s whistle ominously hooting once every five seconds as she had steamed up the harbour. It was a death ship. But whose death?

Shawl-clad women, excited young children and grey-faced men had run down the hill to the pontoon, but not Mam. And she would let neither Hughie, Jim, nor myself go.

We had waited, a heart-sickening wait.

Billie Griffiths, his donkey cart laden with the returning men's empty ration boxes and wooden meat pails, had passed by the bottom of the road. He usually delivered Pa's first, but that day he had carried on up the hill, without turning into Cambrian Road at all.

At last the returning Trinity men had come into view, standing out from the rest of the townspeople in their navy sailor's uniform, the officers with their poke caps and the crews with their rounded hats. Pa had not been among them. We had stood by the front door, the rain drizzling down on our heads, Hughie's and mine, for Mam, pale and calm, had remained indoors, stoically polishing the already gleaming parlour table, when we had suddenly realised that one of the Trinity men was making his way towards us. I had recognised him as Mr. Crawley, the quartermaster of the *Siren* (and unknown to me at that time, I was, little over a decade later, to marry one of his daughters). He had waved, he had smiled, Hughie and I had looked at each other, not daring to hope too much. But still there was no sign of the tall, weather-beaten figure we knew so well.

'It's all right, boys, it's all right,' he had shouted through the gusty rain, long before he had reached us.

'Where's your Mam?' he had asked as soon as he had got within speaking range. 'Your Pa's had to stay for another month's shift,' he carried on. 'Poor old Sam Briggs has gone for ever.'

We had learnt later that Sam, who was to have been Pa's relief, had fallen from the Breeches Boy when attempting to board the lightship. He had disappeared into the swirling seas between the two vessels, and had drowned.

'Why aye, now, it's only another three weeks and your Pa'll be home,' repeated Mam as she took another sip of her broth. Hughie and

I smiled at each other and Lillian began banging her wooden spoon on the table with excitement as she asked what Pa would be bringing home for her this trip.

Carved monkeys on sticks, tumbling clowns, jacky jumpers which somersaulted over their own trapezes by an ingenious arrangement of strings and sticks, Pa always brought something home which he had made while passing the time between his twelve hour shifts. Beautiful sailing ships in bottles, their masts intricately laced with black cotton, thick bristly, hand-knotted rope-mats or geometrically patterned rag rugs—there was always something rolled up under his arm for us, each time he returned.

Scraping the last grain of boiled rice and its eyeful of jam—a sweet luxury in those sugar-short days of the Great War—I rose from the table, made my round of good-byes and set off, once more to the railway sheds. I remember thinking that there was nowhere else I would rather have been going.

* * *

To my pleasant surprise, the afternoon was taken at a far easier pace than the morning. All the rush jobs were out on the road and there was only one loco in the shed, a small tankie, waiting for us to get to work on her. The fire-dropper had tidied up the fire-box and all she needed was a good clean.

'Come on then, lads, all hands on this one, and we'll be finished in no time.' It was Curly Evans who spoke, he seemed to be a leader, of sorts, among the sixteen cleaners who were working in the Shed. Usually four or five cleaners at the most were put to work on one loco, but as this was the only one needing attention we all set to. Like bees round a honey pot, we swarmed all over her. Charlie was down in the pit again, I think he liked it down there, so I jumped down and joined him. I discovered he was sitting on the handle of a short shovel, so I immediately climbed out and found one for myself—you have to learn the tricks of the trade. We perched there, under the tankie, happily cleaning and polishing the bottoms of the motions. The rhythms of our wiping sperm-oiled waste fitted in very well with the raucous songs we sang as we polished!

The afternoon passed quickly and pleasantly. We had plenty of time for chatting, larking about, keeping out of the Chargeman's way and trying to look busy if anyone over the age of eighteen came near us.

We steered clear of the Drivers' and Firemen's Cabin, as they seemed to be a bit of a sober sides to us, either moaning at us for fooling about or finding us extra jobs to do. Yet, when I was eventually to become a driver myself, I found myself treating the cleaners in exactly the same way and thinking of them as young scoundrels who were always trying to avoid doing any work and who grew cheekier every day!

The six o'clock bell came as a surprise to me, the time had slipped by so quickly. Once more I was ravenously hungry, but this time I decided to take the proper route home along with the other returning workmen. As I climbed the steep hill, I thought myself well pleased with my first day with the Great Western Railway.

I soon became accustomed to the regular Mail trains, coal trains, fish trains, and parcels and goods trains which passed the sheds on their way to Carmarthen, Swansea, Llandeilo, Duffryn Yard, Severn Tunnel or Paddington, and like other railway workers I found myself telling the time, not by a watch or clock, but by whichever train was leaving from, or arriving at, Neyland Station.

It was soon obvious to me that the Passenger Expresses and their crews, the drivers in particular, were held in the highest esteem by everyone from the cleaners up to the Foreman. The locos which pulled these trains were the 33 Bulldog class and they were the pride of the Neyland Shed. These were the named engines and each one had its own particular driver which drove that one and no other. They had their regular booked runs, the drivers knowing their passengers personally and taking a fierce pride in the performance and condition of their own special locos.

John Thomas was fanatical about his 3303 St. Anthony, and John Kellick about his 3454 Skylark. Harry Lewis vowed that his 3311 Bulldog was superior to all the others, bearing as it did, the name of the 33 class locos. Bill Osborne would let no other driver near his 3408 Bombay and Bill Llewellyn was as possessive about his Sir Lancelot 3302 as any driver could be. The names of these locos were synonymous with those of their drivers. On duty, you rarely saw one without the other.

These 4-4-0 Bulldogs always received special attention whenever they came into the Shed for cleaning. Not for them the three hours which was the usual time for engine cleaning. An entire day's work was scheduled for the 33's in order to achieve the perfection required by their drivers. Not for them the ordinary cleaner-boy rota. Each driver had his own hand-picked chief cleaner, who, in turn, specially selected those who would be in his team. It was a great day when you were considered capable enough to be trusted to work on these passenger express locos, and you appreciated the honour when you were finally chosen to be one of a team which could send an engine out with every piece of brass and copper gleaming, and every inch of her in peak condition, as sleek as a well-fed black cat.

Sometimes a passenger engine was required for a rush working, and extra hands were needed in order to meet the deadline. This was the chance which the junior cleaners waited for, and each hoped he would be picked to help out on one of these great locos.

Rush jobs were always appreciated by the driver concerned, and rarely did they steam past the Shed without a wave of acknowledgement for the cleaners. A small thing, no doubt, but it meant a great deal to us, and I was to remember this when, years later, I was to take a special out and I saw a line of cleaners watching as I steamed by. They too had their wave of thanks.

I was looking forward to receiving my first wages. It was with ill-concealed excitement I came to work on payday. For the first time since I had started work a fortnight before (as we had to work a week in hand), the morning seemed to go slowly. It was an interminable wait until the Pay Bell sounded at twelve o'clock, and suddenly everyone was full of jokes, smiling as they lined up to collect their check tags from the office clerk. I held my tag tightly in my hand as we waited by the small pay window. This was the first time I had had to queue up outside this dark little office, as, whenever I had collected Harry James' money I had been alone, feeling an intruder in a man's world. But today, I was part of the working complex of the Shed and I was glad I would never be a schoolboy again.

'Morgan, 69,' I announced as I reached the window, almost shouting at the pay clerk in my haste to call my own number for the first time. As usual, quite unimpressed by the sense of occasion, he casually pushed the cylindrical box towards me. There, on the top, was the number 69. I grasped it and walked away. It contained thirteen shillings and sixpence. By hedges, life was good!

2

What the hell was old Kellick doing? I wondered as I glanced inside the fitters' shed. His personal loco, the Skylark, was in for new valves and pistons, and there he was, standing on top of the full tender, slapping whitewash all over the coal! It was the slack time of the afternoon and I was wandering around the yard, chatting here, watching there, asking a few questions and generally being told to clear off! The sun beat down on the back of my neck as I stood at the fitters' shed, completely intrigued by Kellick's whitewashing antics. I knew he insisted on a gleaming loco but he must be *twp* if he was going to start painting the coal. He'll be asking us cleaners to do it next, I thought.

'Hey, you'll never guess what I saw old Kellick doing in the fitters' shed,' I challenged Charlie Matthias, as we were helping to fire-drop one of the locos which had just come in.

'Well, you can't blame him, can you?' he replied when I had told what I thought was an astounding piece of news.

Charlie jabbed the pricker into the bars in an attempt to loosen some particularly stubborn piece of clinker and the choking dust discouraged any further attempts at conversation so I let the matter drop. But it still intrigued me.

My enlightenment came over an unofficial tea break in the cleaners' cabin later that afternoon. It turned out that old Kellick certainly wasn't *twp* after all.

The express drivers on the G.W.R. at that time were paid a bonus depending on the amount of coal unconsumed at the end of a run. This meant that a skilful use of regulator and injector was necessary, and a careful watch had to be kept on the fireman to make sure that he was placing the coal in the best position in the fire-box. A good driver could save as much as one ton in seven with a careful combination of judicious firing and driving. With a driver having to sign for every scrap of coal which was issued to his engine, it was no small wonder that they made very sure that no-one used it but themselves.

And there was Kellick's Skylark, sitting in the fitters' shed, with a three-quarter-full tender of coal, within convenient proximity to the fitters' cabin, the blacksmith's shop, the cleaners' cabin, the charge-man's office and the drivers' and firemen's cabin—each with its fire or stove consuming buckets of coal every day, day and night, summer and winter, all of which had to be carried from the coal pile which was almost a quarter of a mile away.

It really was asking too much of any man or boy to walk past Skylark's tender with an empty bucket. After all, who would miss just a few lumps from the tons which were stacked up there, thought every fireman, cleaner, blacksmith, chargeman and fitter who went to fetch coal. Before long a good few hundredweight would be missing and obviously John Kellick was going to put a stop to any such notions. With the top layer whitewashed he could keep a close check if any was missing and woe betide anyone if a speck of whitewashed coal was discovered in their buckets. One or two intrepid coal fetchers, so Charlie informed me, had surreptitiously tried to remove some unwhitewashed coal from the bottom of the stack, but the resultant collapse of the upper coals was enough to discourage any further attempts at such a tricky operation!

It was not only John Kellick and the other Neyland drivers who took this precaution, however. Apparently it was a custom all along the line, and who could blame them, as Charlie had said?

These express drivers were held in such respect that even the charge-man at Neyland trod very warily, if ever he had to arrange for another driver to take one of the express locos. He waited with apologies to pacify John Thomas, Harry Lewis or any of the other drivers whose engine had been commandeered.

It was cold and damp, with a westerly blowing, the morning that

Harry Lewis was due to take his Bulldog 3311 out with the eleven o'clock Passengers. Just before it was due to leave the shed, sparkling like a new pin, one of the fitters happened to notice a loose tyre on her front driving wheel and there was no alternative but to class her as crippled. Tom John, the chargeman, did his best to have a replacement sent over from Fishguard, but there was nothing available.

'You'll have to take The Anthony, Harry,' he finally admitted with great reluctance. 'What the hell Thomas the Cot'll have to say about it, when he books on, I daren't think, but she's the only one available and you'll have to take her.' And off went Harry Lewis with the 3303.

Poor old Tom John worried all day about how he was going to break the news to Thomas the Cot that his beloved 3303 had been handed over to Harry Lewis, and finally he went over to the Foreman, Rees Jones, and told him that he considered it to be the foreman's job to handle such delicate matters of policy! So now it was Rees Jones who was going around with a worried look. But he was a wily bird and it didn't take him long to think of just the right approach for John Thomas.

We cleaners, for once, tried to keep busy, right up to the last half-hour of our shift, hoping to hear the confrontation when old Thomas the Cot booked on at 5.45. A buzz went through the shed as the news went round, 'Here he comes, and by Gawd, by the looks of him, he knows already!'

John Thomas was short of stature, but a man of grim determined character, his neatly-trimmed moustache giving an arrogant air as he came striding down towards the Shed, swinging his double-homer back and forth angrily. We cleaners got our heads down, spit and polished for all our worth, ears flapping for the grand battle. The Foreman had obviously been keeping a look-out for him, as he came out of his office to meet the enraged driver. We held our breath.

I said Rees Jones was a wily bird and he let old Thomas have his vociferous say without interruption. Then putting a hand on his shoulder he said in a very confidential tone, 'Well, John, it was like this. We had quite a few locos here which Harry could have taken, I even offered him a choice of two from Fishguard, but he refused them all. "Only the St. Anthony is good enough to take the Passenger Express", he insisted, and, of course, I couldn't argue with that, now could I?'

John Thomas stayed silent for a few moments, looking a little more mollified. Praise for his engine was nectar to him and the effect was immediate.

'Indeed, he knows a good engine, does Harry Lewis,' he admitted. 'Always did, fair play.' And he went to take his replacement loco like a lamb.

'Too bloody clever, by half, that Jones,' muttered Billie James in disappointment at the lack of battle, throwing down his cleaning waste in disgust. 'Come on, Bill, let's go to the cabin, that wasn't worth the extra work we did.' And off we went, feeling quite hard done by!

'And what did you think of my engine then, Harry Lewis?' asked Thomas two days later, his voice full of paternal pride.

'The worst damned loco I've ever been blessed with,' replied Harry, waving his hands in apparent disgust. 'Wouldn't pull the skin off a rice pudding,' he went on, and turning on his heel he left a pop-eyed, apoplectic John Thomas inarticulately choking with rage. A devil of a stirrer was Harry Lewis!

These drivers were almost as fanatical about their engines as the old-timers had been. I had spent many an hour on a Sunday afternoon as a very young lad, watching old Georgie Jefferies or Johnny Davis, sitting astride their old brass-domed loco in the siding, polishing and cleaning until the dome gleamed like gold in the sunlight. This was unpaid work, of course, and sometimes they even insisted on their firemen giving up a few hours on a Sunday afternoon in order to get the engine in peak condition ready for the Monday.

But even John Kellick whitewashed the coal in the Company's time and not his own, so times were changing!

The proprietary rights of these drivers with their engines were only possible, however, as long as the twelve-hour working day existed, as it meant that they could work long distances and back, returning with their own loco. When, in the future, the eight-hour day was to be introduced, more relief crews had to take over half-way through a trip and engines often found themselves in strange sheds, sometimes taking weeks to work their way back to their home base.

Some of the old stalwarts were completely shattered by this new arrangement, and perhaps it was just as well that they were soon due for retirement. It was progress, but it was sad even to us, who had never had the pride of ownership ourselves, but who had, nevertheless, taken a personal interest in keeping the Neyland locos looking better than any up the line.

The week following Harry Lewis' remarks about the St. Anthony, I was informed by Tom John, the chargeman, that I was scheduled to take out the call papers for the drivers and firemen on the unbooked turns. The only booked turns, which needed no call papers, were the passenger trains with their regular drivers. All the other trains were worked by a rota system of first one in, first one out.

Elated at the prospect of a few hours of freedom about the town in Company's time, I made my way over to the office where I was presented with a bundle of buff-coloured call papers with the names of the drivers and firemen scrawled almost illegibly in indelible pencil across the top and the times of their turns underneath. In great delight I set off across the lines and made my way to the station.

It was not until I reached the platform that I took a good look at the call papers. Georgie Morgan, Cambrian Road, oh yes I knew Mr. Morgan well, but when it suddenly occurred to me that, although I knew he lived in Cambrian Road, I did not know the exact number, and it was not marked on the call paper either. Quickly I glanced through the remainder of the papers—no numbers on any of them, and some without even the name of the road! Obviously, the call-boys knew these men and their addresses so well, that the clerk didn't bother to fill in all the details.

Mam, I thought, she would know where they all lived, but no, I couldn't ask her, it just didn't seem workmanlike at all. There was no alternative but to go back to the Shed and find the correct addresses. I was furious with myself, as I ran back along the tracks, for not having checked the call papers before. Perhaps I could save my face a little if I went into the Cleaners' cabin and tried to find one of the experienced call-boys to give me the necessary information. As unobtrusively as possible I ran alongside the Shed and darted into the cabin. My luck was in, it appeared, as there, sitting inside having a crafty smoke, was Curly Evans. On seeing a silhouette at the doorway, he quickly clipped the cigarette between his fingers, jumping up looking as guilty as a fox in a hen-coop. His apprehension quickly changed to anger when he realised who it was.

'What the hell do you want? Jesus Jones, I thought it was the gaffer.' I stammered an apology and explained the unfortunate situation I was

C   33

in. Curly looked at me, lit up his dog-end once more and stretched out his hand for the papers.

'Give them here, then, I'll fill 'em in for you.' He grinned at me, and after a few moments handed me the completed slips. Thanking him profusely I dashed out, leaving him lying back on the bench, blowing smoke rings at the roof.

As I raced back to the station I realised that my first trip out on call paper duty was not to be the leisurely walk around the town I had expected. I was a good half-hour late starting and I would have to rush to catch up with myself. I hurried through the station, along the Hotel Gardens, wriggled expertly through the kissing gates and made my way up the hill.

The shops were beginning to bustle and the pavements were being swept ready for a new day as I passed by, sorting the call papers into a delivery order, so that I would not find myself retracing my steps. Cambrian Road, Lawrenny Street, back to the High Street, then up to John Street, across to Charles Street and Kensington Road. Right, I thought, now I am really organised I'll start with Cambrian Road and deliver Georgie Morgan's call paper. This was my own road and for a fleeting moment I thought of calling in to see Mam just to say hello, but I decided to leave it until another day when I had more time. I checked the slip for Georgie Morgan's number, and there it was as Curly had written it. Number 216. My mind went blank for a moment. Surely there wasn't a number as high as that in our road. Lizzie James lived very near the top and her number was less than a hundred, I was certain. The knowledge suddenly hit me that Curly Evans had been taking me for a very big ride. Frantically I checked through the other slips. The numbers on many of them seemed suspiciously high, as I had feared.

The picture flashed through my mind of Curly lying in the cabin blowing his blasted smoke rings and inwardly laughing at my gullibility. No doubt the whole shed would have learnt about it by now—all the cleaners at any rate. I clenched my fists and vowed to get my own back on Mister Evans at the earliest possible opportunity.

I should have realised by then that cleaners were amongst the biggest practical jokers going. As the new boy I had had my share played on me during those first few weeks—oily waste rags in my breakfast box, live crabs slipped in my pocket, earsplitting detonators let off when I was under a loco, errands for non-existent parts—why aye, man, I should have realised by then.

But the pressing decision of the moment was what I was going to do about the call papers. One thing was certain, I was not going to return to the Shed again and give Curly the satisfaction of knowing that his trick had worked. There was only one alternative. Unworkmanlike or not, I would have to enlist Mam's help.

'It's only me,' I called as I went in through the front door. Mam came into the passage with a look of surprise on her face.

'What are you doing here then, Willie?' she asked, her voice full of apprehension. I quickly put her mind at rest and explained the situation. She was at the table drawer for a pencil and sitting down with the slips in front of her, in no time at all.

'Georgie Morgan. Well, Willie, you should have known where he lives—it's three doors down from, no, wait a bit now . . .' and so she went on, working out every drivers' address from who he lived next door to, or who used to live there ten years ago, or sometimes by her own complicated method of tracing back who had married who, where they had lived as newly-weds, tracing them through two or three moves and finally knowing where their present place was! One almost had her beat. 'I didn't know he'd moved to Kensington Road,' she mused. 'That must have been Nellie Harris' place, who went to look after her sister in Llangwm I think it was. Never married, poor soul . . .'

'Oh, come on, Mam, never mind about old Nellie Harris,' I interrupted, 'there's still two more to do.' I looked at the grandmother clock, relentlessly ticking the minutes away, it was nearly an hour since I had left the Shed and not one call paper had I delivered. At last all twelve slips were done, and with my mind full of clues about green curtains, double-fronted houses, broken steps, all of which Mam assured me I could not possibly miss, I dashed out through the passage. Shouting my thanks and giving the door a hearty slam, I raced up to the top of the street.

The next hour was a frantic one for me. I rushed from street to street, knocking doors, stamping my feet in impatience for an answer and cutting short the idle chat from the women who did eventually take the call paper from my extended hand.

'Well, Willie Morgan, fancy you left school and all, growing up fast you are.' Any other time I might have enjoyed the slight look of admiration in their glance, or was it just bewilderment at the speed of passing time?

It was done. I had delivered every one of the call papers and I felt a great weight lift from my mind. I knew I had to return to the Shed as quickly as possible if I was to avoid any enquiries as to why I had taken so long, and as I jog-trotted down through the town I formulated in my mind what I was going to say when I next saw Curly Evans. As I reached Railway Terrace I decided to take the short cut down over the bank, and for the first time that morning I appreciated the fresh breeze in my face. I'll enjoy myself next time, I vowed.

Running a hurdling type of lope across the tracks, I reached the cleaners' cabin. It was empty. Good. Then taking a few slow, deep breaths I dawdled into the shed, hands in pockets, the very epitome of unhurried nonchalance! Everyone looked up expectantly from whatever job they were doing and sly looks passed from one to the other. A few gave a nervous giggle and looked guiltily over at Curly who was up by the smoke-box of the loco in for cleaning. I ambled over to the stand tap. 'It's bloody lovely out there this morning,' I remarked to no-one in particular, taking a long drink from under the tap. 'Suppose I'd better let old John know I'm back,' I added, and wandered off to report my return.

We all played it very cool and nothing was mentioned about wrong addresses, but as the morning wore on I could see Curly becoming more and more edgy as he began to wonder if the men would turn up for their shifts! Those few hours of uncertainty for Curly were prized jewels for me and I enjoyed every minute of them. The relief on his face as, one after the other, the men arrived to schedule, was unmistakable. I caught his eye and he mouthed a string of curses at me as I pretended to doff a cap to him. It was the last of the jokes to be played on Bill Morgan. Now we all awaited another new boy to start so that we could begin all over again!

3

I stayed as Box-boy and Call-boy for five weeks, by which time I felt quite an old hand.

'Foreman's having dictations done this afternoon,' Teddy Morgan informed me the first day of my sixth week. My eyes lit up. Whenever a boy applied to work on the railway he had to write a piece of dictation which was read to him by one of the clerks and had to have a test for colour blindness, which took the form of sorting out various coloured strands of wool. I had done this the week before I had actually started work, so this news meant that by the following Monday, with a bit of luck, there would be someone else starting as box-boy and I would be a fully-fledged cleaner. No extra pay, just status and no fire-boxes!

We never knew the results of our tests, but I presume some notice was taken of them as some box-boys were later directed to undertake more shed labouring and less loco cleaning than others, resulting in their rarely being promoted to firemen. As cleaners, much of our knowledge of steam engines was gained incidentally. It often happened that a loco might need moving from the sheds when there was no-one technically qualified around to take charge of it. The chargeman would give the O.K. to two of the older cleaners and they would be up on the footplate like a shot. An opportunity never to be missed. We all took every possible chance to ride with a fireman or driver whenever locos were moving in and out of the Shed and around the yard. This was sanctioned in the G.W.R. handbook, which encouraged cleaners to take an active interest in steam engines and to learn about the various parts of an engine, supplementing their information by asking questions of fitters, firemen, foremen, drivers, inspectors, etc. We really needed no directives as such, as it all seemed the perfectly natural thing to do anyway. We were all insatiably curious, much to the annoyance of drivers and firemen who were rushed for time at that particular moment.

During that sixth week I heard that another box-boy would start on the line the following Monday, an acquaintance from school, Freddie Griffiths. I felt that this was a great step forward in my career and I looked forward to showing him the inner complexities of the fire-box, just as Charlie had shown them to me.

My first five weeks' wages had been handed over without question to Mam, who had given me one shilling back for myself. I considered this very fair, and I took great delight in planning, each week, the various ways I could spend my shilling. My weekly pay had made a tremendous difference to Mam's household budget. Firstly, because it was obviously a little extra to Pa's money, and secondly, because, unlike Pa, I was paid weekly instead of monthly.

The Trinity Service always paid out on the 24th of each month, when six golden sovereigns would be brought to Mam by which ever light-house-keeper was on shore duty at the time. It used to take all her skill to feed and clothe us five children and herself for a month, apart from buying the food which Pa had to take with him for his two-month turn of duty aboard the lightship. It had been my job, each month, to take one of Pa's wooden pails up to Morgan the Butcher, to be filled with salt meat, either for Pa to take with him on his next trip, or for the relief men to deliver to him half-way through his two-month spell. And sometimes, but only sometimes, that pail of salt meat had to be bought on tick until the 24th of the month came round.

The worst time for waiting for that 24th day was during the month of December. I have seen Mam biding until nine o'clock on Christmas Eve before Pa's pay was brought to the door. It was for-tunate that the Neyland shops remained open until the late hours, as Christmas shopping, for the Trinity families, tended to start late in the day.

Yes, Mam appreciated my contribution towards the family finances, and she made sure that I knew of her appreciation.

However, much to my delight, on hearing the news that Freddie was starting as box-boy, she announced that, as I was becoming a regular Cleaner, I could keep one week's wages entirely for myself, bearing in mind that I would have to buy myself a suit of overalls, the recognised status symbol for a Junior Cleaner as opposed to a Fire-box cleaner, who merely wore any old clothes he happened to have.

The following pay day found me standing outside Biddlecombe's the Drapers, with thirteen shillings and sixpence in my pocket and feeling as rich as Croesus. Bales of serge cloth were artistically arranged between rolls of striped flannel in the crowded window. Every inch of space was filled with button cards—tin, pearl, bone and fancy reels of cotton, twine, and silk, and hanging at the back were the boiler-suits and overalls, stiff and brand-new blue, so unlike the faded, comfortable suits of my work-mates.

Remembering Mam's words that the first wash would shorten the legs and sleeves by a good three inches, I entered the dark little shop prepared to do business. A boiler-suit was out of the question as it just was not the 'in' thing for cleaners to wear! And I was determined to be the same as everyone else. It had to be overalls consisting of separate trousers and jacket, or nothing.

The air inside was stuffy and dehydrated, as if the rolls of material had absorbed every drop of moisture from it. Even sound seemed to be deadened, and the bell gave an echoless ping as I opened the door. Georgie Biddlecombe guessed what I was after, and in no time at all his tape measure had flicked over me. A stiff blue suit was deftly lifted from the window with his long pole, and laid on the counter for my approval. After asking if he had allowed for shrinkage, I decided to close the transaction and handed over the 8s. $11\frac{3}{4}$d. as if I were used to dealing in such large sums of money every day. I emerged, once more, into the fresh air, with a neatly-packed brown paper parcel under my arm and 4s. $6\frac{1}{4}$d. in my pocket. I felt very worldly and very solvent!

The following Monday I turned up for work in my washed-blue overalls. I had flatly refused to wear them in their stiff new state, and had felt indescribably wretched when I had first tried them on and viewed myself in Mam's wardrobe mirror. The sleeves covered my hands and the trousers hung unbendingly over my toes. I think they would have stood up on their own!

'Never heard such nonsense,' Mam had said when I asked her to wash them before I wore them to work on Monday. But wash them she did, when I volunteered to carry the water, light the copper and bale out afterwards. But she still did a fair share of tutting and muttering while the kitchen filled with steam.

Sprawling on the dirtiest seat I could find so that my overalls would lose their newness as quickly as possible, I realised how Charlie had felt, the day I had started as box-boy. No wonder he had done a jig around the stove! It was two minutes past six and a few cleaners started to make their way out of the cabin, but no Freddie hovered uncertainly at the door, and I was beginning to wonder if, after all, he was actually going to start that day. I tried to suppress a sickly feeling of apprehension and disappointment which was steadily building up inside me as the minutes ticked away, when crunching along the ashes came Freddie, and what a glad sight he was! I greeted him warmly, any feelings of superiority smothered by an overpowering gratitude that he had actually turned up!

'Hiya, Bill,' he grinned, returning my greeting, and so started a life-long friendship between us which was to last long after the Great Western Railway had ceased to exist.

I instructed him carefully on the manner in which he was to tackle the fire-box, stayed in with him for half an hour, then leaving him with my flare lamp I backed out of a fire-box for the last time.

Curly wasn't among us that morning as he had recently been up to Swindon and had passed his test for promotion to fireman. He was away pilot shunting empties at Haverfordwest and how we all envied him. I was conscious of the 7.45 Pick-up Goods steam past the sheds on its way to Milford Haven and then on to Carmarthen, and made a mental note that it would soon be breakfast time. So, jumping up onto the footplate I gave Freddie a shout to come out and have a spell. He needed no second bidding and had his head under the stand tap in five seconds flat!

Although I had been a cleaner for a very short time I already knew the various parts of a steam engine. Things I had heard Ernie Perry and Harry James talk about suddenly came to mean something instead of being mere technical jargon. The intricacies of the fire-box I knew only too well, with its brick arch and its sloping floor. When cleaners eventually become firemen, they know exactly where they are placing their shovelfuls of coal because they have actually been there themselves!

They can tell if they have misplaced a feed of coal as they can visualise that it is too far under the brick arch, leaving the firebed uneven, or that the baffle plate is in the wrong position, as they bang their heads on it often enough as a box-boy! Everything is tangible and real, not mere diagrams or instructions in a book, as there is no doubt that, after having spent years cleaning locomotives, you almost become part of them.

Of course I did have my share of book learning to do as a cleaner, because in addition to finding out about steam engines, I had to learn the Rules and Regulations of the Great Western Railway. These included signals, detention of trains, working of trains, protection of trains, prevention of accidents, procedure for coupling and uncoupling, methods of firing and the responsibilities of a fireman.

On reading the regulations dealing with the protection of trains and the setting of warning detonators, I often imagined myself, in highly dramatic circumstances, dashing down the tracks, placing detonators in record speed time, and making the headlines in the local press as 'Young fireman saves lives of hundreds by his prompt action . . .'! But I was obviously no clairvoyant, as I never ever did manage to make the headlines!

* * *

Contrary to what we expected, some of the most enjoyable work as cleaner on the G.W.R. were the night shifts. The late summer found Freddie Griffiths (who had now himself moved up from box-boy) and me, booked together for night shift cleaning for a week. It was considered quite a favour from the Chargeman if you were chosen for night work, as the pay was about a third more than the day shift rate. Both were twelve-hour turns, six 'til six. Night work started at six o'clock on Sunday evening, and that suited me fine for a start, as I could miss the starched collar preparations for attending Chapel with a clear conscience and without black looks from my elders.

There were only two cleaners on duty at night, in contrast to the sixteen who manned the shed during the day, and it was expected that you would turn up on the Sunday evening, in clean overalls, as the first job of work was the delivery of call papers for the Monday workings. Over forty drivers and firemen received their call papers on a Sunday evening, and it was a pleasant way for us to start the shift—always providing, of course, that it wasn't blowing a gale and raining like the devil, as there were few places more unsheltered than Neyland High Street on a wet, stormy evening, with the wind gusting up the hill at force eight!

But that first Sunday evening of night shift was quiet and peaceful, the streets uncannily deserted, as only a Welsh town at chapel time could be. The only ones abroad at this hour were either rag-a-muffins or strangers, with, of course, the exception of the G.W.R. call-boys. Freddie and me.

Apart from our echoing footsteps, the only sound to disturb the silence was the resonant 'hwyl' of the preachers ringing out, as we drew near each chapel, and the harmonic strains of the tenor-laden choirs. It took more restraint than I had to refrain from joining in as I passed by. There's always something about a Welsh choir which makes me want to become part of it.

Sunday evening was the only time of the week when front parlours were used. Chairs were grouped together—near the window, but behind the lace, so that one could see without being seen, ready for After Chapel. After chapel, each Sunday, weather permitting, came the slow parade down the High Street at a stately pace with gracious smiles from everyone. The Congregationalists mixed with the Baptists, the Zionists and Methodists chatted with the upholders of the Church of England, hats were commented on, children's growth remarked upon, and newlyweds were surreptitiously eyed for the first signs of a forthcoming happy event. Those who did not take part in the After Chapel parade around the town, sat ensconced in their parlours, noting and commenting on every example of fashion which swept slowly by. Nothing was missed, from a new pair of gloves to an extra curl peeping out from under a new hat. Occasionally there would be a slight twitch of the curtain, betraying the intense interest of the watcher, much to the satisfaction of the passer-by who occasioned it!

Mingling with the doffing hats and the polite chatter, Freddie and I made our way round the town slowly, feeling in a different world from the Sunday-best dressed friends we met, almost feeling guilty at the commiserations we received from the elders for having to work nights. 'But, then, your Mam can do with the bit extra, I dare say,' they would finish off. Down the hill they would drift, chiding the children for running on a Sunday and worrying whether there was sufficient meat left on the roast joint for the Sunday supper of cold meat, pickles and fried potatoes.

There was no trouble with addresses now. It had taken but a few weeks to get to know where every driver and fireman in Neyland lived, and I could hardly believe I had had so much difficulty on that first call-boy duty. The earliest papers were for the 4.45 a.m. coal empties to Llandeilo junction. The driver and fireman for this train would need a call-boy to knock them up, in addition to having a call paper delivered. That call-boy would be either Freddie or me. This was one of the main duties of night shift cleaners, as there was no actual cleaning to be done, only an occasional engine to be fire-dropped, ready for the day cleaners to get to work on.

We continued delivering our call papers throughout the evening, papers for the early fish train from Milford, mixed goods train to Carmarthen, Cardiff, Gloucester and Paddington, pilot shunting for Johnston and Haverfordwest, parcel trains, milk trains, pick-up goods trains, coal empties and local yard pilot working. The list seemed endless, all the men assigned to a particular train and time, on the principle of 'first one in, first one out'. The express passenger trains were not on any of our call papers, of course. The drivers and firemen of these were the elite whose turns remained constant and who needed no reminding as to when they were due to book on.

Freddie and I stayed together for company for as long as possible, parting only when we had diverse papers for outside town at Honeyborough, Mastlebridge and Llanstadwell, and after four hours of non-stop walking and with all the papers delivered, we decided that we had earned ourselves a break for refreshment.

'It's only us,' I cried, as I lifted the back door latch, immediately catching the delicious whiff of potatoes and cabbage. These were being fried to a golden crisp pancake by Pa, who always cooked the Sunday evening supper when he was ashore. Mam had been expecting us round at about ten o'clock, and the table was laid with large plates, half covered with beautifully carved slices of beef—another sure sign that Pa was home, as Mam usually had little time (or skill) for delicately thin carving. The large earthenware jars of home-made pickles and chutney stood solidly at the centre of the table. It was a feast fit for a king.

The four of us, Mam, Pa, Freddie and I ate our supper with great relish, much to the annoyance of my brothers and sisters who were considered too young to stay up for Sunday supper.

We arrived back at the Shed just after eleven o'clock. Harry Roach, the night Chargeman, told us that he considered we had done very well for a first night, and we agreed with him.

We had walked well over four miles during the evening and Freddie and I were beginning to feel a little tired. The exhilaration of being Chapel-free on a Sunday evening was beginning to wear off, and, what with our filling supper, we were feeling sleepy. But there was work to do. Two locos needed fire-dropping and their smoke-boxes raked out, and although it was not particularly arduous work, by the time two o'clock came round, we were rocking on our feet. It was the first time either of us had remained awake all through the night, and I remembered someone saying that two o'clock in the morning was the worst time. They hadn't been joking.

'Have a breather for half an hour or so,' suggested Roach the Chargeman as he came across us, sitting glassy-eyed on the footplate of the loco we had just finished raking out. Gratefully we staggered back to the cabin and stretched ourselves out on the narrow wooden benches, the gas jet spluttering fitfully, casting a greeny yellow glow over our faces. The stove had burnt low and needed refilling but neither of us could summon up enough energy to bother.

'What time's the first call?' asked Freddie, with a drawn-out sigh.

'About half past-three, I think,' I replied, not troubling to open my eyes. 'Llandeilo double-home, you delivered that call paper, who was it for?'

'Jesus Jones,' remembered Freddie. 'That was right down the other end of Llanstadwell. Why couldn't it have been someone a bit nearer? Just our luck to have the early call nearly two miles away. You go tonight and I'll go tomorrow,' he finished.

'Like Hell, I will,' I answered, eyes wide open now, 'I'm senior to you, so you go first.' In the end it was decided by the Chargeman who was to go. It was Bill Morgan—just my luck!

'You two had better have your tea and bait now,' he added. 'It's quarter to three, so you haven't much time.'

We drank our tea, which was unpleasantly luke-warm because we had let the stove burn so low, and although neither of us was hungry we ate our sandwiches, munching dispiritedly as we stared vacantly into space.

The night shift had definitely lost its glamour. The cabin grew more dismal every minute that passed, the benches grew harder and my eyelids heavier. The next thing I remembered was Harry Roach shaking my shoulder and informing me that it was nearly three-thirty and that I had better get moving if I was to reach Llanstadwell on time. Freddie sat up, bleary-eyed, and stared at Harry Roach with an uncomprehending look on his face. He, too, had fallen asleep, and obviously could not imagine what the Chargeman was doing in his bedroom!

There was a dry, tired taste in my mouth as I stumbled out of the cabin and made my way to the lavatory at the back of the Shed. Of course, there was no light in the small wooden hut, but I knew it was a three-holer, so I sleepily aimed for the centre one and hoped for the best!

The night air was disturbed by the merest trace of a sea breeze as I made my way across the sea-front towards Llanstadwell. Gradually my senses came to life. I breathed deeply and soon found my pace increasing and my awareness sharpening. The water was glassily smooth, broken only by the slightest trace of a wave's ripple as it broke on the shore's edge. The tide was ebbing and the seaweed glistened darkly in the starlight. I remembered hot days when I had wandered the beach searching for crabs and cockles and automatically I jumped down onto the noisy shingle and continued the rest of the way along the shore. I had never had the world to myself before, and the experience was worth every second of night shift which had gone before.

A feeling of elation spread through me as I cross-kicked the loose stones before me—I could do anything I wished and there was no-one to look askance, to chide or to mock. Picking up some beautifully smoothed flatstones I sent them skimming over the water, counting the bounces as they radiated their miniature circular waves out over the flat expanse of sea. Eleven was the most that night, three short of my record. Crossing a small stream by some stepping-stones, I came into the dark shadow of Llanstadwell Church. It stood heavily on the shore's edge, its short square tower outlining itself against the quiet sky. A little further on I left the beach and climbed up the shallow cliff and onto the road. I had reached my destination at last. There before me stood the dark silent house, awaiting my rousing knock. Legal cherry-knocking, I thought with a smile, but no need to run away tonight. I stood squarely in front of the door and gave three hefty bangs with the heavy brass knocker. The noise was so devastating that it made me wince, expecting the entire parish to be awakened. But nothing stirred. I steeled myself to rap again and once more the thunderous knocking rang out. Surely no-one could sleep through that noise, I thought, as the silence closed in again.

The slightest tap of the knuckles had been enough to waken Harry James, I remembered, and although the Chargeman had warned me that this particular driver was a heavy sleeper (along with the rest of Llanstadwell, I should think), this was becoming ridiculous!

I stood back from the doorway and peered up at the blankly curtained bedroom windows. Perhaps a few small stones at the appropriate window might do the trick. But which window? I stared undecidedly at the three windows, mentally eliminating the centre one as probably being on the landing. A sharp click broke the silence as the first pebble hit the glass of the window on the right. I waited for any sign of response. Nothing. Perhaps a handful of small gravel would have a better effect, I thought. Like hail, it sounded, as it hit the glass and for a second I feared that it might crack the window. Success! A faint glimmer of candlelight showed through the curtain, followed by the unmistakable sounds of someone making their way down the stairs. The door opened to a grating of bolts and clicking of locks.

'What the Hell do you think you're playing at?' growled an irate voice through the two-inch opening. 'Nearly broke the bloody window. Use the flaming knocker next time, that's what it's bloody well there for.' And the door slammed shut before I could say a word!

Miserable bugger, I thought. Freddie can come and have a go next time!

The sky was definitely lighter by the time I reached the station, and I recognised the figure of Freddie walking through the Hotel Gardens. 'Where have you been then?' I asked.

'Calling up at Railway Terrace,' he replied. 'It only took a few minutes.' There's no justice, I thought, as we made our way along the tracks and to the Shed.

The following evening, Freddie and I turned up for work at six o'clock, but this time, unlike the previous Sunday evening, we were a little envious of our mates who were just booking off. The novelty of night work had worn off pretty quickly!

'You two have got to meet the Cork tonight, mind,' warned Harry

Roach as we walked into the Shed. 'I did it for you last night, too soft I am. Don't forget, now, 12.30 sharp,' and back he went into his dark little office.

The 12.30 Passengers was still called the Cork, although the Irish steamers it used to link with had long since moved to Fishguard. The only craft still available for passengers was Bill Lloyd's small rowing-boat, which was moored to the pontoon, and which carried any travellers wishing to cross the estuary to Pembroke Dock. The regular large ferry-boat finished its service just after nine o'clock each night, and so anyone wishing to cross over later than this had to knock up Bill Lloyd at 24, Cambrian Road. And this was why Freddie and I had to meet the Cork every night.

Midnight found us idly loafing about the platform. We were rather early, but it was a good excuse for having a break and an experimental smoke. Freddie sported a packet of Goldflake and I had five Woodbines. We had decided beforehand that we would buy different brands so that we could compare flavours and consequently be able to talk with authority about which smokes we preferred. In actual fact I thought both cigarettes tasted horribly acrid and unpleasant, although I would not have dreamt of admitting it to Freddie.

We heard the Cork long before it reached the station, its pulsating beat coming out of the wooded valley at Westfield Mill and floating down the estuary to our ears. I was beginning to regret my smokes and the queasiness in my stomach, being self-inflicted, would evoke no sympathy, so I didn't bother to mention it to Freddie—who, I noticed with chagrin, appeared to be experiencing no ill-effects whatsoever. I made a mental note to smoke my next cigarette with far more caution, inhaling only once every few drags until I was used to it. The idea that I needn't necessarily inflict the unpleasantness on my lungs at all never occurred to me. Anyone who didn't smoke was considered to be a bit peculiar—a real odd character, and that wasn't going to be me, boy. I was one of the regular chaps and I was going to stay that way! So, while still suffering from my last cigarette I was planning how to tackle my next!

'Here she comes,' exclaimed Freddie, heaving himself off the wall and making his way to the edge of the platform. The night was suddenly filled with bustle and noise. Doors slammed, porters shouted, trolleys rumbled and the steam hissed, while passengers hurriedly made their way to the exit, leaving seven indecisive-looking soldiers standing on the platform. They were obviously going to be Bill Lloyd's customers, as the Barracks were at Pembroke Dock.

'You take them down to the pontoon, Fred,' I suggested, 'and I'll go and fetch old Lloydy,' I added, nipping off through the Hotel Gardens, leaving Freddie marshalling the sleep-blurred men with their heavily hoisted kitbags into a straggly line of which their sergeant-major would have been heartily ashamed.

Bill Lloyd was delighted to hear that there were seven fares to be taken across, as it made it worth while turning out. He wasn't too keen if there were only two or three, for, at twopence each, it was small recompense for getting out of bed on a cold night. Freddie and I watched him cast off with his cargo of soldiers, his oars rhythmically dipping into the dark water as he strongly pulled for the opposite shore. Luckily for him, with such a boat load, the tide was ebbing, carrying the little boat along towards Hobb's Point. The row back against the current would be a hard pull, but at least the boat would be empty.

Back at the Shed we seemed to be in a different world from the clean freshness of the waterfront we had just left. We came to look upon meeting the Cork as the highlight of our night shift, and even when there were no passengers for Bill Lloyd, we would take a stroll down to the pontoon for a few minutes of fresh sea breeze, before returning to the grit and dust-laden air of fire-dropping and smoke-box cleaning.

4

After having been earning for a few months, a shilling a week pocket money did not seem such a fortune, so one night, when on duty with Charlie Matthias, we both decided to line our own pockets from the fare-paying travellers to Pembroke Dock, instead of calling out Bill Lloyd. It was a blustery night and there were five passengers from the Cork, waiting to be ferried across. 'By the time you fetch old Bill,' whispered Charlie, 'we could ship this little lot across to Hobb's Point, one oar apiece, and back again, and still have plenty of time to get back to the Shed.'

'And we'd be tenpence better off,' I added unnecessarily. 'Just think what we could buy with fivepence extra each.' Numerous images flashed through my mind in the space of a second: five packets of Woodbines or Cinderella's or Ogden Guinea Golds, a large packet of ten Goldflake, five visits to the picture house at the top of Frederick Street, five sleevers of beer at The Lawrenny Castle or the Coffee House, numerous packets of vinegar-soaked chips from the travelling chip cart, the list seemed endless and the temptation all the greater.

Why not, I thought. I fancied myself as a fair rower and we should be able to manage Bill Lloyd's boat between us, with only five passengers aboard.

'Follow us, Gentlemen,' I announced and led our fares down to where Bill's boat was moored on the pontoon. We weren't sure when to ask for the fares, but we decided to trust them until we arrived at the other side. The crossing was quick although slightly choppy, but we were not certain how much the speed was due to our rowing and how much was due to the current! We were to find out.

I would hardly have reached Cambrian Road by now, I thought, as I steadied the bobbing boat against the sloping side of the landing jetty, for our passengers to alight. Warning them about the slippery state of the stones and pocketing their twopences, we headed back to Neyland. We knew the tide would be against us on the return journey, but just how strong the current would be we hadn't reckoned with. Before we were half-way over, my arms were aching with the effort of pulling the heavy oar against the tide and my back was slippery with sweat.

'*Uffern diawch!*' I gasped, echoing one of Pa's favourite Welsh expressions, 'We're going bloody sideways.' We leant on our oars and viewed the pontoon about five hundred yards away—to our rear! We were indeed drifting downstream, away from Neyland and towards Llandstadwell.

'Come on now, boy,' I said, a bit desperately I admit, 'we've got to pull like hell or we'll be out to sea!' Which was a slight exaggeration as the coast was a good few miles away, but nevertheless our position was becomingly increasingly worrying, as thoughts of not getting back to the Shed on time began to enter our heads.

We rowed like damned galley slaves that night, not saying a word, the only sounds the splashing of the oars, the gasping of our breath and the splatter of the rain, which had just started, just to make matters worse! Gradually the beach drew nearer, all hopes of landing on the pontoon had faded long ago, and we were more than grateful when the bottom of the boat grated on the gravel and seaweed about half a mile downstream.

We sat, hanging over the oars, exhausted, the rain running in rivulets down our faces. 'Five bloody pennies,' Charlie glowered at me, and I glowered back. 'All for five bloody pennies,' he went on. 'What the hell are we going to do now?'

'Blowed if I know,' I answered unhelpfully.

We both sat there, in the blustery rain, glumly discussing the alternative plans of action before us. Either we left Bill Lloyd's boat where it was and dashed back to the Shed, hoping that we hadn't been missed for the past hour, or we took extra time and tried to row it back to the pontoon, keeping close to the shore where we would have no adverse effect from the current, and arrive back at the Shed a good two hours late.

We both looked at our stinging hands. 'Leave the boat,' we decided together, and pulling it up above the high water mark and tucking the oars safely inside, we turned and ran for our lives back to the Shed. Managing to avoid anyone we saw, we nipped into the cabin, grabbed the call papers for the early shifts and disappeared into the night again.

We were cold, wet, miserable and tired, and past caring whether the drivers and firemen concerned were awakened too early for their turns, we just needed an alibi for having been out for so long and for getting so soaked through!

When challenged later by the chargeman about where the hell we'd been half the night, we explained that we had finished all the calls and that we were just about to start on the smoke boxes.

'There'll be ructions if you've called those men too early,' he warned, but that was all, and for the first time since we had marched those passengers down to the pontoon hours ago we both gave a sigh of relief and vowed we would never try to make a few extra pence again. A vow, I regret to say, we did not keep for very long!

The final outcome of our night's escapade was very satisfactory for us, however. The chargeman assumed that we had called out Bill Lloyd to take the passengers over to Pembroke Dock, Bill presumed that there were no passengers that night and that some school kids had been fooling about with his boat and abandoned it downstream, and as the two never came together everyone was happy!

The summer passed quite happily.

My system had become accustomed, by now, to irregular sleeping hours, and I found the work much less exhausting, both mentally and physically. I was well content with the pattern of night work, the Sunday call paper deliveries, the fire-dropping and smoke-box cleaning.

It was only when I cleaned out my first smoke-box that I realised the origin of those irritating ashes which used to find their way into my socks. Now they found their way into my eyes instead, and it was not long before I started to spray a hose on them first in order to minimise the dust and grit in the air. Cat-naps in the cabin, with the stove kept well stoked up so that our tea-cans stayed piping hot, and the dark, foot-echoing walks through the sleepy town for early calls; nipping off when we heard the chip-cart bell for 'a penn'oth of chips to grease your lips', breakfast at tea-time, dinner at midnight, sleeping through the day with kitchen and street sounds filtering through my dreams and weaving themselves into my fantasies, and meeting the Cork—they all blended well together, to give me pleasure at working nights.

One night, Charlie and I happened to glance inside the Drivers' Cabin, something we would not dare do in the daytime as it was almost like an exclusive club. The contrast to our Cleaners' Cabin really impressed us. The floor was swept instead of littered with cigarette ends, old newspapers and other unmentionable rubbish, the table was scrubbed clean, the wood pale and fresh instead of scarred, dog-end burnt and grimy, the chairs and benches were gleaming with polish instead of blackened with oil and coal dust and the walls were geo-metrically decorated with collections of cigarette cards instead of the vilest graffiti imaginable! And, most important of all, it was quite empty, so, from that night on, Charlie and I moved in. We tried to make sure that no-one actually saw us going in, although I am certain now that it was no secret, and we had our escape route well planned in the event of a driver turning up early. The crunching cinders gave us ample warning of an approaching rightful occupant, and before he could make his entrance at the door, we had made our exit through the window on the other side.

Although Charlie and I appreciated the care with which the drivers looked after their cabin, I'm afraid it gave us no incentive to clean up our own! It remained in its dirty, deplorable state for as long as I can remember, waiting to welcome each new box-boy into its grimy, sulphurous interior.

It was during one of our resting spells in the luxury of the drivers' cabin that Charlie and I decided that our pecuniary talents should be exercised once more. We admitted that we had not made a success of our first attempt at private enterprise, but the extra fivepence in our pockets had been very sweet, so we sat there, trying to think of another way in which we could make some money—preferably one in which our muscles would not let us down!

Suddenly, I thought of the old barge which lay, partly sunk, just off the old goods sidings, near the fish stage. At high tide the hold was flooded, but at low tide there was but one or two feet of water at the bottom. This made it an ideal place to store live lobsters, and one of the enterprising local fish dealers did just that. We knew that we could sell a couple of lobsters for a shilling if we were lucky, so all we had to do was to find a way of catching a couple in the old barge. After all, who was to say who they belonged to—they might have just swum in there of their own accord! Somehow, perhaps? Anyway, the possibility was enough to salve our consciences!

It would have been impossible during the day, but working practically on its doorstep throughout the darkest hours of the night, made it a very feasible idea.

'How are we going to pick them up, then?' asked Charlie, trying to iron out all the snags. We thought of thick gloves, but neither of us had any, so I suggested the idea of using a wire rabbit-gin.

'We'll lower it into the water, wait until a lobster is half-way through, then give it a quick pull.' It worked fine on rabbits so I couldn't see any reason why it shouldn't work equally well on lobsters!

The following night I turned up with a rabbit-gin in my pocket and a sack ready to hold our catch. We had our customer already picked out—the landlord of the Foresters' Arms, who, we thought, would be our best bet for a shilling a pair. We were both convinced that this was going to be our big breakthrough in money-making, and we decided to carry out our plan after we had met the Cork, when the tide would be at its lowest ebb.

A stiff breeze was coming in from the sea as we clambered over the old Goods sidings, down the green-slimed ex-sleepers, now used as a breakwater, across the floating bridge and onto the gently rotting barge. Doubled up to aid concealment we made our way to the hold hatchway. It had two draw bolts on it, but no padlock or key—the thought of two such as we had obviously never entered the fish dealer's head! I held a small flare lamp in my hand as Charlie started to draw back the bolts. They fitted badly in their sleeves, rusty and ill-aligned, but with careful rocking to and fro Charlie gradually worked them back. The hatch was heavy, but we managed to lift it fairly quietly between us. We let it down gently onto the sloping deck and peered down into the pitch black hold, listening intently. The unseen lobsters were rustling and threshing, scratching the sides of the barge with their claws. The inky water lapped hollowly beneath us and suddenly it didn't seem such a good idea after all!

'Come on, Morgy,' whispered Charlie, encouragingly. 'We can't give up now. I'll go down first if you come straight after.' We knew that there was a plank slung three or four feet below the hatch and another three or four feet below that. Charlie let his legs dangle into the blackness.

'I've got it, it's quite firm, bit slippery though,' he warned. 'Pass me the lamp.' I handed it down to him but its faint flicker didn't seem to make much impression on the darkness in the hold. I slung my legs over the edge of the damp, rotting timbers and followed my intrepid accomplice.

Immediately we were inside the hulk all the small sounds became magnified, echoing with hollow resonance around us. We sat on the top plank for a good few minutes, straining our eyes down into the rustling blackness below. Gradually it changed from an absolute, impenetrable black to a dark shadowy grey, as our eyes became accustomed to the dark. A few lighter patches appeared as we noticed small holes in the sides, and the outline of the lower plank became visible. We lowered ourselves carefully down onto it. The disturbed water was now but a foot or two beneath us, alive, we knew only too well, with large, angrily clawed lobsters. I was just wishing that there was a longer wire on my gin, so that I would not have to reach down too far towards the water, when, suddenly, there was a loud crash over our heads, the darkness intensified, and the realisation came to us that someone had slammed the door back on the hatch. We immediately heard the rasping sound of the two bolts being pulled over and the patter of feet running along the deck over our heads.

'We're trapped, boy,' I hoarsely whispered to Charlie, then suddenly realising that there was no longer any need for whispering as we had plainly been discovered, I yelled at the top of my voice at the unseen, unknown gaoler. Charlie joined in.

We threatened, we cajoled, we cursed, we pleaded, we tried every form of persuasion we knew, until it came to us that there was no-one listening!

Whoever had bolted us in had left us to our fate. Our immediate thought was of the incoming tide, the water in the hold steadily rising and the lobsters becoming uncomfortably close to our feet! The dank smell of the rotting timbers assailed our nostrils as we painfully slowly, and with the utmost care felt our way back onto the top plank. We could no longer see where the hatch was and I shuddered as my hands fumbled along the slimy planks feeling for the doorway above my head, the flare lamp virtually useless in lighting up our surroundings. The muffled, outside sounds of the shunting engines and clanking wagons mingled with the hollow slapping of the water beneath our feet and the imagined snapping of the lobsters' claws. I won't say we actually panicked, but we did not spend a very comfortable hour sitting damply on that top plank! Our apprehension would have been considerably less if we had known then just how long we were going to have to remain in our murky prison, but as far as we knew, we were fated to stay there the rest of the night, incoming tide, rising water, snapping claws, and all!

After approximately an hour, when we were just beginning to feel really sorry for ourselves, we heard the sound of the bolts being withdrawn. By the time we had scrambled carefully to our feet, slithering dangerously on the fine seaweed which coated every foothold, and lifted the heavy door from the hatch, we were only just in time to see a dark figure running over the tracks to the Shed.

We climbed out thankfully, Charlie looked at me and I looked at him. 'Who the bloody hell was that then?' we both asked each other. I stood up, breathing deeply on the cold, fresh air; after the intense gloom of below, the night sky appeared quite light. The Barrack Hill stood boldly silhouetted against it, the landing stage grew starkly out of the reflecting water, the tracks gleamed like silver ribbons and Charlie's face glistened in the starlight.

I saw everything in the split second of a glance before I bent down to close the hatch once more.

We decided to return as quietly and as unobtrusively as possible, hoping against hope that the Chargeman had not missed us since we had left to meet the Cork. Fate smiled on us and guided us back to the Cleaners' Cabin undetected. It's better to be born lucky than rich, I thought, when we realised that Harry Roach wasn't tearing his hair out looking for us. We sat puzzling our brains as to who had locked us in, but to this day I have no idea who so firmly closed the door on our second money-making scheme! Needless to say we never tried that idea again.

Unbelievable! A few weeks later, a legal way to make some extra money turned up for Charlie and me. The packers who unloaded the fish crates from the mackerel boats onto the railway wagons were short-handed, and the Chargeman told us to go and help out for a few hours during the night. We would be paid one penny for every four crates we loaded. Charlie and I were delighted at this sudden stroke of good fortune, and we lost no time in making ourselves known to the checker, who duly entered our names on his board. Every time we passed him with a crate he would put a mark against our name and at the end of the session they would be totted up and we would be paid accordingly.

We started off at a great rate, dragging and humping the heavy crates. Back and fore we went, mentally ticking up the strokes, dividing by four and counting up the pennies, until our dreams of riches were rudely shattered by a swarthy, fish-smelling packer, who told us, in no uncertain terms, that we were loading his wagon and that ours was a good fifty yards down the line. He didn't look the sort of man we could argue with, far too muscular and ill-tempered, so we walked meekly away. All the wagons seemed to belong to huge, burly fish packers, until we came to the fifth one. We took a quick look around and as there did not appear to be any aggressively-minded owner about, we started again, humping and dragging and clocking up our ticks, taking a little longer as we had further to carry the crates, but nevertheless not doing too badly, until 'What the hell are you two kids doing in my wagon?' and once more we were moved further and further down the line of trucks and further and further away from the fish stage and our penny-counting checker.

When we eventually came to the wagon which we were supposed to be loading we were almost out of sight of the unloading bay and our feeling of dismay was only surpassed by the angry frustration we felt because we were not yet men, and had to take whatever was meted out to us, without complaining. It was now taking us four or five times as long to make one penny, and a devil of a lot more hard work, extra sweat and splintered hands. We were both feeling fighting mad, but at least we had the sense to realise that there was nothing we could do about it—yet—but just give us a few more years and we'd soon see about that!

We made about a dozen long back-aching trips past the checker and then I rebelled.

'This is no use to us, Charlie,' I said. 'We've got to think of a plan

Three young blades of the town.
Bill Morgan is standing on the right, next to Teddy Morgan and Billie Davies.

Lower High Street, Neyland, during the First World War. The Institute, complete with flagpole, is on the left.

Upper High Street.

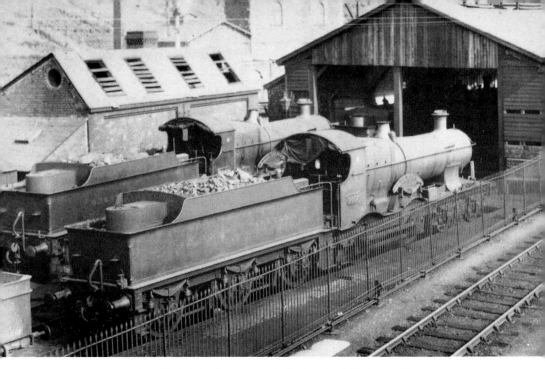

Two of the many faithful 'Bulldogs', photographed at Neyland Shed. 3307 Exmoor and 3448 Kingfisher, June 1926.

'Straight on for Paddington!'
The up-line out of Neyland in 1926 with Bill Morgan's house in Cambrian Road looking down on the Signal Box, the Old Iron Bridge and local coaches in the siding waiting to be 'gassed'—no refinements of electric lights for them!

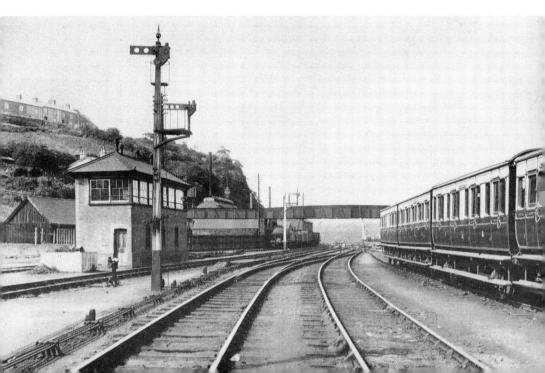

Win Crawley.

Bill Morgan.

Pa Crawley . . . 'That's no schooner, that's a two masted brig!'

of campaign.' We sat on the open-sided wagon, swinging our legs, feeling the sweat grow cold on our foreheads and our fingers begin to sting from the splintery wood of the crates. I stared up at the sky for inspiration. It was nearly dawn and the dark outline of the old Iron Bridge crossing over the railway attracted my attention. A scheme started to form in my mind. . . .

'Come on, Charlie,' I suddenly exclaimed, jumping off the wagon. 'Help me carry one of these fish crates over to the Bridge.' Charlie's puzzled look soon vanished as I unfolded my plan to him. We carried our crate to the bottom of the steps, where the brambles and furze grew abundantly above the high water mark. 'In here with it, boy,' I directed, pushing the fish-packed crate into the furze and bracken, its presence totally concealed by the undergrowth as the brambles closed over it.

'We'll come back for that one later,' I added with a conspiratorial wink, as we returned to our wagon. We continued fetching a few more crates from the unloading bay, looking with envy at the men whose wagons were conveniently placed at the near end of the line. We dragged ourselves back and forth with our heavy loads, until we both decided that we had had enough. When we came to collect our money from the checker, we found that we had carried fifty-six crates down to the wagon—each, and all we had for our back-breaking, skin-splintering work was one shilling and twopence.

'Just think how much we'd have earnt if our wagon had been a bit closer, Fred,' I pointed out. 'I reckon that crate of ours just about squares things up. What d'you say?' Fair's fair, after all!

Later that morning, after we had booked off, we came across the Iron Bridge, retrieved our crate of fish and proceeded to sell them from door to door around the town. The women were delighted at having fresh fish delivered to them at their door and we had no trouble in selling them; in fact, we only just managed to keep a few back for ourselves. Twenty-four shillings profit we made between us!

It was well past one o'clock before I fell into bed, exhausted, but richly content with the day's work. I had a brief four hours of deep, unconscious sleep, undisturbed by banging street doors, home-from-school children, yapping dogs, crying babies or any of the other numerous Cambrian Road noises. Mam's insistent shaking eventually awakened me a mere half an hour before my night shift started again.

I felt more tired than before I had gone to bed, my yawning became almost uncontrollable and the coming night's work stretched interminably before me.

Charlie and I failed completely to hear the approaching boots that night, as we dozed heavily in the drivers' cabin. Our carefully planned escape route lay unused and we were unceremoniously thrown out, with dire threats if we so much as put a foot inside the door ever again!

* * *

I had been cleaning for a little over a year and had been fortunate enough to spend a few of my shifts on spare firing around the yard. The railways were shorthanded at this time, of course, because of the number of men at the Front in France. On one such shift I found myself firing for Driver Bill Llewellyn, on a tankie carrying out pilot work around the sheds. We shunted those fish wagons and empty coal trucks endlessly, it seemed, but I appreciated being out of the gritty gloom of the Shed, and of course I was delighted to be on the footplate, even if it was only that of a small tankie. I was well prepared with my sawn-off shovel, having found on previous firings that the full-length handle was impossible to manipulate in the confined space of a tankie footplate.

It was a breezy summer afternoon and the tide had been ebbing for the last four hours, gradually exposing the green-slimed timbers beneath the fish stage. The scene at high tide, with the trees picturesquely dipping their branches into the water, had been replaced by a landscape of dirty-grey mudflats, black, mussel-coated rocks and a strong aroma of what was politely called 'ozone', but which always assailed my senses as the product of dead fish, rotting crab-shells, and dank seaweed, tinged, perhaps, with a hint of sewage!

There, stranded on the mudflats, was a hundred-and-forty-ton trawler. Bill Llewellyn and I had been observing, with great interest, the efforts of the crew to refloat her. They had missed the full tide and their efforts to use the ebbing tide had been unsuccessful. It was now nearly three o'clock and Bill and I were having a spell, sitting on the footplate in one of the sidings, when we noticed one of the crew of the stranded trawler clamber down over the side, watched attentively by seven or eight others who were leaning over the rail. He dinghied through the main stream, then waded through the expanse of clinging, sucking mud until he reached the barnacled slabs of concrete protecting the base of the fish stage. He disappeared from our interested gaze for a few moments until his head appeared above the seapinks and ragworts which edged the top of the incline which protected the railway from any waves.

Meanwhile, one of the crew aboard had begun waving a lasso round his head. Bill and I continued to watch in silence, completely engrossed by the activities going on before us. Suddenly, the rope came snaking through the air from the trawler, and was expertly caught by our intrepid mud-wader, who began hauling it ashore. Bill puffed thoughtfully at his pipe, shaking his head in silent condemnation of any plan the crew might have.

The other end of the rope was trailing a thick wire warp hawser, which, when it reached land, our friend looped round one of the bollards. He then curled up his rope and made his way back to the ship, where, we could see, he helped to man the winch in an attempt to winch themselves off the mud and into the channel flowing in the centre of the inlet.

The hawser took the strain.

'She moved!' I exclaimed, my eyes aching with concentration.

'Your imagination, boy,' puffed Bill. 'It'll take a deuced sight more power than that winch to shift her off that bank, I can tell you,' he went on.

We watched intently, the men strained, the hawser tautened, but not an inch did she move.

'Go and hail them, boy,' ordered Bill Llewellyn, giving me a push off the footplate. 'We'll give them a helping hand.'

I needed no second bidding. Shouting and gesticulating, I managed to convey the message to the dispirited crew, that we would endeavour to help them by giving them a tow. Great activity and excitement on board followed their understanding of our intentions. Our friend immediately shinned over the side once more and ferried himself over to the sidings, while the remainder of the crew slackened off the hawser and ran to the rail to watch the proceedings. I dashed back to the loco, opened the firebox door and threw a few shovelfuls in.

'Get her up round hundred and twenty,' Bill directed, speculatively tapping the pressure gauge. 'Blower, boy, blower,' he added impatiently, as I stood there indecisively.

Quickly I opened the damper and put the blower on for a few seconds. Gradually the pressure crept up. Bill jumped down from the footplate and went to supervise the coupling of the hawser to the rear of the loco. As we could not manage a direct pull, we still had to use the bollard as a fulcrum, and it took quite a few minutes before Bill was satisfied with the arrangements.

'Must leave a bit of slack, or we'll not move an inch,' explained Bill as he climbed back up, and I nodded, although why that should be, I had no idea!

'We'll give her full regulator in short bursts, boy,' he confided. 'That should do the trick.' I was hopping with excitement and, from what I could see, the crew were too. We signalled readiness and Bill set us off. The tankie strained and skidded, then miraculously the trawler shifted a fraction. Immediately a cheer went up from the men aboard and I felt as much satisfaction as if I had achieved it myself. Bill repeated the process, this time however without any further success, the tankie just skidded violently. Bill shut her down and took a pause, chewing his pipe from side to side and frowning like the devil.

'Right, boy, this time is it,' he prophesied, and grabbed hold of the regulator as if he were going into battle. We really jerked at that hawser this time, the wheels screamed beneath us as they skidded ineffectually, then, with a bone-jarring jolt the entire thirty-five tons of locomotive came off the lines. I was petrified with horror, Bill Llewellyn cursed resoundingly through his pipe and the poor old tankie hissed helplessly askew the track.

There was a stunned silence from the crew of the trawler as they realised what had happened, and our friend hastily unfastened the hawser from the rear of the loco and signalled his crew-mates to winch it aboard. After all you couldn't blame him for wanting to disclaim any knowledge of the incident! Getting rid of the evidence was obviously uppermost in his mind!

Meanwhile, I was visualising myself being booked for being involved in a derailment at the age of fifteen and a half. What a start to my career on the Great Western, I thought with dismay.

I realised, there and then, that this was either something I had to live down or live up to, and being me, Bill Morgan, I decided that I was going to live up to it!

'Fetch the breakdown gang, boy,' sighed Llewellyn resignedly, as he viewed the stricken tankie, 'and don't make too much damned fuss about it,' he warned. 'We don't want the whole bloody yard out here gloating.'

I nipped off to the shed, where Bill Osborne's Bulldog, the Bombay 3408, was ready prepped for him to take out the 4.30 passengers to Carmarthen. The fireman was carrying out the final checks when I hurried up to him and quietly explained the situation, asking if he would fetch the breakdown van for us.

'You did what?' he exclaimed in disbelief. 'This I must see,' he added with a gleam in his eye. He called a few shed labourers over to help out and proceeded to take the Bombay out of the shed to fetch the breakdown van. After a series of shunts in order to get onto the correct line, he arrived at our helpless tankie. Jacks were soon put under the framing and up she came, slowly but surely. I watched apprehensively. Carefully she was side-jacked onto the rails and, suddenly, there we were, as good as new! I could hardly believe it. It hadn't been nearly as disastrous as I had originally thought, and already I was looking forward to telling the tale to my mates—very dramatically, of course, with me at the centre of the action!

A few months after this incident, I experienced a night's work which almost succeeded in making me change my mind about my career on the railway. I came on duty that late autumn evening at six o'clock as usual, along with a new cleaner of only a few weeks' standing. We delivered a few call papers for a couple of unbooked turns for the following day, arriving back at the Shed about two hours later, ready for a warm in the cabin and a hot drink to dispel the damp cold which had managed to seep inside our heavy overcoats. After a short spell, I carried on with fire-dropping two locos which had just come in, while my young helper tackled the smoke boxes. It was a good hour's work and I was just on my way back to the cabin when the Chargeman called me over to his office.

The fireman for an extra coal train which was being run had failed to turn up for duty and there was no-one available at such short notice to replace him—except me. I could hardly believe my good fortune. I completely forgot that a few minutes earlier I had felt quite fatigued. The excitement of having the chance to fire on a main line was tremendous and it filled me with renewed energy.

'You'll be firing with Eskins,' Harry Roach informed me. 'He'll look after you, boy, don't worry,' he added. I felt a bit insulted at this last remark, as I was not in the least bit worried. 'Coal empties, pick up at Milford, then on to Tondu,' he informed me. 'Go and get your tea can and bait, and take it over to the Merlin, she's all ready prepped. There's nothing for you to do, driver's just giving her a few final checks.'

Although not yet sixteen, I felt considerably more experienced than the 'young' fourteen-year-old cleaner who watched enviously as I returned to the cabin for my tea can and food. I gave him a wink, told him not to do anything I wouldn't do and made my way over to the Merlin. She was an old 32 'Duke' class, number 3259, and a great favourite with the men at Neyland. I considered it a great honour to be able to fire her at this stage in my career—and on such a long run too. Tondu was way past Swansea, a good 95 miles away.

'First run on the main-line, is it, then?' queried old Eskins as I climbed up onto the footplate.

'I've done plenty of firing, don't you worry,' I replied quickly, as here seemed another who was doubting my ability to take on the job. 'Over a year, now, I've done spare firing round the yard,' I assured him.

'You'll do fine, boy,' he answered, giving me a reassuring pat on the back, which annoyed me. Confident, I was, up to the ears.

Bill Eskins had already completed most of the checking, so I picked up the long-handled shovel and stoked the fire up a little more, raising the steam to 70 lb, then gave the injectors a bit of a testing. Everything seemed to be all right as far as I could tell.

'How many detonators do we have there?' enquired Bill. I took a quick look in the box and noted that we had a full complement of twelve, and that the red flags, lamps, etc., were all neatly tucked into their compartments.

'Everything's in order, Boss,' I replied cheerfully. There was only one fleeting moment of misgiving and that was when I stood and looked at the tender for a second. There seemed a hell of a lot of coal there— nearly ten ton I estimated—a bit different from the few ton we carried on the tankie.

We eventually steamed out of Neyland Shed just after ten o'clock with just a few empty coal wagons behind us. We were in Milford in under thirty minutes, where we picked up considerably more, making a load of approximately sixty wagons.

We were really on our way now. I built up a steady rhythm of firing, keeping a wary eye on the pressure gauge—no-one was going to be able to say that I couldn't keep up a good head of steam. I could sense that old Bill was keeping an eye on me and I was determined not to slack off, but the damned fire-box seemed to eat up the coal twice as fast as when we were shunting in Neyland Yard, and its interior seemed to be twice as cavernous. Dig into the tender, throw into the fire-box, dig, throw, dig, throw. I tried to remember all I had read about correct placing of coal, but the niceties of firing became unimportant as all my thoughts and energies centred on feeding that insatiable, glowing mouth. Occasionally I found myself off balance, as the swaying of the loco and the play at the junction of the tender footplate and that of the loco was considerable, at speed, making me very wary of the open side of the cab which sometimes seemed ominously close.

We had travelled about thirty miles and I was trying hard not to break my rhythm, but the blasted coal in the tender was getting further away and I was having to take an extra step in order to reach it.

'Have a spell, Bill, boy,' Eskins advised. 'You don't want to make the fire too black, now—let it burn through a bit.'

Gratefully I leant back on the cab side, breathing deeply through my mouth. I had had no time to notice anything outside my world of alternating tender and fire-box, but now I stood watching the dark countryside flashing by. Very few houses showed a light, cattle stood motionless in the gloom and an autumn mist was starting to fill the hollows as we clattered and rattled our way through the night. A cold trickle of sweat started to run down the side of my face and I suddenly felt chilled, where only a few minutes before I had been glowing with the heat of exertion. The cold air outside whistled past, was caught, and eddied around the cab creating unpleasant draughts which seemed all the colder in comparison to the heat of the fire-box.

I started to fire again, the shovel appearing heavier than when I had last used it a few minutes earlier and the coal more awkward to reach. Bill Eskins didn't talk much, he kept a look-out practically the entire time, occasionally glancing at me and checking the gauges. St. Clears and Sarnau went fleetingly past the corner of my eye and I was conscious of him talking to himself, making mental notes on signals. It was getting towards midnight, my back ached, my arms felt too heavy to move, apart from lift shovelfuls of coal, my legs were beginning to tremble from exhaustion, and still that cavernous mouth needed feeding with more and more coal. 'Have a breather,' I heard Bill say and I handed the shovel to his outstretched hand without a word. He fired steadily for a quarter of an hour, the bed had become thin, and it took him all his time and skill to build it up again without losing too much steam. Between firing he kept a look-out and told me to do the same, but my eyes were staring glassily at the approaching signals without comprehension, my mind was numb and it took all my concentration to keep my knees locked to prevent sinking to the footplate. We had covered nearly fifty miles and I had fed that monster dragging its sixty wagons for nearly two hours. The earlier stop at Whitland for water had barely been long enough for me to get my breath back; this had been followed, almost immediately, by a tunnel which had left me gasping and choking from the swirling coal dust and sulphur fumes. Bill had assured me that it had been only a short tunnel, but as I had stood there with my streaming eyes full of grit, I had dreaded to think what a long one would be like.

I had been dismayed to notice that, in spite of all my energies, we had rarely reached a speed of more than thirty-five miles an hour, and on occasions, on some of the banks, we had even dropped to twenty. Bill Eskins reassured me, however, that we had a heavy load behind us and that we were on schedule, but it was small comfort, when I had visualised myself hurtling through the night at eighty miles an hour, with my expert firing being watched by an admiring driver!

The pads on the palms of my hands were stinging with the tightness of promised blisters, my whole body was damp and clammy, and I knew, with despair, that we had reached only as far as Carmarthen Junction and that there were roughly sixty more miles of gruelling punishment before me.

With our water tank once more refilled, Bill took us out of Carmarthen uttering phrases of encouragement. 'You've done well, lad . . . I'll take her for a stretch when we're on our way . . . we've all felt clapped out on first firings . . . have a spell, boy, you've deserved it . . . you've done better than most . . .' He alternately fired and boosted my morale as I gradually recovered my physical courage. With renewed heart, I rubbed my hands on the paraffin waste in my pocket, and thanking Bill for helping out, I took the shovel from his grasp and resumed my duties as fireman. A good five tons of coal had been consumed since we had left Neyland, and the first thing which struck me when I restarted firing was the amazing amount of coal which had disappeared from the tender during the time when Bill Eskins had been firing. We had been double shovelling for the last few tons, as the coal had receded as it was used up, and now only the back half of the tender remained full.

I climbed into the tender and started to shovel the coal forward. Eight, nine, ten, eleven, I set myself a mental target of thirty shovelfuls before I would take a breather. Twenty-six, twenty-seven, each one took an effort of will as I forced my muscles to complete my set target, thirty, at last, and one extra just to prove I could. I leant on the shovel handle, grit and dust blew in my face as I closed my eyes and swayed with the motion of the tender, feeling the cold air pierce the weave of my overalls. I savoured it for a few moments until it changed from a cooling pleasure to a shivering clamminess once again.

The glowing heat from the fire-box hit me as I climbed back onto the footplate. Bill turned his head as I reappeared and gave me a conspiratorial wink. I felt as if we were in battle together—it was us against the fire-box and steam pressure. Llandeilo Junction was about five miles away and I worked like a slave again, reshovelling the same damned coal I had shifted only a few minutes before. I attacked it like an enemy. My new surge of enthusiasm and energy, however, was soon spent, and as we drew into Llanelly for water and examination of the train, I felt that another mile would kill me. Yet I knew with heart-sickening despair that Tondu was another thirty-five miles of uphill firing ahead of us.

It was half-past one in the morning and it was not only the firing which had contributed to a sense of exhaustion, I was just plain tired. I had been up since three o'clock the previous afternoon, when I had taken a walk down to the pontoon to watch the fishermen, returning up the hill for tea at about five. I had signed on for duty at six, walked roughly three miles delivering call papers and fire-dropped two locos, all before firing the Merlin all the way, well, nearly all the way, to Llanelly! Suddenly, I decided that I would not shovel another lump of coal, even for the King himself. I reckoned I had done enough work for one night!

With a nerve in my leg twitching uncontrollably, I sat having my bait at Llanelly, listening to Bill congratulating me on how well I had

E   65

managed. Suddenly I announced my intention of going no further. He looked at me in disbelief, his sandwich halted half-way to his mouth.

'You can't do that, Bill boy, why no now, you can't do that,' he exclaimed with a stunned look on his face. 'I'll help you out, don't you worry yourself. We'll manage to finish the run between us. Mind you, now, there's a fair bit of uphill work, but we'll manage, you'll see.'

I shook my head, nothing and nobody was going to make me change my mind. I was going no further. There's a state poor old Eskins was in now, when he realised how adamant I was. He dashed over to 'phone Control at Swansea to explain the situation, and I think he must have impressed upon them my lack of years, because they finally agreed that I could be allowed to remain at Llanelly. However, I still had to work! A Llandeilo man who had been pilot firing there was to exchange shifts with me. He would fire with Bill Eskins to Tondu and I was to finish his turn of firing at six o'clock in the morning.

'I was told to caution you, Bill, that this must never happen again, and that it was highly irregular to exchange shifts,' warned Bill Eskins as I climbed down from the footplate to make my way to the sheds. I thanked him for all he had done for me, bid him cheerio and made my way along the line.

Half-way to the sheds my heart sank as I thought of starting firing again on a strange loco with an unknown driver, and I decided there and then that I had done enough work of any kind for one night and I was damned if I was going to do any more. I about-faced, walked back along the tracks and defiantly strode onto the down platform, where, by absolute, wonderful chance, stood the Mails from Paddington to Neyland. I opened the door of an empty third-class compartment, sank into a corner seat and drifted into the blissful oblivion of utter exhaustion as the train pulled out and carried me back, through the coming dawn. I awoke only when the guard's voice, mingling with my dreams, brought me back to consciousness at seven o'clock on Neyland Station.

With sleep-blurred eyes, I made my way up the hill, still in a state of dazed weariness. Mam commented that I was a bit late coming home and I told her briefly that I had been firing to Llanelly, but I was too tired to appreciate how impressed she appeared to be. After a quick swill I fell into bed and went straight back to sleep.

But I had unwittingly forgotten to book off at Neyland Shed and ten o'clock found the Chargeman hammering on our door in great consternation. As far as the Company was concerned I had simply disappeared at Llanelly! Fears of my lying dead on the track had been running through his mind; either that, or I had run away to sea!

Consequently, instead of praise for my first long distance firing, I had a telling off from Mam for being so thoughtless, a reprimand from the Chargeman for not reporting for duty at Llanelly shed, and a stern warning that it had better not happen again!

Then the unbelievable happened. I was sitting in the cleaners' cabin two nights later, after having just delivered the call papers, when in came Harry Roach the Chargeman to inform me that the same fireman had failed to report for duty again! I stared at him in dismay, my stomach dropped, surely he wasn't going to ask me to fire that damned train and its cursed wagons to Tondu again?

But he did just that.

I dug my heels in and blankly refused, with all the determination that a fifteen-year-old could muster. The Chargeman stared at me in silence, turned on his heel and left. Within half an hour he was firing the Merlin to Tondu with Bill Eskins, and I was left in charge of Neyland Shed!

5

The news spread through Neyland like wildfire. Someone had seen the letter lying on the foreman's desk—the entire crew of a German submarine, which had been captured off the Heads, was being transported through Neyland that very morning and was going to be put on the 10.45 Passengers to Paddington. In no time at all the entire yard knew about it, and one of the men surreptitiously slipped off to share this interesting titbit of information with everyone he could see on his way up The Hill through Neyland.

By ten o'clock the station yard and platform were packed with gossiping, inquisitive, excited folk, necks craning to catch the first glimpse of an actual German. Of course, all the cleaners, including myself, were amongst them, and an almost festive air reigned over this unusual diversion. More curiosity than animosity showed in people's faces as they awaited the arrival of The Enemy.

A murmur went through the crowd as two covered lorries drove into the yard. Armed soldiers jumped down from the rear, followed, more slowly, by a group of grey-faced seamen, mostly dressed in high-necked, coarse-knit jerseys, grey trousers and plimsolls. Their officers wore naval uniform which I viewed with great interest. My eyes travelled up over the gold braided jacket and the insignia on the shoulder, until I found myself staring into the steady grey eyes of the owner.

Immediately I felt a hot blush stain my face, and I recalled the

68

embarrassed feeling I had experienced on entering the Penny Peep Show at Pembroke Fair, in order to see the Fattest Lady in The World. I had walked round her with my eyes fixed firmly on the ground of that stuffy little tent, finding that I could not stare at her as if she were a mere object. I now sensed the same indignity about my German officer. I quickly looked away from those calm grey eyes, making some stupid remark to Freddie, who stood near me, about how I had always thought all Germans were blond.

They were supposed to be our enemies, but they resembled our own Trinity men too much for my peace of mind.

Suddenly, the attention of the crowd was caught by the sound of raised voices coming from the platform. The driver of the 10.45 Passengers was not so kindly disposed to the prisoners, it appeared. I recognised the voice of John Thomas, shouting bitterly that he drove a fine engine, that he had fine, regular passengers which he carried in fine compartments and that he wasn't going to have it all despoiled by having to take German prisoners on his fine train.

He raged up and down the platform, finally retreating to his cab, muttering and fuming under his breath, but he took the St. Anthony 3303, looking her best, out of Neyland Station, on time, with the German officers in one of the First Class compartments, and the remainder of the crew in three of the Third Class compartments, accompanied by their armed guards. I often wondered if my German officer ever returned to his homeland and whether he had understood what the driver had been shouting on Neyland Station that morning, for even if he could understand English, I doubt if he could have unravelled any meaning from Thomas the Cot's Carmarthen-Welsh accent. Perhaps it was just as well. But at least we had allowed him the privilege of riding behind the St. Anthony, and beautiful she had looked too.

Freddie Griffiths often found himself on special night duty whenever the Anthony had to be cleaned ready for the morning Mails. John Thomas insisted that only Freddie could be entrusted with his 3303 and it took him all night to clean that loco on his own, but, of course, Freddie regarded it as a privilege and discounted all the hard work involved.

I discovered that at sixteen and a half I could cope with firing ten ton of coal without any assistance from the driver. Any request for emergency main line firing I now accepted with great enthusiasm. It's amazing the difference twelve months can make to a boy's muscles!

Like Freddie, I, too, was sometimes chosen to give a Bulldog a special night clean. It was Osborne's Bombay 3408 I was working on that night when Alec the call-boy came rushing into the Shed, face white, eyes widely staring, gasping about ghosts and stammering that he was never going to go calling in the middle of the night again. The Chargeman tried to calm him down a bit as we endeavoured to find out what was the matter, and we eventually gathered from his garbled account that he had been walking up the Hill on his way to Frederick Street, when a white, swirling figure had appeared at the corner of Lawrenny Street and had 'floated' across the road. Alec had been transfixed with fright, but when the apparition had seemed to disappear he had tried to gather his wits about him and continue on his way, telling himself that it was just his imagination.

He never reached Frederick Street, however, because as he had drawn near to Lawrenny Street, he saw, to his horror, that the ghostly figure had not, in fact, disappeared, but was hovering and weaving its way along the road. This had been too much for Alec and he had immediately about turned and had run down the Hill as fast as his legs could carry him, back to the safety of The Shed.

The men tried to reason with him that there was no such thing as ghosts and that it must have been washing blown off a line, smoke swirling from a chimney, or cloud shadows blowing across the moon, but there was not a breath of wind, just the clear, cold sky, icy-bright with stars.

Damn me, we had no sooner managed to calm down poor Alec when in ran the second call-boy, who had been out calling at Llanstadwell. In he rushed, looking half-frightened out of his wits and shouting about a ghost hovering by the Hotel Gardens.

I can tell you, there's a commotion there was! We were all thoroughly perplexed, as it was obviously not a put-up joke by the two lads, because of the state they were in. But what other explanation there could be, we just did not know.

One thing was certain. Alec was not going to venture up Neyland Hill again that night, not for anyone. He was still swallowing hard and looking over his shoulder even in the reassuring company of The Shed.

'Leave your call to me, boy,' volunteered one of the firemen just come off duty. 'I'm just on my way home now, and I'll give the tap for you.' We didn't believe that it was a ghost which the boys had seen, but nevertheless we were all very mystified by the strangeness of it all, and we three cleaners talked of nothing else for the rest of the night.

The following morning, the body of Mrs. Peters, wearing her long white nightgown, was found drowned at Hazel Beach at Llanstadwell. Poor soul.

* * *

Then came the date on which my life, along with the lives of all other Great Western Railway employees, was considerably altered. The eight-hour day arrived.

The two twelve-hour shifts had to be replaced with three eight-hour shifts and we found ourselves working a forty-eight-hour week instead of seventy-two. It had been anticipated for some time but its realisation seemed too good to be true. We had leisure time which we hadn't experienced since leaving school and part of every day took on the flavour of a holiday. The early morning shift of 6 a.m. until 2 p.m. seemed so short that we joked that it was hardly worth going in for! The afternoon shift of 2 p.m. until 10 p.m. seemed like a half-day with an extra bonus of lying in bed until whatever time we chose, and the night shift of 10 p.m. until 6 the following morning seemed so short that no sooner had we booked on than dawn was almost breaking—or so it seemed to us in contrast to our twelve-hour shift. No longer were the streets of Neyland empty of men during the day. Hitherto, only Granfers and children populated the town with the women, the men either at work or asleep, but now, young and middle-aged men mingled with the shoppers and gossipers, standing in groups still slightly dazed with all the leisure time they had suddenly acquired.

Allotments flourished, cricket teams practised, quoits were thrown for endless hours, farmers were besieged with requests for shooting rights in exchange for offers of help with haymaking, harvesting, or potato picking. The pubs prospered, the clubs thrived and the fish in the river rarely had a minute free from some angler's line. More babies were conceived, more blackberries picked, more roses pruned, more gardens dug. Whist drives, socials and dances were better attended than ever before and children were surprised to find that their fathers had more time for them.

There was more time for spending, more time for courting, more time for journeying, more time for wearing clothes other than overalls and more time just to stand and stare.

Some wives complained about having their men under their feet half the day, some immediately found dozens of jobs around the house which suddenly needed attention and some wives just thought it was wonderful. 'There's lovely it is,' said a beaming Mrs. James.

For me, it meant that, for hours, I could wander through the woods shooting for game. I had graduated from an air-gun for potting at crows to a shot-gun for rabbits, pigeons and the occasional pheasant. Rabbit-gins were often successful in providing a good meal for the family but they could not rival the kick of a shot-gun against your shoulder as you fired at a moving target of fur or feathers. Freddie's cousin was a local farmer and consequently we had free access to his land at any time. Now, at last, we had the time to take advantage of it. Cartridges were cheap and the rabbits healthy and plentiful. No shadow of myxomatosis marred the hunter's horizon, the world was ours, with an open field before us, a gun tucked under our arms and a dog at our heels. What more could we ask?

Shooting, fishing, courting and quoits, I suddenly found ample time for them all, although not necessarily in that order! Fortune was certainly smiling on us and we received her bounty with open arms. It was good to be alive.

* * *

Promotion had been very erratic for the past few years and its incon-sistencies had created unrest among the men. The Great War and the introduction of the eight-hour shift had caused a severe manpower shortage in the railways and, at first, young cleaners had been allowed to pass for firemen after having worked for only two and a half years. However, when it had come for my age group to benefit from this fast route to promotion the war had ended and the servicemen returned from the forces to their work on the railways. There was now no need to recruit young cleaners as firemen. A new ruling was issued that no cleaner could put in for fireman until he had reached the age of eighteen. This meant an extra two years' cleaning for Freddie, me and others like us, and this was a great disappointment as we had been hoping to be firemen before we were seventeen. But there was nothing we could do about it.

Firemen gained rapid promotion to drivers as the demand increased with the return to peace-time working, but we cleaners, once again, could not take advantage of the chance of fast promotion, as the ruling regarding eighteen as the qualifying age still stood. The only way the railways could surmount this problem of replacing firemen was to employ newly-recruited cleaners from the continuing stream of returning soldiers. These cleaners were older than us, of course, and were promoted to firemen after a very short time, some as early as three months. We could not help feeling antagonistic towards them, yet we knew, in our hearts, that only a year or two before they had been risking their lives for us. We watched them take a prized place on a footplate as qualified firemen after a few months in the shed, knowing that we had more knowledge of steam engines in our little fingers than they could possibly have acquired. We became bitter. We feared saturation point, which would keep us as cleaners, waiting for vacancies and on low pay, into our twenties.

We all awaited our eighteenth birthday with a wary eye on the fireman vacancy list.

During my last year as a cleaner, never a week seemed to go by without some fracas involving inexperienced firemen. In fact, I think the drivers tried to rival each other about the incompetence of their particular footplate partner.

'Solid with clinker she was, man, not a breath of air could get through . . .'

'Prepare an engine? He wouldn't know how to prepare a duck for a thunderstorm . . .'

'. . . opened the front damper at 50 miles an hour, man, the blast could have killed him . . .'

'. . . damn me, he nearly slid off the footplate twice before we'd reached Johnston!'

'. . . smokescreen wasn't the word for it, mind you, the fire-box was like the hole of Calcutta . . .'

'I applied the brake and all the damn tools shot off the rack . . .'

'. . . not a scrap of an idea as to how to change a gauge glass, not a scrap, indeed . . .'

John Thomas even went so far as to parade up and down Carmarthen platform, apologising to his passengers for any irregularities in their usual smoothly-run journey, 'Look what they have given me, gentlemen—a Navy man for a fireman. The Anthony and I have done our best for you, gentlemen, but a Navy man . . .' and he threw his hands in the air as words failed him.

Of course, it was not only the new firemen who were inexperienced, there was a fair sprinkling of newly-appointed drivers who had rocketed up the promotion ladder after the war, after very little time firing on the footplate. But as the months went by experience was gained and soon the railways were manned with confident crews.

* * *

May 10th, 1920 dawned dull and uninspiring. Nevertheless I was up and dressed before six, feeling a stranger to myself in my best flannels and stiff-collared shirt, instead of my usual blue overalls. The previous evening had been spent reading up the rules and regulations, in preparation for the great day when I was to take my test for promotion to fireman. Feeling quite confident, if a little nervous, I made my way to the station to catch the eight o'clock Passengers to Swindon.

I slammed the carriage door shut, placed my trilby and my packed dinner on the rack, pulled the leather to drop the window and leisurely surveyed the platform scene as I leant out. The good-luck wishes of the family still rang in my ears as the guard's whistle blew and we were away. Gaining speed as we pulled away from the platform, I spied them, the gang of waving, whistling cleaners, standing outside the Shed derisively cheering me on my way. I gave them a fist shake in reply and watched them grow smaller and more insignificant as we steamed away, even The Shed seemed to lose its air of importance.

Neyland was the Shed's third siting. Previously it had stood at Chepstow and at Haverfordwest. Its wooden structure, resting on its four-foot-high, stone base walls, was thick with the layered years of creosote and tar, and I recalled as the eight o'clock Passengers carried me away, how I had almost set the entire place alight through placing a burning flare lamp on top of the four-foot stone wall! I had soon learnt that all flare lamps had to be placed on the floor or well away from the highly-inflammable wooden walls. It was a constant miracle that it never actually did burn down!

Under the old Iron Bridge now, past Billie Darkie sitting huddled in his little rowing boat, waiting for a few early shoppers and school children to ferry across from Barnlake. Round the bend, through the cutting and Neyland finally disappeared. The day was still dull, and the cool damp air rushed against my face, as swaying gently with the motion of the train, I watched the scenery glide past.

Over Westfield Mill ford, no-one waiting to cross the line, only Tommy Harrison, the crossing keeper, leaning over the gate, his hand slightly raised in acknowledgement as we swept by. I caught a glimpse of a double-barrelled shot-gun propped up against the corner of the gate. No doubt he would be rabbiting up the line before we reached Johnston.

Technically, it was Harrison's wife who attended the crossing, from their solitary little cottage sited in the wooded valley down by the ford. The occasional cart meant that the gates were opened once or twice a week. But often days went by without a soul coming near the isolated little place, so Mrs. Harrison had plenty of time for her roses and chickens and baking.

There were three small crossings along that stretch of single line from Neyland—Westfield Mill, Upper Rosemarket and Lower Rosemarket, and it was amazing just how many large lumps of coal managed to slip off the tenders of passing locos, landing just in their back gardens!

Tommy Harrison worked as a shed labourer and coalman in Neyland Yard, and was renowned for his philosophical sayings which he uttered in the broadest Pembrokeshire dialect which can only be heard to be believed.

'How b'ist th'?' was his invariable greeting, and each new cleaner was eventually cornered by his wagging finger and indoctrinated by Tommy's maxim, 'Hard work never kilt nobody, boy, only medd'em goa deaf—an' bai Gaw', boy, ai'm a-goin' deaf!'

He always scorned an overcoat, no matter how inclement the weather, and when the pelting rain blew in from the Atlantic, Tommy Harrison could be seen walking down the line to the Shed, wearing his three clean flour sacks, judiciously tied around him according to which way the driving rain was blowing. One tied around his hips, one around his chest and the third, with one corner pushed in, was placed on his head and draped over his shoulders. He garbed himself in the same fashion whilst shovelling coal on the coal stage, and a more effective outfit against the Pembrokeshire weather I have yet to see!

He prided himself on his never catching cold, but that might have been due to his wearing a piece of tarred rope around his neck throughout each winter, and the fact that he never had even a touch of rheumatism was no doubt due to the potato which he always carried in his pocket!

Old Harrison claimed that he was the last man in the county to partake of 'bundling'. This was the old custom of an engaged couple spending the night together in the same double bed, separated either by a large bolster, or by each participant being enclosed in an empty bolster case!

'And a mighty-fain boolster it was, boy!' he often reminisced with a sparkle in his eye. Personally, I think it's a shame the custom ever died out! As Tommy was later often heard to maintain, 'The man who invented them there wireless sets was a clever man, but the man who invented a bed beat'n holler!'

Wooded Westfield Mill disappeared behind us and we steamed on our way up the bank to Johnston. I had the compartment to myself until Haverfordwest, when two elderly ladies (who, on reflection, must have been at least thirty-five), climbed in and settled themselves into the opposite corners of the compartment, with a great deal of skirt arranging, hair patting and brushing off of real or imaginary smuts from lapels. They proceeded to ignore me, except for a disdainful sniff when I started to roll a cigarette, having graduated from 'tailor-mades' more than a year before. The silence suited me quite well, however, as my mind was full of a medley of facts. Hand signals, fixed signals, procedure for coupling and uncoupling, working of trains and protection of trains, water gauges and steam chests, injectors and clacks, valves and pistons, fusible plugs and cranks—they all circled through my mind in time with the rhythm of the wheels beneath us.

Clarbeston Road, Clynderwyn, Whitland, St. Clears, Sarnau, Carmarthen, Llanelly; we bustled at each station and then on our way again until we drew into Swansea. My two travelling companions left without speaking a word and without sparing me a single glance, for a moment I had an absurd feeling that perhaps I was invisible! This fear was quickly dispelled by a vociferous Welsh-speaking family, carrying large wicker baskets covered with white cloths, who invaded my domain with smiles and apologies. They were very friendly, but I could understand only the occasional word as they incessantly lilted to each other. Neyland and its environs was English-speaking, for South Pembrokeshire was well named 'Little England Beyond Wales'. We were proud of being Welsh but shied away from being too 'Welshy', we left that to those who lived in the valleys.

The crew was changed, a new engine coupled to the rear of the train and we were ready to steam out of Swansea cul-de-sac. Neath, Cardiff, Newport, through the Severn Tunnel and on we raced to Swindon. I ate my packed meal with relish, sinking my teeth into the home-made, spicy bread pudding, its close texture deliciously moist with fat, juicy sultanas. I wondered, as I sat munching, whether Win would turn out to be as good a cook as Mam. Win Crawley and I had been courting for a few years now—off and on, that is. She was good fun and had a zest for living . . . but I did just wonder whether she would be able to cook. I liked my food and I would have to give the matter serious consideration!

We pulled into Swindon station on time.

Twenty-four of us sat awaiting our turn in the hall of The Manor House the following day, having spent the previous night at the G.W.R. Hostel. Each one of us was an aspiring express driver.

First came the medical. I entered a small room where an insignificant little clerk stood operating a lamp at the far end, his hands clutching a selection of coloured filters. These he placed in front of the lamp, requesting me to state each colour in turn. Everything went smoothly until we reached the last filter.

'Puce,' I stated in a loud, clear voice.

'I beg your pardon?' queried the little man.

'Puce,' I repeated, a little more loudly. There was a short pause, then, taking a quick glance round at the front of his lamp, the little chap stammered.

'I'm afraid that isn't quite right, Mr. . . . um . . . Morgan.'

'That colour is puce,' I reiterated more firmly.

'I'm afraid we don't have . . . er . . . puce . . . Mr. Morgan, would you like to try again?' he offered helpfully. 'I'm afraid I've never heard of that shade before.'

The little man seemed to be afraid of everything, I thought. Fancy not ever having heard of puce, a lovely rich purple it was. 'Call it purple, if you like then,' I suggested with a shrug of my shoulders. The perturbed look left his face and he beamed at me with relief. I think I had made his day!

We then proceeded to the eyesight chart, and I knew that it would present no problems as my long sight was extremely good. I could quite clearly read the names of the boats moored in the Dockyard on the other side of the Cleddau at Pembroke Dock, so a few letters on a chart just the other end of a room was child's play.

A few minutes later I was back with the other waiting cleaners in the Hall. We sat there, chatting amongst ourselves, all boasting that this was just a formality as we had all, it appeared, been spare-firing expresses for years! No-one believed anyone's stories of the various firing feats, but we pretended we did, and I must admit, we all sounded damned convincing! Names were called, and one by one they disappeared into my puce-less little clerk's office.

I suddenly realised that my name was being called from the other side of the hall, by an extremely officious-looking person in a white coat. I hurriedly clipped my cigarette, slipped it into my waistcoat pocket and walked over to the doorway in which he was standing waiting impatiently.

The room I entered was entirely different from the insignificant eye-testing room I had been in previously. It was large and lofty, the clinical whiteness fighting with the rich, polished mahogany red for dominance. The whiteness won as far as I was concerned and I felt as if I were in a doctor's surgery which immediately put me ill at ease as only a panel patient could be.

My weight was recorded, my height measured. Heart, lungs and blood pressure were listened to, echo-tapped and pumped up. I was scrutinised for flat feet, varicose veins, overlapping toes and any other abnormality of my nether regions. Legs and feet had been the downfall of many a promotion aspirant, but fortunately mine didn't let me down, and when it was confirmed that there was no tuberculosis in the family, no history of 'blackouts', and that I didn't wear glasses, the examination ended. My examiner had been a man of extremely few words and had managed to retain his superior air of refinement, even when viewing my feet at close quarters. I must give credit where credit is due!

Sitting in the hall once more, I relit my clipped cigarette and waited for the final call. This would be to face the examiner on Railway Procedure, who turned out to be a tall, spindly gentleman, impeccably dressed, with a heavy gold watch chain glinting from beneath his black jacket. I followed him into his domain, impressive with glowing mahogany, where he motioned me to sit at the long table in the centre.

'Mr. William John Morgan from Neyland,' he stated in a flat tone as he took his place opposite me. 'Now, Mr. Morgan, tell me what you know of Hand Signals.' He leant back in his chair, stared at the ceiling and waited.

I was on home ground now and quickly rattled off descriptions of signals for caution, danger, move away, move toward, create vacuum, etc., all the while waving my arms about in a rather flamboyant fashion in my efforts to give an exact description of each Hand Signal. I suddenly realised that my demonstrations of the signals were useless as the examiner wasn't looking at me anyway, the ceiling still having some strange fascination for him, so I forcibly kept my hands still and endeavoured to continue with the remainder of the signals in a verbal manner only. Hell, it was difficult, like trying to describe a spiral staircase without using your hands!

I was interrupted before reaching the end of my list, however, and I was extremely relieved.

'Tell me, Mr. Morgan, what do you understand by Fixed Signals bearing the letters C, W or S?'

Aha! I thought, I'm not going to be caught out with that one. Every cleaner at Neyland Shed was told the tale how one unfortunate lad had failed for Fireman because he had thought that the W stood for Wait and the S for Stop.

Confidently, I spoke up, 'C is Calling on, W is Warning, and S is Shunt ahead.'

There was a long pause. The gold-watched gentleman cleared his throat. 'Of course, you know all about protection of trains, Mr. Morgan?' I agreed vehemently that I did. 'And working of trains?' he added. Once more I emphatically agreed that I did.

'Yes, of course,' he sighed. 'Yes, of course you do.' Another long pause. 'I can take it that you are familiar with coupling and un-coupling?' he queried with a raised eyebrow. I assured him that he could take it. He took a deep breath, rose from the table, thanked me for attending the examination and asked me to be so kind as to wait in the hall.

I felt rather disappointed that I had not been asked any other questions; it seemed rather ridiculous just to take my word that I knew all about protection of trains, etc. I would have taken great delight in proving to him that I really did know all I should, but apparently he had great faith in human integrity and believed everything that anyone said! On this assumption, it was a wonder that anyone ever failed, although I often wondered if a secret report had been sent from the foreman of each candidate beforehand.

Yet only eight of the twenty-four cleaners passed the examination, so I presumed that perhaps some of them did answer no to the examiner's questions after all! It was either that or a preponderance of flat feet, hammer toes, colour blindness, and lack of stature!

We fortunate eight, for I was among the successful few, were taken back into the medical room, now stripped of its clinical trappings, the only reminder of its previous use being the scales tucked into a corner. There, on a long table, was a mountain of G.W.R. overcoats, all neatly folded and sized. We eight were about to be issued with our first free article of G.W.R. uniform. It was a great occasion. It took but a few minutes to fit us out and soon the room seemed to be full of young men in heavy black serge overcoats, single-breasted with large black buttons and G.W.R. embroidered on both sides of the collar in bold red lettering. We stood there admiring ourselves, clutching a Rule Book in our hands, which had been issued along with the overcoats. But there was relief mixed with our exhilaration. Not only because we had successfully passed the examination, but because a vacancy for a fireman had turned up when we reached the age of eighteen.

I arrived home that night with The Cheap, pulling into Neyland station at 9.15.

'You made it then, Morgy,' shouted one of the porters, pointing at the heavy overcoat hanging over my arm. No-one ever needed to ask whether you had passed for fireman, as the overcoat was tangible proof of your success. Half-way up the hill I saw Win running down to meet me. I waved the symbol of my success in a sweeping circle over my head and she waved delightedly back, recognising what the coat stood for. I was a fireman at last.

We celebrated that night, first at my home and then at hers. The home-made wine and ginger beer popped their corks and flowed lavishly, and I decided that after all I would take the risk of Win's turning out to be a good cook or not! I didn't say anything to her, but I had made up my mind that I was going to marry her.

F

6

Receiving my Company Number when I had started as a cleaner and seeing my name on the duty roster for Firemen and Drivers for the first time were the two most satisfying experiences I can recall from my early working life. Both symbolised goals achieved after years of waiting.

I was now in the First Link at Neyland Shed, which consisted of four different types of shifts—preparing engines, Yard Pilot, Haverfordwest Pilot and the 2.10 Carmarthen Goods, which included two hours of shunting at Carmarthen.

The heavier, more powerful, 43 Class, 2-6-0 Locos were coming into Neyland now, replacing the old 33 Class on the heavy loads. The first five of them came down in one batch, serial number 53s they were, and when the signalman at Haverfordwest Bridge saw the first one approaching he had immediately slapped on the signal and refused to allow it over his wooden-decked bridge!

There had been a confrontation. Nothing as heavy as this had ever come down to Neyland before and the signalman was taking no responsibility for the bridge collapsing under the weight!

But across it came and we had our 53s—and there's powerful they were, a joy to fire and a delight to drive.

The 2-8-0 R.O.D.s found their way to us as well. These were the locos which the G.W.R. had acquired from the Government, after the

Great War. They had been used a great deal in France, and now their low wheels made them excellent Goods engines for South Wales—workmanlike, strong and reliable, not glamorous, not record-breakers, but a great engine to have before you when you had sixty wagons of coal behind.

Billie Vaughan and Georgie Lewis, two of Neyland's drivers, did not know whether to be glad or sorry to see the R.O.D.s make their appearance, however, as they had both been driving them in France during the War and their memories were not too pleasant, but they had to admit that they were an asset to the South Wales lines.

Neyland was a terminus, which meant that every engine arriving there had to be turned. This took place 'up the Rock' on a heavy, hand-operated turn-table, a good 500 yards up the line near a rocky cutting—hence the name. At one time the turn-table became so difficult to move that the help of a donkey was enlisted for a number of months until the foreman could arrange to have it properly balanced again.

Taking engines for turning made a pleasant break when on the Prepping shift of the First Link. It was good to get out of the atmosphere of the Shed for an hour or so and to take a short light-engine trip up the line, giving a wave to the children on the old Iron Bridge as we effortlessly steamed beneath them, and there was usually one or two of them waiting for a ride on the turn-table when we arrived there!

It took us about an hour to prep an engine ready for its crew. I collected the key from the storeman in order to unlock the necessary prickers, shovels and fire-irons while the driver checked the oiling, and started other routine prepping jobs. There was usually a small, but bright, fire in the fire-box, as we had a good lighter-up, and I would set to and rake the hot embers evenly over the bars, spreading a few shovels of fresh coal over them. With repeated use of blower and careful placing of coal I would gradually build a healthy fire and a climbing head of steam. Check water levels, injectors, sand boxes; there was no way of rushing through prepping, everything had to be done and it all took time. At first the list seemed endless, but it soon became routine.

If a crew were on a short run, with no fear of their making overtime, then they prepped their own engines. It was only the ones on the longer runs which we prepped for, so that they could book on and be away almost immediately.

My wage had risen considerably with my promotion to fireman. I was now paid £3 11s. a week, and it remained at this rate for many years.

I stayed in the First Link for three years, and it was while on the 2.10 Goods to Carmarthen shift that I spotted them. Six perky-eared rabbits, sitting up as pretty as you please, fearlessly watching us steam by. The wooded and brackened slopes and adjoining fields between Neyland and Johnston made ideal rabbiting terrain, and it riled me to steam past and see the little devils sitting up and watch us go by, without even flinching. I thought of rabbit pie, rabbit stew, roast rabbit, and I decided that something had to be done about it, and I was just the chap to do it!

'Slow her down a bit, mate,' I asked a surprised driver the following day as we approached the embankment.

'What's up then, Bill?' he quickly asked, shutting off the regulator and applying the brake.

'Stop her just by here for a minute, and I'll show you,' I replied, turning to open the storage box and taking out my .22 rifle.

'*Arglwydd Mawr!* What you got there then, boy?' he gasped. By now we had come to a stop and, just as I had thought, there they were again. I could almost see them twitching their little noses as they stared inquisitively at us.

'My dinner, man—over by there, see them?' I pointed down the embankment at our furry friends.

'Don't be long now, Bill, we can't keep these fish wagons waiting for ever.' I grinned appreciatively at him and climbed down from the footplate.

The line from Neyland to Johnston was a single track which meant staff working. As long as we had the staff (which authorised you to use the track) in our possession no harm could come from stopping for a few minutes along the line!

I quietly slid down the embankment, pausing for a second to load the .22. I had two beautiful shot-guns at home but I thought that they might be a bit too noisy to fire from the footplate, and besides they were a bit bulky to get onto a loco without discovery! The .22 was just the right size for concealment.

Stealthily I crept towards the hedge and carefully took aim. What a moment full of anticipation that is, just before you squeeze the trigger, willing your prey to stay for a few more seconds. In less than two minutes I was climbing back onto the footplate with tomorrow's dinner hanging limp, warm and furry at my side.

'One for you tomorrow, mate.' I winked at my driver, after all I had to keep him happy!

After that it just became a habit, for the next twenty years, for me to take my .22 Winchester repeater or my 4.10 rifle on the footplate with me, whenever the turn and the driver were suitable! I have even, on occasions, been tempted by one or two fields of enticing, succulent, white mushrooms. It only took a few minutes to stop the loco and pick enough for the driver, the guard and myself—and they tasted beautiful with rabbit pie!

'I hear that wild mulberries grow up near Swansea, Willy,' said Mam thoughtfully, as she gently simmered the mushrooms in a sauce-pan of milk. 'If ever you happen to pass any, growing wild-like near the line . . .' she looked queryingly at me. But even I had to draw the line at stopping the Duffryn Yard Coal Empties on the main line just to pick mulberries!

Our family had now reached the total of seven—myself, Jim, Hugh, Anne, Lillian, Leonard and Dorien. We would eventually make the grand total of eight children, but Alfred hadn't made his appearance as yet.

Hugh, who was four years younger than I, was destined to become a teacher, and at the time when I was working the first link he took a post as pupil teacher at Rosemarket before going to College. This meant a walk of four miles every morning and evening, and with the blustery Pembrokeshire weather it was very hard going at times. I was working the 8.45 goods to Carmarthen when I had the brilliant idea of taking Hugh on the footplate as far as Rosemarket embankment each morning. It was just too good an opportunity to miss and with the empties behind us it would be no trouble to stop on the bridge over the road leading to the village.

The drivers I was working with on this link were all amenable rule-benders like myself, and there was no difficulty when Hugh turned up at the coal-stage those wintry mornings and climbed aboard the foot-plate with us. It took us but a few minutes to reach the bridge, where we slowed to walking pace and Hugh left us with a grateful wave as he scrambled down the embankment to the road below, a mere quarter of a mile from the village school.

Unfortunately, although I racked my brains, I could not devise a way of transporting him home as well. Short of flagging down an Express, there was nothing I could arrange, and even I thought better than to ask an express driver to keep an eye out for my brother on the Rosemarket Embankment!

I did manage, however, to arrange continued footplate taxi-service for Hugh each morning, even after I had moved on from the 8.45 Goods to an afternoon shift. A quiet word in the appropriate ear and the occasional partridge, pigeon or still warm rabbit in the appropriate box ensured a welcome for Hugh on the footplate from each successive crew. My shot-gun has always provided me with currency for barter or bribe and I would feel lost without it.

It was round this time of the early 1920s that our local G.W.R. blacksmith, by the name of Giles, found himself in great demand from the firemen, and in the fortunate position to make a nice little sum of money on the side. This golden opportunity arose because there were no seats on the footplates at that time, and although firemen were kept busy, there were a few occasional minutes of rest when a sit-down would have been much appreciated, but out of the question, of course.

Everyone accepted this as an inevitable condition of footplate work, driver and fireman alike. That is, until one character, recently de-mobbed from the army and working as a fireman at Neyland, stated, quite unequivocally, that it was bloody ridiculous not to have a seat on an engine and that he wasn't going to stand throughout a long run for anyone. He promptly contacted Giles the smith to make him a portable seat, which Giles did forthwith, for the fee of five shillings.

The Shed buzzed with the news, and many eyes watched the intrepid fireman as he turned up for duty the next day. There it was, strapped to his box, his very own custom-built, bespoke seat. It was a beautiful piece of work, a tip-top design which hooked onto the bar at the side of the cab. It took up little room when in position as the wooden seat projected but eight inches, and when not in use it canti-levered up flat against the side of the cab, and took up virtually no room at all. The functional design could not have been better.

Unfortunately, the fireman's driver that day was none other than John Thomas! We waited for the sparks to fly.

'You can remove that bloody contraption off my engine as soon as you like,' stated John Thomas flatly, hardly believing his eyes. The fireman blankly refused.

Everyone in The Shed from the Box-boy to the Chargeman listened with bated breath.

The story of the battle which followed was retold from Shed to Shed up the line. The language was unrepeatable, but repeated it was and with great relish! The tale grew with the telling, and by the time it reached Whitland it was rumoured that both Thomas the Cot and his fireman had to have hospital treatment for black eyes and broken knuckles!

In actual fact the fireman was thrown off the footplate by an enraged John Thomas, closely followed by the offending seat!

But it was not the end of the battle, and much to our surprise it was the fireman who won by reasoning and brute force, suitably inter-mingled—plus the fact that the 7.45 Goods to Carmarthen should have left ten minutes ago, and John Thomas had never been late in his life. He capitulated, scowling and muttering about 'they'll be bringing their beds with them next'. So the 7.45 Goods left Neyland a quarter of an hour late with a victorious fireman giving the thumbs up to everyone as he steamed by, his prototype seat fixed firmly to the cabside behind him!

This was all that was needed for Giles the smith to be inundated with orders for 'five-bob seats' from every fireman in the shed. The test case had been won and now there was nothing to stop us! Eventually the drivers began to realise that if you can't beat 'em, join 'em, and they too started to put in their orders, giving old Giles a roaring trade, which left very little time for his regular work!

The Shed Foreman threatened him with regulation after regulation if he found one more seat being made in Company's time, but everyone knew that Giles was the best smithy this side of Cardiff and that the Foreman wouldn't risk losing him, so he carried on making his 'five-bob seats' until the demand was met, and the Foreman decided that he might as well save his breath and just look the other way!

At first, everyone jealously guarded his own particular seat, and it was a common sight to see each driver and fireman going to and from work with his seat slung over his shoulder or hooked onto his box. No-one would take the risk of leaving it in a cab after a shift was over, but gradually, as the years went by, newer engines came into use with seats already fixed in the cabs, some of the older ones were modified in the same way and our original, little bespoke seats found themselves no longer required.

New Year's Eve, 1922 found Win and me at the Church Hall Social and Dance. The hall was decked with flags and streamers and buntings galore, dominated by three enormous Union Jacks which wafted slowly and majestically from the centre of the ceiling. Win's father, being a Trinity man, nearly had apoplexy every year when he would invariably find at least one Union Jack suspended upside down! 'An insult to the King!' he would rage, and there would be no peace for anyone until the offending flag was rehung correctly. Mr. Crawley ruled his family with an almost Victorian strictness, but it was tempered with kindness and a rare flash of humour.

The Hall was packed with laughing, dancing couples, watched by the older folk who sat around the edge of the dance-floor commenting and gossiping to their hearts' content. Satin shoes twinkled, amazingly short skirts swirled and bobbed hair bounced—all the girls looked wonderful and the blades of the town, including me, thoroughly appreciated them. Everyone was set for a good time, although Win and her sister Margaret were conscious of their elder brother's wary eye on them: Archie was a fitter on The Western, a handsome, high-cheekboned lad, whose good looks had set many girls' pulses racing, but he was very wary of anyone setting either of his younger sisters' pulses a-going! Win was a match for him, but Margaret, who was quieter, took more heed of his cautionary glances, or, at least, she pretended to.

Both girls had special late-night extensions in order to see in the New Year. Normally, both had to be home before the gun on the Barrack Hill at Pembroke was fired at its customary nine-thirty each night. That cursed gun was the bane of my courting life.

The local four-piece band was playing a ragtime as I glanced at my pocket watch, it was quarter to midnight.

'Come on, Win, fetch your coat,' I whispered. 'We're off down the Shed.' Always ready for anything adventurous, Win unobtrusively disappeared for her coat as we danced past the cloakroom. I glanced round to see where Archie was, but he was quite safely engrossed with his new bride, Gwen. Win's father was busy talking to his cronies and Margaret was sitting by her boyfriend Dan, a fireman like myself. Dan looked up and caught my eye; he knew what I had planned and gave me a conspiratorial wink and a nod.

Win and I made our way to the door and pushed our way through the rather tattered crowd of lookers-on who always thronged there whenever any festivities were taking place. 'Old Gran' grinned at us with her one tooth and hugged her much prized army great-coat round her thin self, Lily Fullpelt (so called because she was always in a tearing hurry) gathered her brood out of our way and gave me a leering wink which made me shudder, and Old Daffy made way for us without taking his bemused eyes off the colourful scene behind us.

Down the Hill we raced, the sound of music gradually fading away and the working noise of the railway yard taking its place. Our flying footsteps echoed under the glass roof of the station, then out into the cold night air again, along to the end of the platform and down to the shed sidings.

'Hurry up, Morgy, it's nearly midnight,' called Tom Francis, beckoning us from the footplate of the waiting tankie. Satin shoes full of splintery cinders, Win was unceremoniously pulled up onto the footplate, the heat from the fire-box scorching our faces as we stared pantingly at my watch.

'Now, man!' I shouted to Tom. A ship's siren started to wail, another joined it, the Barrack Hill gun burst forth and the tankie slowly started to move.

'Hold on, Win!' I warned, but my words were drowned by the sound of the first detonator exploding beneath us. Win shrieked, I laughed, Tom cheered, another detonator exploded and another and another. The track was laid with twenty and each one unfailingly took Win by surprise!

'Blow the whistles!' I yelled over the pandemonium of noise around us, pointing to the chains. Win needed no second bidding and the shrieking blasts added to the other ear-splitting noises building up around the harbour and yard.

Other engine whistles joined in, the cleaners' own specially rigged detonators started to explode and every boat seemed to be in fierce competition with the locos to see who could make the most celebratory noise. The ships' Very-lights lit up the sky, the water sparkled with their reflection and someone lit a bonfire on the Barrack Hill.

'Happy New Year!' we shouted at each other with hugs and kisses above the joyous clamour.

'Happy New Year, Morgy!' bellowed Tom, giving me a clap on the back which nearly sent me reeling off the footplate, as gradually the celebratory sounds died down, ending with a few whoops from a small fishing smack which was obviously determined to have the last word. The quiet returned.

It was 1923.

* * *

The screw propeller of the ferry steamer slowly started to turn, ropes were cast off and thrown onto the pontoon, a late workman came racing down the ramp, took an unhesitating leap over the gradually widening gap between boat and pontoon, and I turned up the collar of my issue coat against the biting early morning wind which suddenly blew more fiercely as we drew away from the shore.

The six o'clock boat was packed with dockyard men, two dozen or more huddled below in the dark, evil-smelling cabin, the remainder standing, like me, with their backs to the wind, waiting for the short crossing to pass. A few lucky ones leaned with their backs to the warmth of the engine room. It was supposed to be early summer, but only the calendar said so—more like March that wind was.

In our wake, the Llangwm boats skimmed silently by as we turned to approach the Pembroke Dock slipway. A couple of dozen men to a boat, rowing with an almost mechanical precision, they headed straight for the Dockyard, their high-prowed tar-black boats as dour as the men who rowed them. Llangwm was a small village a few miles upstream from Neyland, and a deadly rivalry existed between the two places. No Neylander would dare to trespass into Llangwm alone for fear of being stoned or besmirched with clods of earth and mud, thrown by the clannish villagers—male and female alike! And Heaven help the Neyland All Blacks football team if they won their away match at Llangwm! I had more than once been stoned out of the village, my coat thrown over Win's head for protection, after watching her brother Archie help the Neyland All Blacks to victory over the Llangwm Wasps. Devils they were!

I watched them row past, neither looking to left nor right, giving no hint of awareness that their work-mates from the Dockyard were within hailing distance. No hand was raised in morning greeting, no smile broke across the grim, stone-grey faces. We were 'the foreigners' and as far as the Llangwmers were concerned, we were nothing.

The heavy black boats glided silently away into the sea mist and I mused on the stroke of fate which had brought me onto the early morning ferry to Pembroke Dock that unseasonably cold morning.

Poor old Jack, a local fireman, competent and well experienced, had only the previous week been unfortunate enough to forget to pick up the staff on a single line working. The particular stretch of line was the single track from Whitland to Narberth, which lay on the main line from Swansea to Pembroke Dock. This was the route of the Pembroke Coast Express, complete with decorative headboard emblazoned on the front of the engine. Jack hadn't given the Whitland staff a thought until they were steaming into Narberth station and he suddenly realised, to his horror, that he didn't have a staff to hand in to the signalman. The commotion it caused was understandable as another train could possibly have been coming in the opposite direction with disastrous results. At the ensuing enquiry Jack had been immediately suspended for six days and so there I was on the ferry, on my way to take his place on the footplate of the Pembroke Coast Express. It was out of my link, but I was the only fireman available at such short notice. At least, I flattered myself that I was the only available fireman competent enough to be entrusted with the Pembroke Coast Express!

I picked up my box and made my way with the rest of the workmen to the boatrail. We were all up to the top of the slipway before the ferry had even been tied up, as the passengers started to disembark as soon as the pier was within jumping distance, and we were soon all making our way along the bleak, windswept Pier Road towards the town. I soon reached the station where Driver Georgie Nash greeted me warmly, and we both spent the next hour prepping the 53 class loco for its run to Swansea. It was a stopping train, and eight staffs had to be picked up before we even reached Whitland! Pembroke, Manorbier, Tenby, Saundersfoot, Kilgetty, Templeton, Narberth and then Whitland. Firing the 53 was child's play and I gave all my attention to remembering each and every staff. As we approached each station, there was the signalman standing at the end of the platform, waiting to hand me the staff for the following section. I returned the staff from the previous station to him with one hand and took the new staff with the other. It all went very smoothly. This procedure was repeated until we were approaching Whitland.

'Get the staff ready, Bill,' warned Georgie Nash. 'Hang her on the horn as we pass—and don't miss it,' he added jokingly—I think!

The previous stations were very small and the signalman doubled as porter, which was why they were able to be on the platform with the staff. At Whitland, however, the signalbox was further away from the platform and it required a full-time signalman to operate it, so the staff was placed on the horn further down the line, away from the platform, and the fireman helped himself as he went by. If he was travelling from Narberth he slipped the ring of the staff onto the horn, and if he was going towards Narberth he would lean out and loop his hand through the ring and take the new staff off. This method enabled non-stopping trains to keep up good time, and it was this ringed staff at Whitland that Jack had forgotten to take, on his return journey to Pembroke Dock.

The staffs had to be directly associated with the signalmen as they were the only ones in direct link with the next station and both signalmen had to release the staff at the same time as a safeguard.

Whitland came into view and there was the horn waiting for me. We were slowing down and I reached out and hung the staff ring on without a hitch. We had reached the end of the single line workings and now it was plain sailing to Carmarthen, Llanelly and Swansea, with one short decrease of speed at Ferryside for us to lower the troughs and take on extra water as we went by.

We ran into Swansea at eleven o'clock, easing our way gently onto the buffers. Our first task was to uncouple from the train, as one of the new Castles was taking the Express the remainder of the journey to Paddington, and she coupled up at the rear, adding a few extra coaches and a diner.

As soon as our train pulled out and our road was clear, we steamed slowly down to the turn-table, and then left our loco ready for call at 1.30, when we would take the Pembroke Coast Express down to Pembroke Dock. Meanwhile Georgie Nash and I took a window-shopping tour of the town and I bought a toy canary on a stick for my new baby brother Alfred, our family now being complete!

'We ought to have the headboard on, Bill,' remarked Georgie as we made our way back to the station. 'I couldn't find a blessed one at Pembroke Dock this morning,' he went on. 'Blowed if I know where they all go, but they're sure to have one in the Inspector's Office here, so nip down and fetch one for us,' he suggested.

I walked down the platform and poked my head round the door of the office; there they were, three beautiful headboards lying on the floor in the dusty gloom. I picked up the top one and held it at arm's length. 'Pembroke Coast Express' it read, the letters boldly etched in gold, gracefully curved, ready to add a touch of grandeur and importance to any engine.

'Where the hell d'you think you're taking that, then?' came a challenging voice from behind me. I turned to face the local Inspector whose outline was framed darkly in the doorway.

'Driver Nash asked me to collect a spare for the down Express to Pembroke Dock,' I explained.

'Where's the one you came up with then?' he queried. I proceeded to tell him that there was none available at Pembroke Dock, when he interrupted with, 'What the bloody hell do you do with the bloody things down there? Bloody well eat them?' I gave a shrug of the shoulders.

'Well, can I have it or not?' I asked, the heavy headboard still in my hands.

'There must be at least half a dozen lying around down there somewhere,' he went on, ignoring my question. 'Check at Whitland Shed on your way back and see if any locos have gone in with the boards on. This is the last one I'm letting go down the line,' he warned. 'Now clear off and don't lose that one.'

I carried my prize off under my arm and made my way back to our 53 where Georgie was waiting on the footplate. It was surprisingly heavy and I was glad when I could put the thing down.

The tantalising smell of frying bacon came to me as I drew near our idling loco, which was gently hissing and patiently waiting in the siding.

'Did you get it?' asked Georgie, not taking his eyes off the sizzling bacon neatly layered on the hot shovel in the fire-box. I told him of the fuss the Inspector had made.

'We don't lose the damn things on purpose,' he muttered to himself, carefully turning over the slices of bacon. 'They must be lying around somewhere, nobody would pinch one, they're no value to anyone, not like a shovel now,' he added.

If we only knew then what we know now . . . there would have been a few in my attic for a start! But the idea of Great Western Railway equipment being of value to future connoisseurs of 'Railway antiques' was as remote from our thoughts as the idea of going to the moon. We certainly lived in a different world, back there in the 'twenties.

The salty Welsh bacon was delicious. We sat there on the footplate, contentedly munching our doorsteps of bread with the thick slices of bacon between, shielding ourselves from the parky wind and feeling our faces turning red from the heat of the fire. Our tea bottles were carefully wedged between the hot pipes and I thought what a good life it was.

'Here she comes,' remarked Georgie suddenly, as the Express from Paddington thundered powerfully towards us, Pembroke Coast Express emblazoned proudly across the front of the engine, which served to remind me that our board was still propped up against the wheel!

Savouring the last lick from my fingers, I climbed down from the footplate, took the headboard round to the front of the 53 and secured it safely to the handrail and smokebox.

'Stop admiring your handiwork and come and give me a bit more steam!' shouted Georgie above the noise of the clattering empties nudging each other along the next siding. A few shovels of side-firing, a couple of minutes of the blower and we were ready to steam up and couple to the rear end of the Down Express. The diner and extra coaches were at the front of the train this time so that we could un-couple them and leave them behind at Swansea and take the remainder of the train on its way to Pembroke Dock. Georgie took us in slowly, tender first, and even those few yards made me glad that we weren't going tender first all the way to Pembroke Dock. I had some very chilly recollections of tender first journeys from Whitland to Neyland and I was in no hurry to repeat the experience.

As soon as we were given the Right-away by the guard we took the Express behind us, out of Swansea dead on time. We didn't need water by the time we reached Ferryside on the return journey, but we slowed up to have a top-up from the trough anyway, to make sure that we would have enough water to reach Pembroke Dock.

'Staff, Bill,' reminded Georgie as we approached Whitland. No fear of my forgetting it, I thought to myself, not after what happened to poor old Jack. We had a short stop at Whitland and as soon as the signal came off we steamed away once more, with me at the ready, half-hanging out of the cab in my determination to make a clean gaff at the staff as we passed the Instrument where it had been placed. With it safely on board we carried on our way and arrived at Pembroke Dock at 3.45 without incident. But by hedges, I knew I had done a day's work. I could feel it in my shoulders; they seemed to remember every shovelful of the twelve ton of coal I had fired. But at least I had the satisfaction of knowing that I had been personally responsible for the 53 travelling with the Pembroke Coast Express that day.

'*Mae'n bwrw gwlaw, y fe?*' I remarked with a shiver as Georgie Nash and I made our way from Pembroke Dock Shed through a damp drizzle which was settling in for the rest of the day.

'*Aye, dipyn bach,* man,' he answered, which more or less exhausted our conversational Welsh on the subject of the weather!

'See you tomorrow, then,' I called as we went our separate ways. Georgie raised his hand in acknowledgement and I started to make my way to the ferry.

Walking along the Pier Road, my mind happily fancy free, I suddenly found myself smiling as I recalled an earlier walk along the same road nearly a decade before during the Great War.

Mam had kept Jim and me home from school one afternoon in order to fetch some turnip and strawberry jam, which she had heard they were selling in the Pembroke Dock Star. Two blessed hours we had queued in order to buy that turnip jam, as I am sure there was very little, if any, strawberries in it! We had carried it back carefully along the Pier Road in the earthenware jug which Mam had provided, both having a few finger dips and licks on the pretext of hooking out the bits of straw which were mixed in with the jam! Disaster had struck as we were standing on Hobb's Point waiting for the Ferry; the jug had simply slipped out of my hands, the smashed earthenware mixing with the sloppy pale brown jam on the seaweed-covered stones!

I chuckled to myself as I recalled, with vivid awareness, that horror-struck moment, when Jim and I had stood transfixed, staring at the ghastly mess, and at the memory of young Jim suggesting that perhaps we could put it in our pockets! What a telling-off we had from Mam that day.

But today my luck was in, and a boat was waiting when I arrived at the slipway. It meant a good three-quarters of an hour wait if you just missed a ferry, and I didn't relish the thought of that on this windswept promontory.

When I arrived home there was a delicious Welsh 'cawl' being kept hot for me in the side oven, and baby Alfred thought his toy canary was lovely.

I remained on the Swansea run for the whole week, and by the third day I was perfectly at home with the routine. We had been on time on each run and everything was going smoothly . . . until the fourth day on the return trip.

About a quarter of a mile after we had left Whitland, my hands suddenly went clammy and my heart dropped into my boots as I realised with sickening certainty that I had forgotten to pick up the staff!

'Stop her!' I yelled at poor old Georgie, who wondered what the hell was the matter.

'The staff! The bloody staff!' I shouted at him.

'We can't just stop, boy,' he said, staring at me unbelievingly.

'Stop the bloody thing,' I insisted. 'I'll go back and fetch it.'

Reluctantly, he brought the 53 to a halt.

'It can't be more than a quarter of a mile,' I remarked hopefully as I climbed down from the footplate.

'I'll go and protect with detonators in front,' I heard Georgie shout, as I made my way along the track, trying to ignore the opening windows and questioning looks from the passengers and forcing myself to walk calmly past the carriages towards the guard's van. He looked as puzzled as the passengers, straining his eyes along the line to see if there was any obstruction!

'I missed the staff,' I said to him with a shrug of the shoulder, implying that I hadn't really forgotten it!

'I'll have to lean over a bit further next time,' I added over my shoulder as I broke into a run. Aye, I thought to myself, and a bloody sight further too! I glanced back and saw Georgie Nash bending to fix the second detonator to the rail, a few hundred yards along the track, and by that time I was almost half-way back and could make out the staff, prominently displayed alongside the track. The sidings at Whitland were always busy and no-one had noticed that the staff had not been taken, but I went cold at the thought of what might have happened if the staff had not been there on my return. It would have meant that it was still in the instrument, and consequently another one could have been taken out at Narberth to give another train the right of way of the same line in the opposite direction. But this would be most unlikely as we had had the signal, which the signalman would not have given us if he hadn't already placed the staff for our collection. These double safety checks minimised any possible danger on single track workings, so that even if one check failed there was always another safeguard.

I jog-trotted back to the Pembroke Coast Express in a happier frame of mind. I endured more enquiring glances as I passed by the carriage windows, hearing one passenger making a jocular remark about 'bits falling off the engine', as he noticed the metal staff in my hand!

We steamed off once more, exploding detonators as we went, the wheels skidding round as old Georgie tried to get us off to a quick start in an endeavour to make up for lost time. He wiped his brow on his waste, as I did a bit of fast firing, saying that he was pretty certain we'd had the road, but it was still reassuring to have the staff on board.

In contrast, I have known a crew steam off with two staffs on board! Of course this just had to happen to me too. It was all the fault of a friendly signalman-cum-porter. He was a nice chap and liked to have a bit of a chat with us every time we passed through his station, sometimes climbing up onto the footplate for a warm, if the weather was a bit on the chilly side. I had already exchanged staffs with him, but unknown to us, he left his on the front of our tender when he climbed down to give us the Right-away.

We didn't discover it until we reached the next station, when we found that we had two of the damned things to hand in!

Of course, this meant that the stretch of line we had just passed over was now completely out of commission, until the staff could be returned to its correct instrument. Finally we had to send a tankie back with the extra staff—at least he was sure that he wouldn't meet anyone travelling the same road!

Those blessed staffs! Either you didn't have one or you had one too many, it seemed.

By the time I'd finished that week's working with Georgie Nash, with its sixteen staffs per day, I was dreaming of the gallus things!

G

7

It was a sparkling, crisp evening, the air unusually still for Neyland, where a sea-breeze almost invariably blew draughtily around the streets. It must have been well below zero and I was not relishing my trip that night. Along with Jimmy One-pint, I was taking the ten o'clock passengers as far as Whitland, where we would link up with the Paddington–Fishguard train. It was the thought of the return journey, however, which made me shiver. The turn-table at Whitland was too small to take our 33 Bulldog, and this meant that we had to steam back to Neyland tender first. Knowing from past experience what it was like travelling at speed through icy face-aching air, without the protection of the cab, I checked that I had not forgotten my long khaki scarf which I kept especially for such occasions. A scarf was something which I always scorned to wear—and still do—but the elements, when encountered tender first, needed to be treated with respect.

My breath condensed in vaporous clouds before me as I made my way down the Hill, the metal handle of my box biting into my hand with the intense cold and my boots ringing out on the frozen air of the deserted streets.

The Shed was a haven of warmth as I walked over to the office to book on. Jimmy and I had a few hours of shed work before our trip to Whitland and I passed the time of day with a few of the shed men, the freezing weather being the sole topic of conversation. 'Don't envy you tonight, Bill,' remarked old Lampie, 'a blue icicle you'll be, boy, by the time you get back here,' he added. 'Pity it is we're not all like old One-pint there,' nodding across to where Jimmy was just striding into the shed, open-neck shirt, summer weight overalls and no overcoat. 'Never feels the cold, man,' Lampie went on in a marvelling tone. 'Never feels it a bit.'

Jimmy One-pint was a big genial chap whose bare-chested philosophy seemed to be, 'cheerfully ignore the weather and it won't bother you!' His son, who was a cleaner at the Shed, was already known, of course, as Jimmy Half-pint, but I don't think he inherited his father's scorn of the elements.

Our shed work completed, we set to, prepping the 33. Jimmy went on with the oiling while I built up the fire, tested the water gauge, checked the lamps, took a quick look in the sand-boxes, examined the smoke-box, re-stoked the fire and carried out the other numerous tasks which, by now, were second nature to me. We were all set to steam out of the Shed at 9.40, and the cold night air hit us as we slowly moved towards the platform where we coupled up to the waiting coaches. We got as much steam through to them as possible in order to give our passengers a warm, comfortable journey to Whitland.

The twenty-seven mile trip was effortless and uneventful as usual, and after warming ourselves up with a tea-break, we collected our new passengers and started on our return journey with 'the Cork'.

As we were travelling tender first, it was no longer possible for us to heat the coaches. We had managed, however, to build up as much heat as possible on the up-journey, and the unfortunate passengers travelling to Neyland had to make do with what was left, but at least, it was better than nothing. Mind you, there wouldn't be much left by the time we reached Neyland, I can tell you. So we, on the footplate, were not the only ones to suffer by travelling tender first!

And so, with my khaki scarf wound round my head and across my face, as many times as it would go, leaving a mere slit for my eyes, I was all prepared for the icy journey home. It was bad enough in the summer, when all you had to face was the equivalent of a force eight gale, blowing coal-dust in your eyes, but in winter it was like a knife cutting through you.

There was no place I could protect myself from that remorseless, frozen blast. Even when actually firing close to the fire-box, the radiant heat was dissipated before I could reap any benefit from it. I was slowly turning into that blue icicle that old Lampie had predicted, and by the time we reached Clarbestone Road I started swearing in an effort to warm myself up by cursing the elements. But it had no effect. Mentally I was a little less numb but physically I was as frozen as ever, in spite of an extra pair of overalls, pullovers and my khaki scarf!

I glanced over at One-pint, his shirt was as open-necked as ever and his thin overalls flapped around his large frame as he stood there defying the rushing, icy air. Damn me, he looked as if he was enjoying it!

We pulled into Neyland Station on time, the passengers disgorging from the rapidly cooling compartments and grumbling about the lack of heat in the carriages while I stood, almost frozen to the footplate, my teeth literally chattering with the depth of the cold which I felt in my bones, and the hollows of my sinuses aching with a deep intense pain. It seemed I would never feel warm again.

'Bit on the chilly side tonight then, Bill,' remarked One-pint, wiping his hands reflectively on his waste. I just stared at him in disbelief as he gave a little shrug of his shoulder as if a small breeze had sprung up on a summer evening.

Even now the words 'tender first' make me shiver!

*   *   *

The weeks and months went by and the routine of the Shed went on. But some of the unfortunate cleaners who were still waiting for a vacancy in order to be made firemen were becoming disheartened. A few, who despaired of ever gaining promotion, reluctantly left the G.W.R. and decided to go to sea with the fish trawlers from Milford Haven, and one or two left to go to work in the Dockyard at Pembroke. But the majority stuck it out and waited.

I was still taking home good pay of £3 11s, and was saving hard to get married. Win and I had set the date for 21st January, 1925, which was Alfred's first birthday, and we were to be married at Llanstadwell Church. Everyone must look back on their wedding day as one of the greatest days in their lives, and I am no exception.

Win and I had spent the previous few weeks decorating and furnishing the two rooms we had rented from the District Nurse who lived at 36, Lawrenny Street. Wedding presents were installed, bed and mattress from Win's parents, bedroom suite from Auntie Annie in

Porthcawl, a much-prized Crown China tea service from Mam and Pa and numerous other gifts showered on us from relatives and friends.

There's excitement there was in the two households during those few weeks. Special arrangements made with Jones the Baker to allow us to use his large ovens to bake the three tiers of the wedding cake, Morgan the Butcher agreed to boil a huge ham and press a tongue, and the amount of sewing that went on was nobody's business! Never in my life have I heard so much debating about whether one thing 'matched' another!

At last everything was ready and the 21st of January arrived, cold and blue-skied. No cloud came rolling in from the sea to dull the frosty sparkle, it was just perfect. Two o'clock found Dan James and me waiting in the old church of Llanstadwell, the guests rustling and fidgeting behind us. The traditional musical accompaniment struck up and the bride arrived followed by the two bridesmaids, Margaret and Anne. The actual ceremony is a blurred mixed memory of my own wedding and of the numerous others I attended before and since.

Any similarity between our wedding and that of others, however, ended when we eventually came out of the church and made our resplendent way home in imposing hired cars. Our journey was to prove to be rather costly!

The first roped barrier across the road was but a hundred yards from the church. A cheering gang of children and youths on either side of the narrow winding road greeted us with home-made confetti, an impassable rope across the road, pulled taut by the two biggest boys, and a dozen open palms waiting for the toll money! Dan and I had filled our pockets in advance with halfpennies, pennies, silver threepenny bits and a few sixpences, and some we threw out to our captors—who, in exchange, allowed the three cars to pass by to the accompaniment of even louder cheering. We had expected to be 'roped' once or twice as was the custom, and Win, in her ice-blue brocaded satin dress helped to scatter the money with the largesse of a Lady of the Manor!

We soon began to realise, however, that 'once or twice' was not to be the case on our wedding drive! We found another three roped barriers obstructing our progress before we had even reached the main Neyland road at Church Lakes, and we were beginning to regret having been quite so generous at the first hold-up.

We did manage to pick up some speed along the Front, however, but rounding the bend at The Hotel we noticed another rope half-way up the hill and yet another near Railway Terrace. My pockets were feeling ominously flat and jingle-less as I leant out of the window and shouted to Dan in the car behind, to find out how much money he had left. But his answer was drowned in the shouts and cheers of our new captors.

I was a bit dubious about the cars stopping on The Hill as I hadn't much confidence in their ability to start off again on that steep slope. I know what it was like on a loco if you stopped on a bank and I couldn't see that it was much different with the internal combustion engine! Win and I quickly sorted out as many halfpennies as we could so that they would make as much noise as possible when they hit the road, then we flung them as far away as we could and as soon as the rope was dropped in the scramble for the rolling coins the three cars made a noisy, high-revving hill-start. Off we went once more, making a quick get-away before it was discovered that there was no silver amongst the ransom money!

All told, we were held up seven times before we eventually managed to reach our reception, and even then, there was a diminutive three-foot rope across the doorway of 37, Frederick Street, supported on either side by two grinning urchins with outstretched palms!

I think our wedding broke all records for ropings in Neyland—that's the trouble with having so many friends—or enemies!

As soon as the guests had arrived, all the available dining chairs were hastily carried out onto the pavement, ready for the arranging of the Wedding Photograph, with Win's Mam, conscious of the eagle-eyed crowd of spectators outside, trying to give each chair a quick run over with the duster as it was carried through the passage.

The photographer viewed us professionally as we took our places on the pavement in front of the house. Margaret arranged her hand-beaded, panelled dress to more advantage, Mam told Anne to sit up straight, the photographer tidied up the gutter a bit, I made sure that my genuine velour trilby, which I had paid over half a week's wages for in Swansea, was suitably prominent, Win adjusted her fur stole more artistically, and suddenly it was all over and everyone began to complain of the cold as we all jostled our way indoors with the chairs, ready for the Wedding Feast.

The platform was packed with well-wishers when Win and I made our way down through the Hotel Gardens to catch the 6.30 Mails that evening. There could not have been a single man or boy left in the Shed as every cleaner, fireman, driver, fitter, and shedman seemed to be there on the platform waiting to see us off in style. Family and friends in their best wedding finery jostled and joked with the blue-overalled railwaymen. Lily-of-the-valley mingled with the sulphur on the evening air, satin shoes nudged against heavy, black boots and soft kid gloves clasped waste-wiped hands as Georgie Perkins, the Guard, led us with great ceremony amid the flying ribald remarks to the specially reserved compartment. It had been previously locked, and was now unlocked with a flourish as we were bowed into a first-class compartment, accompanied by tumultuous cheers, limitless pats on the back and more ribald remarks! There, hanging from the luggage rack were a large working boot, it must have been at least a size thirteen, a lady's dancing shoe and a tiny baby's bootee. The floor was soon deep in confetti and the crush was almost unbearable! I managed to get my hand into my pocket to reach a pound note and a ten-shilling note which I gave to Freddie Griffiths with shouted instructions to treat all the lads to a drink at The Hotel when the train had gone. Another ten-shilling note I managed to press into Georgie Perkins' hand and asked him to treat the driver and fireman of the train to a drink, when they reached Carmarthen. I had lost contact with Win by this time, but I assumed that she was in the compartment somewhere!

The Guard blew his whistle and everyone reluctantly started to step down out of the compartment, some needing a push or they would have ended up coming with us! There was a flurry of last-minute farewells, good wishes, kisses from the family, more confetti, piping eyes, waving hands and the 6.30 Mails steamed out of Neyland Station with two exhausted honeymooners!

Being a railwayman I should have been prepared for it, but we were both just about to sit down with a sigh of relief when we hit the first detonator! In the excitement I had forgotten the traditional send-off awaiting us, which I had, so often in the past, rigged for other newly-wed Western men leaving Neyland on their honeymoon.

Explosion followed explosion as we steamed past the Shed, under the Iron Bridge and on to Westfield, battering our ears and those of our fellow passengers on the train for a good three-quarters of a mile. Each one we thought would be the last—but it wasn't! A very modest estimate would be fifty detonators exploded under the wheels that night —supplies in the Shed must have been very low that week!

8

The summer of 1926 was Strike Summer. Unlike others less fortunate than myself, I did not suffer any great hardship. Win and I had over sixty pounds saved and with strike pay of £1 a week we managed to live quite comfortably, our larder well-stocked with the usual rabbit, pigeon, and partridge, provided by my double-bore, mackerel and rock salmon (which sounds more appetising than its usual name of dog-fish), provided by my line, fat bacon, eggs and the occasional chicken provided by Billy Jacobs the Farmer for services rendered in the 'fields' of duty, runner beans, peas and new potatoes provided by my allotment, which left very little in the way of provisions which had to be actually bought with hard cash—apart from the rent of course.

I felt pity for the miners in their industrial homesteads with no natural resources to fall back on. Jim, my younger brother, was on strike from the mines at Ammanford and he turned up one evening and told us a tale of life far different from our own, where hardship and shortage of food was all too real.

Jim managed to make a little money by buying trees in Neyland Wood for a half-crown, felling them, sawing them up and then selling them from door to door. Even after the strike was over he never returned to the mines, but instead, followed Pa into the Trinity Service and became a lighthouse-keeper, spending the rest of his life on the wild, lonely rocks around our coast.

I whiled away those warm, workless afternoons with Dan and Archie, firing an air-gun in the back garden at a target backed by a wet sack and sand. We could not afford to buy pellets so we used the same ones over and over again, as the noses were undamaged because the wet sack absorbed the impact.

Each time, we tossed up to see who would have first shot at the matchstick, propped up twenty yards away at the top of the garden, and we each put a halfpenny in the kitty for the winner. The trouble was that if Archie won the toss he almost invariably won the bet, as his accuracy rarely failed him and he split that matchstick in two, nine times out of ten! Dan and I were good—very good by most standards, but Archie nearly always ended the richer in spite of all the extra practising Dan and I put in.

Of course quoits flourished more than ever. Strike meetings, held most evenings at either Neyland or one of the nearby villages, always had a precursory quoits match. The evenings were long, light and warm and it was an ideal opportunity to challenge other village quoits teams to a tournament. We travelled by horse and cart or by char-a-banc to Johnston, Rosemarket, Sardis, Milford, Haverfordwest and other villages and towns. We met in Chapel Halls, Oddfellows Halls, Workingmen's Clubs, barns and even in the open fields for our strike meetings each evening, in order to hear the latest developments in the nation-wide strike.

I can still recall standing in the Oddfellows Hall at the top of Neyland, where an enormous eye, which was painted on the ceiling, stared down at me surrounded by the words 'The Eye of the Lord See-est Thou'. Those words used to chant through my head and mingle with the announcements of collieries closing, pickets making stands and reports of hardship in the Valleys. The Eye of the Lord and the 1926 Strike remain forever allied in my mind.

It was not only in the industrial valleys, however, that there were cases of hardship. Many drivers and firemen in Neyland and the surrounding district had families to support and no savings to fall back on, but with careful management they somehow survived the lean months.

Even when the strike was over, it took time before the railways were running full power once more, and as luck would have it Dan and I were the last two firemen to be reinstated in Neyland. It was two months after the official ending of the strike before we were paid for a single day's work. Every day the two of us would go down to the Shed to see if we could be started, but the answer was the same each day—if someone went sick we could have a start, but everyone made mighty sure they didn't fall sick. After thirteen weeks of strike no-one dared think of being ill. Dan and I were without work for twenty-one weeks and we were beginning to think that there would never be a vacancy for us.

Being out of work along with the remainder of the men had been bad enough, but when we found ourselves out on our own, for those extra eight weeks, it was soul-destroying. Everyone else had work, even if it was for only three or four days a week, but Dan and I kept waiting.

But at last the rail traffic increased and the demand for men rose. We were reinstated and started working for two days a week. It felt good to be back.

* * *

Light engines are always in a hurry. There's no getting away from it. They are either trying to beat a Mails in order to avoid being held up at stops, or they are trying to keep pace with an Express so they can slip through a junction while the Express is at the station, or they are endeavouring to take a staff before they are due, commandeering the track so that the train at the other end of the single line is kept waiting instead of themselves. Light engines are nearly always on their way home, usually at the end of a shift and with a feeling about them of not actually being on Company's business at all! It's that great emptiness behind them that does it, no goods, no passengers, no wagons, nothing. Just the light engine, fancy-free, tootling along the track all by itself without a care in the world. Without a care in the world? Then how did Tommy Francis the driver with Dan firing, manage to end up on a light engine in the middle of a field? I'll tell you this, it could have been any of us for that matter! It was undoubtedly the light engine the-world-is-mine euphoria which must have been the cause.

Dan and Tommy Francis had been effortlessly steaming along the single track from Templeton to Narberth, bringing their loco back to Neyland after having worked a passenger train to Pembroke Dock. Work for the day was finished, God was in his Heaven, all was right with the world. There was always a staff ready on the return run from Pembroke Dock, so no need to come to a halt, thought Tommy, just exchange staffs at ten miles an hour, save time, home early, quick tea and a spot of gardening.

But the staff which was always there, was not. The signal which was always off was on. The points which were always set for through-traffic were not, and Tommy Francis and Dan James found themselves heading straight for a set of bumpers at the end of an unpleasantly short siding! The loco ploughed straight through them, plunged down a slope, through a fence and into an adjoining field where it buried itself up to the footplate in the soft earth. The tender, aided by the slope, stood on end, sliding tons of coal into the cab, half-burying Dan and pinning Tommy against the scalding pipes. Fortunately, because the accident happened close to the station, help was quickly at hand and both survived without too much injury. Dickie Davies also succumbed when returning a light engine from Landore. He and his fireman had worked a double-banker on a heavy fish train from Milford to Landore and were travelling home light. They were trying to keep pace with the passenger Express from Swansea, so that they could slip through Carmarthen Junction while the Express stood in the station. Unknown to Dickie however, the Swansea Express had a banker in front that day, and had to make an unscheduled stop at Cocket in order to take the banker off and continue single-engined. The approach to Cocket Station is through a tunnel, and as the Express was too long for the platform, its rear coaches were standing in the tunnel while the banker was uncoupled.

Dickie had had the road from Landore for the first section, and had naturally expected a clear run to Cocket, not dreaming that the Express would stop there. He hadn't noticed that his next section's starter and distant signals were on, and he unsuspectingly entered the tunnel. By a stroke of good fortune, however, the Express was just on the move and the guard's van took the reduced impact. Miraculously, no-one was hurt, but the light engine and the last coach of the Express were derailed inside the tunnel, and at the following enquiry, Dickie found himself temporarily suspended from Mainline driving. There's a stir that had caused in Neyland Shed, I can tell you.

Another incident, in a much lighter vein, however, occurred a few years later, when Sid Lloyd, finding himself driving home on a light engine, had a sudden irresistible impulse to play one of his practical jokes. Leg-pulling was second nature to him and everyone in the Shed was automatically on their guard if Sid was about. The trouble was, he would behave himself for weeks and lull everyone into a false sense of security! He seldom planned a leg-pull, he just seemed to dream them up on the spur of the moment, as, for example on this occasion, when he was driving back light from Carmarthen after having worked the empties from Milford.

Now the road from Carmarthen divides at Clarbestone Road, the one leading to Haverfordwest, Johnston and Neyland and the other going to Fishguard. On reaching Haverfordwest, although he was signalled straight through, Sid pulled to a halt outside the signal-box. One of Sid's fiendish plots was about to unfurl.

'What's the matter then, driver?' queried the surprised signal-man who had been expecting the light engine to steam straight through.

'Just wanted to check that this road to Fishguard was clear,' replied a serious-looking Sid. (What the hell his fireman must have thought, I can't imagine!)

The signal-man looked puzzled for a moment and then obviously decided that this called for his descending from his box and having an explanatory chat with this rather confused driver, who, if he thought that this was the road to Fishguard, must have missed the points at Clarbeston Road! Hurrying up to the stationary loco, he started to explain to a straight-faced Sid that he was on the wrong road, etc.

'Don't be bloody ridiculous!' interrupted Sid in a belligerent tone, 'I know the road to Fishguard like the back of my hand and THIS is the right road and THIS is the way I'm going!' The signal was still off, and without more ado and cutting short the poor signal-man's protestations, Sid opened up the regulator and steamed off, leaving the bewildered signal-man running behind, still vainly trying to tell him that he would never reach Fishguard on that road! The poor chap then immediately raced back to his box where he telephoned Johnston about the mad-man who was bringing down a light R.O.D. in the mistaken belief that he was on his way to Fishguard!

'Stop him!' he ordered frantically. 'He doesn't know where the hell he's going. *Twp* he must be!'

When Sid approached Johnston he found the signal against him and the red light in the box on. The signal-man, who by sheer chance was not a regular otherwise he would have recognised Sid and guessed what he was up to, was already waiting by the track. More futile arguments followed about whether this was the road to Fishguard (with the fireman wisely refusing to be drawn into the dispute) when the two exasperated, shouting men were interrupted by the telephone in the signal-box. It was Control, who, having been informed by the Haverfordwest signal-man of the strange behaviour of one of the drivers, now wanted to speak to the driver of the R.O.D. Cool as ice, Sid left the loco and went to talk to them, still not backing down from his mad plot! Control wanted to know who he was and where he had come from. I think they were beginning to think that someone had taken an R.O.D. from a shed for a joy-ride! Sid gave a fictitious name and told them that they had been misinformed and that he really was on the correct road to Fishguard and that in his opinion the signal-man at Haverfordwest was out of his mind! He then rang off, leaving Control in an uproar of confusion and tumult. Bells were ringing along the line trying to trace where this madman had come from, and Neyland was warned to be on their guard as an R.O.D. was loose on the line with an unknown, unauthorised driver in charge! Instructions were given to arrest him on the spot if ever he did reach Neyland! In the meantime, Sid had climbed down from the signal-box and returned to his waiting loco.

'Have I got the road ahead?' he asked the worried signal-man, who by this time was beginning to be a little wary of this stranger.

'You've got the road, but it won't take you to Fishguard,' he replied in despair, not knowing how to deal with this man who swore black was white.

'Is everyone around here mad?' shouted Sid loudly as he climbed back up onto the footplate. 'Of course this is the road to Fishguard.' And he steamed away once more, leaving a bewildered signal-man behind him.

How he ever had the nerve to arrive at Neyland at all, I'll never know, and the look on the foreman's face when he saw who the 'unknown, unauthorised' driver was, was indescribable.

Sid was most pained when he learnt that he was suspended for one day without pay. 'Only a bit of fun, man, that's all it was. They can't take a joke that's their trouble!' he grumbled. Perhaps that light engine should take a little of the blame . . .!

9

We sat in the dark, our ears strained for the first sound we would hear. Win, her father and I had come up to Swansea on the 2.20 for this sole purpose, having decided that it was worth using two of our free passes in order to be the first people in Neyland to hear the 'Talkies'. The canvas and wooden shed at the top of Frederick Street which acted as the cinema in Neyland did not boast such refinements as sound, apart, that is, from Hilda Journeaux, who provided dramatic musical accompaniments on her pianoforte. The ingenious way in which Hilda could alter her basic arrangements in order to suit the mood of the film was a constant marvel. Sometimes, during the winter performances, however, her attention was distracted from the screen by young scoundrels, who, after having surreptitiously undone the canvas sides of the 'cinema', proceeded to throw snowballs onto the tortoise stove which glowed a few feet from Hilda's nimble fingers (which were more often than not, in woollen mittens). She would mis-cue a scene and the William Tell Overture would be accompanying a romantic love scene until her attention was recalled by the raucous whistling from the stalls —or benches to be technically correct!

But there was no Hilda Journeaux here in the Capitol at Swansea. It had also cost us ten times as much for the seats, but at least there were no splinters in them and we didn't have children banging on the walls with wooden sticks, raising clouds of dust from the old canvas!

The screen flickered into life. The film we were about to see was 'The Wreck of the *Hesperus*', which was the sole reason we had managed to persuade Win's father to come with us. Being a Trinity man, who had spent all his working life on sailing ships, he was keenly interested to see this exciting, dramatic film—with *sound*.

We heard the roar of the wind, we heard the splash of the sea and we saw the good ship *Hesperus*. The commentator's voice suddenly interrupted the wonderful sounds of sea and wind, and we marvelled that we no longer had to read the commentary.

'You are about to witness the dramatic story of the schooner *Hesperus* which . . .' but we didn't hear the remainder of the poor man's announcement, however, because Win's father was on his feet exclaiming to the audience in a thundering, indignant voice, 'Schooner? Schooner? That's no schooner! That's a two-masted brig.' He gesticulated at the screen in violent accusation, 'Any fool knows that could not be a schooner,' he shouted in exasperation to the amazed audience. 'Just look at the masts, look at the masts!' He waved his arms about, turning to all directions in an endeavour to correct the misinformation which the audience had received! 'That's a two-masted brig . . .' he carried on in exasperation, while Win and I did our best to shush and quieten him. But the reality was spoilt as far as Pa was concerned, they obviously knew nothing about ships and he considered the entire Swansea trip to be a complete waste of time and money! He sat throughout the film muttering about schooners and two-masted brigs, and the rather obvious buckets of water which were thrown over the deck of the *Hesperus* to create the impression of a storm at sea didn't help matters much!

But in spite of the short-comings, Win and I were completely won over by sound movies and we were soon to become firm addicts, travelling back and forth to Swansea until our passes were used up and we had to change to privilege tickets. Needless to say, Win's father never set foot inside a cinema again in his life!

It was on one of our cinema trips that Win spotted a piano in a shop window at Swansea, and so, taking advantage of the new sales method, called Hire Purchase, we decided to buy it!

It was a beauty with a lovely soft tone. Nearly seventy pounds we paid for it but it was worth every penny. I couldn't read music, but I played quite well by ear, keeping a good vamp going with the left hand.

I found the key which used mostly black notes and proceeded to play solely in that key. Well, I didn't want to get the white notes dirty, you see, with my work-soiled hands.

I still play solely in the key of C sharp—old habits die hard!

Blenheim won the Derby, MacDonald was Prime Minister and Win visited No. 10, Downing Street as a Labour Delegate from Neyland. The fact that she was also on the local committee for the Conservative Party was immaterial! The year was 1930 and we had just moved into the Institute with Win's parents, her father now having retired from the Trinity Service and taken the post of Caretaker of the 'Tute. It was an imposing building, situated half-way up Neyland Hill. Iron railings surrounded the premises with the door at the front leading to the billiard hall and reading rooms, although I never ever saw anyone actually reading in them, cards being the preferred way of passing the leisure hours, with nap, pontoon and poker being the three favourites. The side door led to the private portion of the house where we lived and it was here in July 1931 that our daughter Bette was born.

Life settled into a comfortable pattern. Work was good, holidays with free travel passes were spent in Porthcawl with Win's relations or on the Isle of Wight with my family. Pa had gained promotion and had been moved with the rest of the family, to Cowes, where he was Master of the Calshot Light. It was a long journey to visit them, but the free passes made it possible to keep in touch, and to keep them up-to-date with all the Neyland gossip.

We were so busy living our own lives to the full that we had little time to reflect on the miserable existence which people were experiencing in the South Wales valleys and the mining areas of Tyne and Tees in the North. Unemployment was still up in the millions and the poverty which went with it was appalling. True, we sympathised from afar, as we read of the Prince of Wales visiting the depressed areas of South Wales. Poor things, we murmured, as we looked at the pictures of him being cheered by half-starved colliers and their families. Let's hope he can do something for them as he promised. But their poverty did not really touch us, we were fully employed and that made us almost a race apart. Assuredly we had a few misgivings when the Labour Government resigned in August 1931 because of the financial emergency in the country, but Win was busy arranging the date of the christening of our new daughter and I was busy building wireless sets

Bill Morgan and Freddie Griffiths - two young GWR cleaners. (Bette Meyrick)

Neyland looking towards the High Street. The buildings on the immediate right are the end of the Company (Railway) Cottages. On the left the white building is The Institute, but known locally as 'The Tute'. This was where Bill Morgan's daughter Betty was born. (Bette Meyrick)

Bill Morgan shortly after starting work for the GWR,. Photograph taken circa 1916/7. (Bette Meyrick)

Neyland Fireman in the 1930's. Back row L-R, Teddy Morgans, Arthur Evans, Jim Hitchens. Front row L-R, Jack Benjamin, Jack Sutch, Billy Townsend. (Collection Richard Parker)

Bill Morgan and brother-in-law, Archie. (Bette Meyrick)

The Company Cottages on Neyland Hill. (Bette Meyrick)

Looking down Neyland Hill towards the Station. (Collection Richard Parker)

Bill Morgan, Win and daughter
Bette. (Bette Meyrick)

Bill Morgan, Bette, and Bill's brother Alfred, seen on Neyland Promenade and setting off for a days rabbit shooting.
(Bette Meyrick)

The family home, Bill Morgan's bungalow on Neyland Promenade.
(Bette Meyrick)

Neyland Promenade. Bill Morgan's bungalow is the first on the right.
(Collection Bette Meyrick)

Z.6. The Promenade, Neyland.

'Dean Goods' No. 2413 at Neyland circa 1930. L-R, Ben John,(Shunter), Gilbert John (Carriage Cleaner) Bert Davidge (Carriage Cleaner), Albert Blackmoor (Driver). (Collection Brinley John)

The railway from Barnlake Pill. The line of lime-washed cattle wagons were probably being used for the Irish cattle traffic. (Collection Richard Parker)

8

Contemporary advertising for the Hobbs Point steam ferry.

Spectators to the aquatic sports in 1911. (Collection Bette Meyrick)

The loco shed and area. (Collection Richard Parker)

Neyland Signal Box and the engine shed. (Collection Bette Meyrick)

with Archie, each one more sophisticated than the last. The problem of buying enough batteries was of more importance to me than the nation's finances. After all, I could do something about the cost of a 120 volt battery but I could do nothing about the country's expenditure.

It was rumoured that the King himself would actually speak on the wireless on Christmas Day and when that time came I wanted to be ready with the best receiving equipment I could make. Archie and I were experimenting with a three-valve set at that time, and a C.A.V. loudspeaker. Jones the Baker charged our accumulators for us for two-pence, but the necessary 120 volt battery presented a problem as it was much too expensive for us. We eventually solved the problem, however, by arranging $4\frac{1}{2}$ volt batteries in series until they built up to 120 volts. We needed to replace only the last two batteries each week in order to keep a good charge flowing and this proved a cheap way of running the wireless equipment. I had solved my financial problem, but the government still had theirs!

Our wireless sets were not listened to indiscriminately all day as they are now, however. It would have flattened the batteries far too quickly! Programmes were always carefully selected and everyone settled comfortably before the actual switching on took place. These sets with loudspeakers were a great improvement on the crystal sets which we had been making previously, as only one person at a time could listen to the programme through the head-phones we had rigged up. We did manage to overcome this to some extent, however, by placing the head-phones in a large pudding dish which amplified the sound somewhat and enabled the surrounding circle of straining ears to pick up the faint sound of the broadcast. By the time we were making loudspeakers we considered ourselves to have reached a height of sophistication in wireless building!

'We definitely need a higher aerial, Bill,' announced Archie, staring at the maze of red, blue and yellow wires sprouting from the rear of our latest set. We had worked on it all the evening by the light of the gently hissing gas lamp above us, only the occasional pop of the fitful jet and the steady clicking of Win's knitting needles breaking in on our concentration. The air was blue with cigarette smoke and acrid with burnt solder and flux.

'Gallus atmospherics,' muttered Archie in annoyance as another burst of harsh interference crackled on our chosen wavelength. 'A

H   113

higher aerial we must have,' he repeated adamantly. I pulled deeply on my Woodbine and thoroughly agreed with him.

'Leave it to me, Arch,' I suddenly announced with confidence. An idea had suddenly come into my head.

'What are you up to now?' asked Win suspiciously. I think she was psychic where some of my ideas were concerned! After assuring her that there was nothing particularly illegal in my plan for obtaining a taller aerial, Arch and I returned to tackling our 'atmospherics' once more.

I was unable to put my plan into operation until the following week when I was on the Haverfordwest Pilot with old Jimmy One-pint. A beautiful grove of pine trees grew near the sidings at Haverford, belonging to a private estate nearby, and I had already ear-marked the young pine which would suit my purpose exactly. I waited until we had just half an hour left before finishing our turn and returning to Neyland, before asking One-pint to take us over to the far siding which ran next to the pine grove. A stone wall lay between the track and the estate and I was soon over it with my newly-sharpened axe and chopping away at the base of my prize. One-pint hung over the side of the cab watching my exertions. My pine fell beautifully. First with a resounding crack which was surprisingly loud for such a slender tree, and then with a sigh, as it prostrated itself on the bracken-covered earth.

I quickly denuded it of its branches, looking up only in answer to One-pint's impatient blast on the whistle.

'Right you are, man, I'm just coming,' I called and made to pick up one end of the tree in order to drag it towards the wall. Blow me, there's heavy it was! I couldn't lift the blessed thing, leave alone drag it! The weight was unbelievable for such a young tree. I had to call to Jimmy for assistance and between us we managed to stagger back over the wall with my thirty-foot wireless mast! How we heaved and pushed that damned pine in order to stack it on the tender, but eventually, after much cursing and panting we stood back and viewed our achievement. The top of the trunk was overhanging the rear of the tender by a good twelve feet!

'There's a beauty of a mast that will make, Bill,' remarked Jimmy appreciatively, 'once you've got it up like . . .' he added thoughtfully!

I blew a crow to attract the signal-man's attention, and as soon as he gave us the road, off we set for Neyland with my prize, and by hedges

I was relishing seeing the admiring look on Archie's face when he saw it up in the garden. There'd be no more 'atmospherics' after this!

Strengthening wires were the next items I required, as a mast of this height was a flagrant challenge to the Pembrokeshire elements! Many a lesser pole had succumbed to a Westerly gale before now and I didn't fancy my pine crashing down onto the roof of my greenhouse, or the roof of the house, come to that—the slates had enough to contend with with the gales themselves without having to cope with errant pines as well!

After having booked off, Jimmy and I staggered up the hill with my thirty-foot-long pole—always ready to give a hand was One-pint, fair play. But by the time we reached the 'Tute, even after numerous spells, we were almost in a state of collapse, so it was over to the Lawrenny Castle for a drop of liquid refreshment to revive our flagging spirits.

'*Diolch yn fawr*, Jim,' I gasped gratefully, raising my glass to him in heartfelt thanks for his muscles, '*Diolch yn fawr*, man,' I repeated fervently. Well, there's a weight it had been.

Only when my new possession was safely installed in my own back garden, its stubble tip projecting well over my neighbour's wall, could I relax and turn my thoughts to the problem of how to acquire the strengthening wires. I had thought of looking round the Shed that evening before coming home, but I had not dared risk taking my eyes off my precious mast for any length of time, or, sure as eggs, it would have vanished by the time I came to look again! It's not that we were a light-fingered lot in Neyland Yard, but we all had an uncanny instinct for finding just what we wanted 'lying around'!

Now for the wires. On returning from Haverfordwest the following evening, I stayed on at the Shed after booking off, in order to see what I could find lying around in the form of wire. I searched everywhere but without success. It wasn't often that I was beaten, but there was nothing available at all. I didn't mind buying something like a piano, which I couldn't possibly make or just find lying around, but when it came to odd bits of equipment which I might need from time to time, I drew the line at the idea of actually going into a shop. These sorts of things had to be acquired—it was a matter of pride and principle. To buy something was the easy way out, make do and adapt was my motto.

I had only three weeks left before Christmas and the wire situation was becoming desperate. There was the King ready to speak to the entire nation on Christmas Day by means of the wireless, and here was I without supporting wires for my new mast. Win's father would have apoplexy if King George's voice was distorted by those atmospherics, a great respecter of Royalty was Win's father. Something had to be done.

Inspiration came to me while shunting the Fish Empties in Neyland Yard the following day. I was firing away on the footplate and was about to dampen down the coal-dust with water from the pet-pipe when I happened to notice the strong wire wound round the flexible pipe. It was the answer. The only problem now, was how to get the stiff wire unwound. This was the type of challenge I thrived on.

Shunting Fish Empties became the most unimportant thing in the world from that moment on. George, my driver, tucked us into an inconspicuous siding and we set to work with pliers and pincers. After half an hour of frustrating manipulating we ended up with a few feet of crinkled, twisted wire which was absolutely useless to anyone, for try as we would we could not straighten it out. Time was going on and old George was eyeing the long line of empty wagons still waiting attention.

'Listen here, Bill, I'll go and get a cup of tea,' he offered. 'You stay by here and see what you can do.' And off he went back to the Shed leaving me sitting on the footplate wrestling with the stubbornest wire I had ever met. Whoever made those pet-pipes didn't intend that anyone should ever unwind them again, that was for sure. Having a spell and a smoke, I racked my brains trying to fathom an easier way of unwinding the wire and an efficient way of straightening it out. The answer was obvious. I could use the power of the loco.

Neyland Yard was on the slightest of inclines, running down to the buffers, consequently, wagons or carriages in the sidings were often left (unofficially) without brakes or blocks as the slight slope prevented their running back. At the Iron Bridge, however, the gradient sloped in the opposite direction and any coaches on this side of the bridge had to be firmly braked or they would be off on their travels in no time.

An empty carriage happened to be sharing my siding that day and it conveniently gave me a fixing for one end of the pet-pipe. I secured it firmly to the coupling of the carriage and fixed the partly unwound end onto the coupling behind the loco. It was so simple it was ridiculous! Quickly climbing back onto the footplate I let the brake off and took her slowly down the line for a few yards. I couldn't see if my plan was succeeding behind me, but I just kept going until I estimated that the entire wire was unwound. I slapped the brake on and dashed back to view my handiwork. There, trailing across the sleepers was the straightest, finest wireless mast support you could wish to see. I coiled it into loose loops and carried it triumphantly up onto the footplate where I stowed it safely away at the back of the tender. I didn't want anyone spotting it 'just lying around'! Checking that the engine was secure I jumped down and walked over to the Shed and made straight for the stores.

'Replacement pet-pipe, mate,' I requested from the storeman. 'Damn things are a bloomin' nuisance, always leaking all over the place,' I grumbled, taking the new pipe with what I hoped was concealed glee! I hung the replacement pipe around my neck as I searched all the odd corners and scrap dumps around the Shed for cast-off pet-pipes which had genuinely been discarded because of leaks. To my delight I found five in various places where they had been cast aside, and I was soon back in my private siding with my trophies, where I immediately coupled one of the pipes to my attendant carriage, flinging the new one up onto the footplate to replace the one I had 'borrowed'. I gave all my attention to the task before me.

It was not long before I had two more lovely straightened wires, looped and stacked on the tender. By now I was really getting the hang of things and was not nearly so cautious with the speed as I had been with the first attempt. But, misjudging the distance I had travelled with the third wire, I discovered when I went back to fetch it, that it was still taut between the loco and the carriage and it still had a few more feet to unwind. Back I climbed onto the footplate and went a few more yards in order to complete the procedure and to loosen the wire from the pipe.

A few intrigued, dirty-faced urchins were watching my activities from the Iron Bridge, their faces jammed against the railings, looking down on me in the silence of complete enthralment. When I steamed under them they dashed to the other side to view my progress from a different angle, obviously wondering what this new G.W.R. technique was all about!

The fourth pet-pipe was coupled up ready for stretching, and throwing a few more shovelfuls of coal in, I raised a bit more steam and set off merrily down the line. I didn't want the bother of finding that I had stopped short again, as I had done with the third wire, so I steamed away under the bridge, giving a wave and a short crow to my silent observers above and continued down the line a good few yards further. With the brake hard on because of the incline, I was just about to jump off when I heard the rhythmic click, clickety click of wheels behind me and there was my carriage following me under the Iron Bridge! It reached the apex of the gradient and started to gain speed as it rolled down the other side towards me and my stationary loco. The boys on the bridge started to cheer and wave excitedly, obviously thinking that I had been endeavouring to achieve this all along! By hedges, there was a bit of panic I was in for a few moments! I got the loco moving as quickly as I could, determined to avoid a hard collision at all costs, but the gap between me and the chasing carriage was closing rapidly. Fortunately the road before me was clear, but I gave a few blasts on the whistle just in case, and I set off trying to match my pace to the rolling carriage. Closer and closer it drew until it started to nudge my buffers giving me the chance to apply the brake and bring us both to a halt—uncomfortably near the closed points to the neighbouring siding! I gave my brow a quick wipe with my waste before putting the loco into reverse and slowly and gently pushed my unwelcome companion back up to the apex of the incline once more. The gentlest of nudges and it was over the top, where it picked up a lazy tick over down the other side, coming to rest with a solid thump on the siding buffers. Back where it started, thank goodness!

My watchful friends above were more puzzled than ever. I appeared to have achieved nothing to them and when I climbed down from the footplate in order to find my wire, that is exactly what I had achieved, as it was severed in three places where it had caught under the wheels of the runaway carriage. It must have been a good wire, that one. Instead of breaking off as the others had done when fully extended, it had taken on a fifty-ton carriage! A noble wire, such a shame it was, I could not use it to fight those Westerlies!

It wasn't long before half the Shed was busy pet-pipe stretching and the authorities must have been extremely puzzled as to the failure of a host of pet-pipes at Neyland Shed during the next few months. Leaks sprung unaccountably in almost new pipes and extra replacements had to be ordered from Neath. No doubt they thought it must have been a bad batch, but the wireless masts throughout Neyland had never been so secure, and the Fish empties had never been so neglected!

Christmas Day 1932 found me ready. Archie and I had been checking and re-checking every wire and connection in our latest set to ensure that nothing could go wrong, and our high aerial was the best in Neyland. Accumulators were well charged up, with a spare tucked in the pantry, and batteries were almost new. Only the best was good enough for King George.

Our hours of preparation were well rewarded when His Majesty's voice sounded loud and clear in our very own, Christmas-decorated, front parlour. Win and I were very impressed and Win's mother marvelled at actually hearing the King speak, while Pa insisted that we all stand to attention while the National Anthem was played! It was a great day, and my pine tree and pet-pipe wires had those atmospherics beat hollow!

* * *

I had changed turns with Jimmy Clarke for a day off and I thought I had the best of the bargain until he called in that evening on his way home from work. He was beaming all over his ruddy, coal-dusted face.

'You missed it, Bill, you missed it, boy!' He chuckled at me gloatingly. 'Look at this then,' he went on, pulling from his back pocket a pound note which he waved tauntingly before my eyes. Win stood there, bouncing Bette up and down on her hip in order to keep her quiet while Jimmy disclosed his intriguing piece of news. I racked my brains to think of a means whereby Jimmy could have made an extra pound on the Carmarthen Goods, while he continued to wave the pound note before my face.

'The Hunt!' I finally shouted at him in disbelief. 'The Blasted Hunt. You lucky . . .' and words failed me because Win was there. 'Well I'm damned. And it was my turn you took. Where did they cross you then?'

'We were coming round the bend at Sarnau when I spotted the hounds, see. Coming over the hill they were. The Carmarthen Hunt I expect. They were running parallel with the line, about two hundred yards away.' Jimmy's face glowed with the recollection of the excitement. 'Well, of course, we eased ourselves off a bit,' he went on, giving me a knowing wink. 'Just kept pacing them we did, and blow me, our luck was in and the scent changed direction and the pack heeled round at right-angles and headed straight for the line. We slammed on the brakes and the wagons came jolting into the back of us like ramrods, I can tell you. Then they crossed the track, howling and yelping more like a pack of wolves than dogs. I don't mind telling you, I wouldn't like them to be after me, boy,' he added, with a shudder at the prospect. 'Right in front of us they were,' Jimmy went on. 'I tell you, Bill, if we hadn't worked it right, we'd have been too far ahead and they could have crossed behind us!' He frowned at the thought of what a missed opportunity that would have been! 'Anyway, down came the huntsmen over the field, all touching their caps in thanks as they took their horses across the front of our loco. And we just touched our caps back and kept our fingers crossed. Sure enough, the last one to cross, rode his hunter up to the footplate, a bit skittish it was, didn't like the hissing I don't think, but he handled it well, fair play. "Thank you, driver," he said. "Appreciate your thoughtfulness, please accept this on behalf of The Hunt," and he took out two quid from his wallet and handed it over—as true as I'm standing here,' concluded Jimmy. 'So we split it down the middle and here's my share to prove it!' He waved his crumpled note in the air once more.

'You lucky . . .' I said once more, as much in envy of the actual experience as the cash bonus. It was quite a rare occurrence to stop for a Hunt and I would have loved it to have been me. It takes a great deal of skill to be at the right place at just the right time—as Jimmy well knew. It is so easy to be that little bit too soon and the pack can cross harmlessly behind you! Well, that's no good, now!

I spotted many Hunts in my career on the railway, but, unfortunately, none showed any inclination to cross my track, in spite of my careful pacing. I had missed my opportunity and my chance never came round again.

Although I never had any actual contact with a Hunt when on a loco, a few months after Jimmy Clark's profitable encounter, I had a most frightening and unpleasant experience with a pack of hounds while I was on foot.

It was a beautiful late spring morning and as it was one of my rest days I decided to take my new young spaniel out for a day's gun training. He was a lovely little animal, really keen, but still a little gun-shy. I knew that eventually he would make a good gun-dog, but it would take hours of patient training before that day arrived.

Up the line was one of my favourite rabbiting terrains and that is where we went that glorious spring morning. Mack and I. We walked down past Railway Terrace and on over the Iron Bridge. Mack

The Great Day.
Bill and Win Morgan, surrounded by their family and friends, face the camera for their wedding photograph.

An aerial view of Neyland.

Fireman Dan James with Express Driver Ernie Perry, about to steam out of Neyland with the 4.40 passengers to Carmarthen.

The South Wales train at Paddington General Station during the 1926 strike.

running ahead, then back for reassurance that I was following his chosen path. I had left my Winchester Repeater at home, having decided that my double-bore would be more suitable that day and the bulky cartridges bumped awkwardly in my pockets as I strode along.

The Yard clattered, clanged and whistled beneath our feet as we crossed the bridge, the smoke, grime and dust rising to sully the clear air above. I liked my work, but I liked hunting better!

The discordant but friendly noise of the Shed and Yard gradually died away as we set off up the line. An occasional loco would whistle us and busily shunt a few wagons back and forth, but soon we were on the single track to Johnston. A warning cry to Mack whenever he attempted to cross the line soon discouraged him and he contented himself with exploring the fascinating scents along the Westfield Mill side of the track.

On reaching the first cutting, I automatically pushed two cartridges into the barrels, put the safety-catch on and kept my eyes peeled on every bush, tree, frond and fern ahead. Pigeons were often a good bag from Neyland Woods above us on the other side of the line, but it was too early in the day for those wily birds. Rabbits today. I gave Mack a quiet whistle and he came expectantly to my heels. I knelt and let him sniff the gun, 'That's my beauty,' I whispered as I gave him an affectionate pat on his sleek, puppy head.

We were deep in the country now, the only reminder of man's intrusion being the two gleaming rails, spinning their way remorselessly ahead around every bend. We kept up a steady pace past Westfield Mill crossing and as we rounded a curve I saw that the distant signal was off and I whistled Mack to heel as Dan James steamed noisily past us with the Pick-up Goods to Milford. The signal swung back on and we were left undisturbed once more, until, very faintly at first, then becoming progressively louder, the baying of hounds filtered into my consciousness. They suddenly appeared over the hill, splashes of white and tan on the green fields, the huntsmen still, as yet, unseen. Down the hillside they poured, yelping, baying, barking, ravaging the peace with their blood-thirsty clamour.

We were right in their path. The realisation suddenly hit me as I heard Mack begin to whimper. He cowered round my legs, his tail down and his whole body quivering with fright. I felt the hair on the back of my neck prickle with fear. Not for myself, but for Mack. They would rip him to pieces if he was on the track of the fox's scent, and his fear became a tangible thing which communicated itself to me through his cringing, whimpering little body.

Quickly, I picked him up, his claws scratching my face in his eagerness to be as far away as possible from the terrifying aloneness of the ground. Buttoning up my coat I hurriedly pushed him inside and started to run. The distant signal was only twenty yards away and I made straight for it, Mack bouncing awkwardly inside my coat as I held him close with one hand and carried the gun in the other.

The hounds drew nearer, their baying becoming more frantic as they heard the sound of their huntsman's horn encouraging them. I leant the gun against the base of the signal and started to climb, making comforting, cooing noises to Mack to try to pacify him and to prevent any thought of jumping from entering his little head. He wriggled dangerously and I tightened my grip as I climbed upwards. I reached the top and held on for dear life.

A pack of wolves Jimmy Clarke had called them a few weeks earlier, and the phrase came back to me at that moment. The remainder of the Hunt appeared over the hill, the horses slithering and sliding down the slope just as the first of the hounds reached the signal. They circled wildly around the base, baying and howling up at us, climbing and jumping over each other as they stood on their hind legs and pawed the sides of the signal. I yelled every curse I knew at them, Welsh and English, and held Mack more tightly as he started to struggle at the sensed proximity of his assailants.

'Steady, my beauty!' I repeated over and over again to him, holding his head down inside my jacket. If only he would stop wriggling. There's a hefty sigh of relief I gave when the Huntsmen rode up and took charge of the situation. But it took them a good five minutes before they could achieve any order among their canine ranks. Eventually the pack was taken off to a safe distance while two Huntsmen remained behind apologising profusely. They sympathised with poor Mack, stroking and comforting him, trying to give him back some of his confidence, but he quivered anew at every yelp he heard from the departing hounds, and I knew there was only one thing to do, and that was to take him home and call it a day.

And what a day!

10

In spite of Neyland's being an important terminus for the Great Western, we were definitely in the backwoods as far as progress was concerned. The number of houses which could boast of having running water and sanitation could be counted on one hand, with fingers to spare! Most households in Neyland had their own rain-water tank for both drinking and domestic water—that is, except in a dry spell in the summer when water had to be fetched from one of the pumps dotted around the town.

The domestic rain-water tanks were stone built and the size of a small room. In fact, decades later some of the tanks were converted into bathrooms! And each summer the scrupulous took advantage of the low level of the water in their respective tanks to scrub the interior walls, remove the odd worm or other foreign body which might have had the misfortune to fall in during the winter, and then to lime-wash the walls and floor ready for refilling at the first rainfall. It was not a particularly pleasant task, climbing through the small trap-door in the top into that dank, dark interior. Flare lamps were always unaccountably in short supply and G.W.R. overalls invariably sported a rash of white lime spots, every June, as each master of the house 'limed his tank'.

Sanitation was completely primitive. Euphemisms such as 'going out the back' or 'going down the garden' or 'up the garden' depending on which side of the street you happened to live, were no joke, especially in the middle of a wild, wet Pembrokeshire night. But, on the other hand, it could be an extremely neighbourly act. This was due to the fact that the small stone-built lavatories were always sited back to back with the one next door, and many an interesting discussion has been conducted with the two participants sitting back to back with but a thin plaster wall between them to ensure some degree of privacy. Or, if feeling even more neighbourly, you could leave the door open and conduct a conversation with your other neighbour who would then be facing you! This latter practice, however, usually died out as the interested parties reached the age of eleven or twelve and then recommenced as the age of approximately seventy or seventy-one was reached! The weather, of course, also played a large part in governing the frequency of such neighbourly chats. It was snug on the leeward side but decidedly rugged on the windward!

The Ash Cart (another euphemism if ever there was one), patrolled the back lanes each week, emptying the lavatory buckets, obtaining access through small doors, approximately two-foot square which were sited at ground level in the back wall and which opened directly beneath the seat of the lavatories. A stranger, walking along the back lane, might imagine that half the population of Neyland were midgets—one large door, one small door, one large door, one small door!

These miniature doors, however, presented a great temptation to the local young varmints out for devilment. The calamine lotion has been known to have been called for more than once, after unfortunate encounters with cunningly-placed stinging nettles, and the devilishly clever positioning of small gorse bushes have been known to inflict serious damage to the vocal chords in some instances! Briars and goosegrass were also among the hazards which had to be taken into consideration when answering a call of nature in Neyland. The proverb 'Look before you leap' (or something very similar) may well have originated 'out the back', 'up the garden' or 'down the garden' behind the terraced houses of that Great Western terminus!

We fought back, of course, with locks and bolts which could only be reached from the inside. This was very effective in giving peace of mind and undisturbed stretches of contemplation, but proved to be more trouble than it was worth if, by some chance, we

forgot to unlock the door ready for the weekly visit of the 'Ashcart'!
Life could be very difficult at times.

* * *

No new houses had raised their walls for over twenty years in the town,
and the words 'building plot' were simply not in our vocabulary. That
is, until Win and I decided that we were going to build a bungalow.
There's a commotion that caused, with everyone shaking their heads at
our rashness and telling us that we would be wasting our money. We
had managed to save £120, which was originally intended for the purchase of an Austin Seven, but which, on reconsideration, we decided to
use as a deposit on a £500 bungalow. Win and I walked miles viewing
every field around the town with the prospect of building on it, and,
eventually, we chose a site bordering on the shore along The
Promenade, which was completely undeveloped.

Apart from the glorious views across the estuary there was the
unique advantage (for Neyland) of the availability of piped water. This
water had been laid on decades before by the Great Western, for the
convenience of troops during the Great War, the shore fields being the
site for their canvas camp. The soldiers had long since gone, but the
piped water was still there.

Win and I decided that this was a great waste so we bought our plot
of land from Osborne the Farm, and simply tapped the Company water
supply and no-one asked any questions! The problem of piping water
to our bungalow had been solved, and by 1935 we were the proud
owners of a handsome bay-windowed residence complete with bath-
room. The woodwork had been lovingly grained by Dickie Hughs the
Builder, the wood itself 'acquired' from Strumble Lighthouse, when
it had been dismantled in readiness for the construction of a stone
one.

'St. Neot's' was our new home and we named it after Win's father's
birthplace.

The success of our venture encouraged others and soon Bob and
Alice May built a sister bungalow next to us. Bob was a booking clerk
on the Great Western and Alice hailed from Llangwm where the
villagers had almost disowned her for mixing with the Neyland
foreigners. Fortunately, Alice was of a more enlightened generation and
Win and I became life-long friends with both Bob and Alice. Old Mr.

May moved in with them, he was a guard on the Western and a devil of a fine rabbit-gin setter he was too.

Joe Nicholas the Draper built next. He owned the drapery in the High Street and travelled round the nearby villages doing a roaring trade in Welsh flannel shirts and long woollen combinations.

Neyland now had three new bathrooms. There's progress for you. Of course, we still had to rely on the High Tides in order to empty our cesspits, and even if it meant getting up in the middle of the night in order to catch the tide at its peak, it was still progress! Definitely a step up from the 'Ash cart'!

* * *

Ivor Williams was a hell of a case. A good driver to work with, as long as you watched him, otherwise you would find yourself doing more than your fair share.

We were on a small 14 class tankie, achieving some order out of the confusion of shuntings around Haverfordwest sidings, when he announced at about 2.30 that he thought he had better take a stroll up to the hospital for them to take a look at his wrist which he had sprained the previous day.

'You can manage without me for half an hour or so, can't you Bill?' he suggested smilingly as he gave me a clap on the back.

'All right then, Ivor,' I agreed, 'but don't be too long, we'll be needing water soon mind,' I reminded him, nodding towards the water gauge behind him. There was no water column at Haverfordwest Station and the nearest supply was Clarbeston Road—a few miles down the main line. The tankie could only hold enough for a few hours shunting, then we'd have to take her for a refill.

Ivor started to climb down from the footplate, when he hesitated with a thoughtful look on his face. 'What's coming now then?' I thought to myself.

'Look here, Bill, I don't suppose you'd mind if I had my boots soled on the way—there's a good cobbler just up the hill and he'd only take a few minutes, I dare say.' He looked appealingly up at me.

'Aw, all right. Now clear off and don't you be too long,' I warned again. To my surprise Ivor started to climb back up onto the footplate. I looked queryingly at him.

'Well, Bill, boy,' he started, 'you see, now, I've only got this one pair of boots like, so do you think you could lend me yours?' Hurriedly adding, 'It'll save time see, if I can leave them at the cobblers on the way up to the hospital and collect them again on the way down.'

Fair play, you had to give him credit for his cheek, he was so plausible it made you sick! Capitulating without argument, I proceeded to remove my boots.

'It's too bloody slippery up by here in my socks, man, I'm telling you straight,' I announced, as I experimented moving around the footplate in my stockinged feet.

'Take your socks off, Bill,' suggested Ivor helpfully. 'You'll have a nice grip then.' I glared at him, but once more complied with his suggestion.

There's daft it was! The hot metal near the fire-box was impossible to stand on and the grit and coal-dust were like splinters of glass.

'Now just you listen to me, Ivor,' I gasped as I hopped wincingly from one foot to another. 'Either you get me a large piece of sacking— thick sacking, or I'm having my boots back.' I delivered my ultimatum with the finality of one who could be pushed no further!

Of course, Ivor was only too willing and dashed off to the Goods Shed to obtain my temporary carpeting. I had a few sarcastic comments from Shunty who was directing the wagons with me, but apart from that I don't think anyone else looked at my feet—except me. Damned unpleasant it was, even with a sack spread on the footplate. I'd swear it felt as if there was clinker between my toes, and when a large lump of coal fell off the shovel onto my unsuspecting foot, I tell you, it was the last straw!

Three-thirty came and went with no sign of Ivor—of course, and the water gauge was getting dangerously low.

'We'll take a spell!' I shouted down to Shunty, explaining the water shortage and the non-appearance of Ivor. Four o'clock and a long line of wagons still needed shunting. There was nothing for it but to take the tankie up the line to Clarbeston Road. It would be impossible, however, to get out onto a main line with only one man aboard the footplate, so I enlisted the presence of Shunty, who climbed up beside me and leant over the cab side with a most professional air! After all, as long as there were two Company men on the loco, who was going to bother to check if one was actually the driver!

I blew a crow for the signal-man, who immediately gave us the road and off Shunty and I steamed to Clarbeston Road. We returned half an hour or so later without mishap, expecting to see Ivor waiting for us— but not a sign of him was there. Shunty climbed down and I started my barefoot, solo shunting once more. An hour went by, two, three, until the last wagon was shunted into place, and who should walk up along the track, all smiles, but Ivor, remarking on the lovely weather we'd had all day!

When I eventually recovered my power of speech I demanded the return of my bloody boots, and where the hell did he think he'd been all day?

'Now, now, boy, don't fret about it. I wasn't long at the hospital, but there was this little nurse who was just coming off duty, see, so I walked down by the river with her for a spell and then we strolled back to the yard, but I could see that you had obviously gone for water, so there was no point in my just hanging around like a lump. Back up to the hospital gardens we went to have a bit of a sit in the sun—lovely and warm it was. We could see you from there, Bill, I was explaining everything you were doing to Maisie see and the time just went by. Got a bit chilly when the sun went down, so here I am,' he concluded with a matey clap on the back.

I shook my head in despair. 'Take us home, Ivor,' I sighed, tenderly massaging my blackened, splintered feet. 'I've had a busy day.'

* * *

It wasn't my year for successful shunting at Haverfordwest. I came to this conclusion a few weeks later when I was on a similar turn with Jimmy One-pint. The only difference being that this time we were shunting in the pitch dark, and with a trainee ground shunter at that! It was only his third week at the job, the previous two having been spent entirely on observation of methods of lamp signalling, points turning, coupling and uncoupling. The layman might think that shunting wagons is an undemanding, simple operation requiring the minimum of skill. Nothing could be further from the actual fact.

A train of fifty or sixty mixed goods wagons, consisting of oil-tankers, perishable goods, mixed goods, G.P.O. parcel wagons, empties, coal wagons—(perhaps for three or four different coal merchants) could be waiting attention. The wagons were never in the correct order in which they were required to be berthed—even down to the empties which were needed the following day and those which were not required for a week. The oil-tanks were just as likely to be stuck in the middle, when it was imperative that they were first in the sidings in order to connect to the coupling pipes.

After various uncouplings, shuntings, recouplings, the oil-tanks would eventually be extricated from the centre of the train, it's true. Unfortunately, in the process, you might just find that you have somehow anchored down your perishable goods between next week's empties and a parcel wagon! While struggling to rescue your perishable bananas with more fantastic permutations of shuntings, you eventually breathe a sigh of relief when it is safely in its correct siding, only to realise with dismay that you have split a coal merchant's four wagons, and now one of them is berthed at a rival's coal stage!

I have seen experienced drivers helpless with laughter, tears rolling down their faces, as they watched the antics of new shunters trying to achieve the correct order from a sixty wagon train. After an hour they have been in a worse muddle than when they started!

Such was not the case with One-pint and myself, I must hasten to add. Experienced we were, to the last degree. We permutated shuntings with sidings to perfection, it was a work of art. We used the time-honoured practice of knocking back in order to avoid having always to reverse and come forward. This meant that as soon as the points were changed to suit the required siding, the wagons to be berthed were uncoupled and we gave the entire train a hefty jolt, sending the uncoupled wagons merrily on their way along their chosen track, while the remainder of the train moved but a few inches. It needed, however, good cooperation between the driver and the ground shunter who changed the points and uncoupled the wagons.

Simple 'Right-o's' were insufficient as the distance was usually too great, except, of course, towards the end when the load was diminished. Communicating in daytime shunting was achieved by means of flags and hand-waving, but night shunting consisted of a more complicated arrangement of red, white and green lamps signalling. This was further complicated, of course, if the track was on a bend!

Perhaps the layman's picture of a half-asleep driver, lazily steaming back and forth, taking it easy as he jogs along doing a bit of simple shunting, is beginning to change!

I can still recall in my early shunting days, the exasperation on reaching the final wagon and discovering that it should have been berthed at the front of a particular siding, which by then was full of wagons! The number of operations necessary to place one errant wagon in its correct berth can be quite surprising:

1. Change points.
2. Knock back offending wagon into spare siding.
3. Change points.
4. Steam into required siding.
5. Couple up to wagons.
6. Pull out wagon train.
7. Change points.
8. Steam to single wagon.
9. Couple up.
10. Reverse out of siding.
11. Change points.
12. Shunt all wagons into original berth.

And that is merely one misplaced wagon. The chaos arising with an inexperienced crew with three or four stray wagons sandwiched in the middle of a siding full of already shunted wagons, must be seen to be believed! Tempers can run very high and frustrations reach exploding point!

As it was often necessary to overflow onto the main line in order to shunt a long wagon train, there was also the added frustration of constantly having to clear the line and stop work for a quarter of an hour or so, in order to let an express or goods through. No wonder shunting took so long!

Well, there we were, One-pint, myself and our ground shunter with his trainee anxiously awaiting instructions in Haverfordwest Yard that drizzle-dark evening.

'We'll knock out the empties first and loaded back, driver,' announced Shuntie. Haverfordwest Yard was an ideal place for knocking back because of the slightly falling gradient to the sidings. Just trickle in they would. 'A trainee we've got tonight, boys,' he went on. 'But I'll do the uncoupling for him just to give him a bit of help.' The trainee stood in the background looking suitably grateful, fiddling awkwardly with his white lamp and scuffing his boots.

'Up to the points with you, then,' Shuntie ordered. 'Empties out first now, mind,' he repeated to his apprentice who replied with a quick understanding nod. 'I'll shout "All Clear" and if they're clear of the points you give me a white light when you've changed the points back for the next lot loaded back. Got it straight now, have you?' More quick nods answered him, and off our trainee shunter scurried into the dark, wet mist, eager to commence his first duties. Well, he should find them easy enough—after all, he didn't have to bother with the uncoupling as well. Throwing a few curses at the miserable weather our Shunter disappeared into the darkness, while Jim and I sat in the cab and had a quiet smoke, keeping an eye out for our first lamp signal. We had already pulled all the wagons out of the siding, and by extricating all the empties it would make it far easier to sort out the loaded wagons later. We had about fifty wagons on and we'd pulled a good bit ahead so that we could hit the first few up hard. After a few minutes, I spied our white lamp, widely swinging, signalling us to hit 'em back hard, so clipping my cigarette I opened up the regulator for a few seconds, giving the train a hefty jolt, and slammed it shut again immediately. The first wagons must have cleared the points all right as we were given the following red light acknowledging successful completion of the manoeuvre. The next white light we received was swinging slightly less vigorously, so I concluded that Shuntie must have noticed that the wagons had rolled into their appropriate siding just a shade too fast, so I eased up on the force of my next knock back. Jim offered to take over, but I suggested that I might as well finish knocking out the empties, so he carried on with his smoke. We repeated the procedure several times, and everything seemed to be going smoothly, although I could make out nothing in the darkness ahead, just wet and miserable it looked. I was thankful that I was in the cab and not out by the points. A ground shunter's work in winter was no joke.

I'd already had one green light signalling me to pull up a bit before knocking any more wagons back, and now I received another. We had been shunting for about half an hour or so, and I was rather surprised at receiving a second green light so soon after the first. Surely I didn't need to pull up any more yet, but 'Proceed on Caution' it meant so I did just that, expecting the usual red light to stop me after a few yards so that we could get cracking with the knocking back once more. But it kept on slowly swinging, until I found myself almost drawing level with it. I couldn't think why Shuntie had decided to stop knocking back as we had about fifteen to twenty wagons still on. Jim hung over the cab side to try and see what was going on as I slowly steamed up to Shuntie. His face glowed eerily in the glistening reflection of his lamp and we could see by his expression that all was not well.

'What's up then, mate?' Jim asked, as I drew the loco to a halt beside the damp, drooping-shouldered figure.

'Do you know what that dull bugger's been doing down at the points?' Shuntie asked in despair. 'Everyone of those blessed wagons is back in the siding where we took 'em from. . . . Every . . . blessed . . . one!' he finished on a note of indescribable pathos, shaking his head in disbelief, as a raindrop trickled off the end of his nose.

Our new trainee had been so anxious to make sure that the wagons had cleared the points, so that he could signal his confirmation to Shuntie's 'All Clear?' that he had completely forgotten to change the damn things! So there we were, not back where we started, but a deuced sight further back than that, as all the wagons had to be recoupled again in order for us to pull them all out and start again— after we'd had a cup of tea, boy, after we'd had a cup of tea!

He never did get the hang of it, our trainee. Hopeless shunter he was. In fact, he ended up as a porter, but there's one thing I must say, fair play, he could play the piano lovely!

* * *

Mishaps were not solely confined to Haverfordwest Yard, however, and not many weeks later I found events running none too smoothly at Neyland Shed. Tommy Stickie and I, well, Tommy Davis, really, but no-one ever used his proper name, had been prepping a loco for the Llanelly men to take out from Neyland to Llandeilo.

'Let's take her out then, Bill,' said Stickie, slowly moving us the few feet to the Shed exit. We usually took the prepped engine across into the sidings and coupled up ready for the crew to take over. A few feet from the Shed limit was a hand-operated set of points which led either to a buffered line where locos awaiting prepping were berthed, or to a short length of track with a catch-point half-way, operated by the signal-box and indicated by a low dummy signal. It was this length of track which led to the main line and across to the main sidings where the 5.20 Goods were awaiting us.

The procedure for any prepped engine to leave Shed was for the driver to bring her to a stop at the shed limit. The fireman then set the hand-operated points away from the waiting-road and onto the road leading to the main line, while the driver blew the appropriate whistle code, which was five and a crow, which informed the signal-man that there was an engine waiting to leave Shed. The signal-man then closed the catch-point along the track leading to the main line and the road was then clear for the waiting loco to steam out.

On this particular day, I was just jumping down from the footplate to operate the points when the relief Llanelly fireman (a chap we called Sinbad, because many years before he had run away to sea for a short time), came over the tracks towards me with a friendly wave.

'All set then, Bill. I'm a bit early so there's no need for you to bring her over,' he suggested. 'I'll take her from here, boy,' and he climbed up onto the footplate by Stickie who was just blowing five and a crow, while I pulled the hand points over.

'Right-O!' I shouted to Sinbad, meaning that I'd moved the points for him. Stickie must have heard me and thought I meant that the entire road was clear and steamed out.

I was just about to have a spell in the coalman's cabin when there was the most almighty earth-shaking crash from outside. I dashed out of the cabin and there was the loco, steaming violently, laying on her side, derailed at the catch-point, with Stickie and Sinbad staggering dazedly about on the tons of tipped coal which was still rolling from the tender.

Accusations started to fly left and right. Stickie accused me of giving him the 'Right-O' when the catch-point was still open. I hotly denied any such thing, trying to explain that I had been giving the O.K. to Sinbad that I had changed the hand points for him, and accused Stickie of not checking the dummy signal that the catch-point was closed. Stickie insisted that I had given him the all-clear and so the shouting match went on! Soon the entire Shed, cleaners (excited and delighted), labourers, fitters, firemen, drivers, and of course the Chargeman, gathered around us and the crippled loco, with poor old Sinbad looking as worried as hell and busy telling everybody that it was nobody's fault, man—it just happened like, and cursing the Fates which had made him turn up early for his shift, and Stickie and me shouting and gesticulating at each other, in white-hot rage.

Of course, there was an Enquiry.

The following week found me sitting apprehensively in the

Foreman's Office at Neyland, facing the Superintendent from Neath.

'This is a serious matter, Mr. Morgan,' he opened, shuffling the papers on the desk before him in an authoritative manner. We spent the next fifteen minutes going over all the circumstances and he admitted that he could see how easily the misunderstanding had occurred, but he remained adamant that blame had to be attached and finally informed me that I would have a registered caution. The words were like a death sentence. It only needed two registered cautions in a career, which might span half a century, and you were automatically taken off all main line workings for good. I could not see the justice in this sentence at all and I dug my heels in.

'I refuse to accept it,' I stated in a flat but determined tone, realising that this would mean that the enquiry would have to be referred to higher authority, but it seemed the only thing to do—a Registered Caution for a friendly 'Right-O'—never on your life, I thought.

This, of course, extended the interview for a further ten minutes, and after considerable discussion, the Super eventually decided to change the Registered Caution to a Verbal Caution.

I took a deep breath and once more refused to accept it. After all, I thought to myself as I stared across the desk into the Super's grim face, a Verbal Caution could be brought up against me in ten, twenty, or thirty years time—it would always be there, on my record. It just seemed too big a price to pay for letting old Sinbad know that I'd changed the points!

'In that case, Mr. Morgan, I'll have to refer this matter to Headquarters,' concluded the Super with an air of finality. 'Please send in Mr. Davis on your way out.'

Mr. Davis, I thought, who the hell is Mr. Davis? Oh, of course, old Stickie. 'Your turn,' I nodded to him as I went out. There's a grim day that was.

The threat of having to appear before Headquarters hung over me like a cloud for the next few days. But the days drifted into weeks and the weeks into months and never another word did I hear about it!

Stickie and I bore no malice, of course, and before the year was out we were talking about it as a joke, 'Hey, Morgy, remember the time. . . .' But I've been very careful with my 'Right-O's' ever since!

11

I had been firing now for fifteen years, and along with Freddie, Dai, Dan and others, I was ready for promotion to Passenger Fireman. Neyland had comparatively few passenger trains and consequently required few Passed Passenger Firemen. This was offset, however, by the fact that Neyland carried the Head Foreman—Whitland, Pembroke Dock, Tenby and Cardigan all being controlled by Neyland. Very often, relief drivers were required at these stations and Neyland men were sent, leaving temporary vacancies for Passed Passenger Firemen to take their place at Neyland as drivers. This grade of Passed Fireman permitted us to be put in charge of an engine and to work trains for which we received drivers' pay. It was the lowest grade drivers' pay, but it was still very acceptable, along with the experience.

This examination for Passed Fireman was compulsory and was carried out by the Inspector sent down from Neath, which was the head station in South Wales controlled by a Superintendent. These Inspectors were men who had been selected by the Head Staff, and had worked their way up from cleaners. They certainly knew their job and all that was required of the firemen who were applying for promotion. This was not to be the walk-over I had experienced in Swindon when interviewed by my golden-watch-chained superior who had loftily assumed that I knew all that I was supposed to!

These Inspectors had spent their lives with steam engines, as we had, and we held them in great respect. No-one would dream of trying to pull the wool over the eyes of an Inspector—Heaven help him if he did!

Classes were held at each station with rule books and diagrams supplied by the Company for study. The Instructors were mostly drivers who gave their time freely in order to prepare cleaners and firemen for promotion examinations. Our examination consisted of rules and working of the engine, with particular emphasis on what to do in the case of a breakdown as it was essential to know whether to move a loco or whether fitters had to be sent for.

After having taken the verbal examination, the Inspector would arrange to meet each of us on duty in order to see how we handled an engine. He came with us on the footplate and watched intently as we drove, making notes on the use of injector, regard for signals, etc. Many good firemen reached this stage but no further. They were given three trials on the footplate, spaced over a few months, and if they were still not up to standard they were reduced to shed men, which meant taking a job of coalman, fire-dropper, lampman or general labourer.

This might seem a ruthless way of dealing with men who had proved over ten or fifteen years that they were good firemen, but who, nevertheless, just could not reach the standard required for Driver. This had to be, however, otherwise they would be blocking the way for promotion of other up-and-coming men who were still cleaners, by filling a fireman's post. This was why the Examination was compulsory.

It was, therefore, no light-hearted affair, with success almost guaranteed merely because we had put the time in as firemen. Many hopes were dashed at this stage and some felt such despair at the prospect of demotion that they left the railway altogether and tried to find alternative employment at the Milford Docks. The Dockyard at Pembroke Dock no longer offered employment to hundreds of men as it had done. It had closed down in 1926 along with other victims of the General Strike, its closure helping to put one more nail in the coffin of Neyland's industrial prosperity. The first had been hammered home when the Irish Boats with the passenger and cattle trade had been moved from Neyland to Fishguard, and another when the Ice Factory had closed when the Fish Trade was moved to Milford Haven.

But there were no failures that year and Neyland Shed was the richer by six Passed Passenger Firemen—and good ones at that!

Double-home had been an established and accepted part of my

working life for the past fifteen years. The double-home boxes were obtained by sending away to Grimsby to an Ironmongers and Tinsmiths by the name of Hildred, who supplied our characteristic domed boxes. It was more or less assumed that once you became a fireman you set about obtaining your Grimsby Box, or it might be thought that you were not really going to take the railway seriously as a career!

Of course, it goes without saying that I didn't exactly buy mine—I acquired it, you might say! It was a Grimsby Box, all right, but a second-hand one. I had bartered three months' supply of weekly rabbit for it, guaranteeing delivery every Friday evening. This had been back in 1921, not long after I had been made fireman, and the elderly Haverfordwest widow, whose husband had been the original box owner, had had a good rabbit roast every Sunday without fail for three months. I took good care, of course, always to let her know whether it was trapped or shot as, if the latter, she would keep a wary eye out for lead pellets embedded in the flesh. I didn't want any complaints about broken teeth!

It was a beauty of a box, high domed, with my name engraved on a brass plate screwed onto the lid. W. J. MORGAN.

Double-home meant spending one night away from home at either Swansea, Llandeilo, Landore, Severn Tunnel or Gloucester. The 5.45 a.m. Goods to Milford, taking coal empties to Llandeilo Junction and Duffryn Yard, returning with coal for the Milford trawlers, was a typical double-home shift, the round trip taking thirty-six hours away from home. But the 5.20 p.m. Goods to Llandeilo was a different kettle of fish and could be managed within the eight-hour shift. This was because the Down Goods to Neyland from Llandeilo met the Up Goods half-way—which was roughly St. Clears. The two crews then exchanged trains and worked back to their home station. A very convenient arrangement, which, however, brought out the worst in us! Everything ran smoothly at first, when each train arrived at St. Clear's at roughly the same time, but soon the Devil's own game of 'delaying tactics' gradually crept in!

It all started one night when the Llandeilo crew, on arriving at St. Clear's, found no exchange Goods awaiting them, as we had been unavoidably held up at Clarbeston Road. They were given the road, and had to take their train on to Whitland, where we exchanged with them. The seed had been sown! From then on it was a waiting game we played, with each crew endeavouring to delay their arrival at St. Clear's, thereby making the rival crew work a longer journey and ourselves a considerably shorter one! Not only did the loser have to take his train further in order to meet his wily counterparts, but he also had to work the exchange train back along the same extra distance—the stakes were high, indeed!

On one occasion when we were on the losing side (which happened very rarely), we found ourselves signalled on through St. Clear's to Sarnau, where to our dismay the signal was still with us and no sign of the Down Goods, and we eventually found ourselves at Carmarthen Junction before we encountered our opponents! What we called them would not stand repeating, but we had to give them credit for their skill! We didn't make it back to Neyland by one o'clock that morning, but at least we managed to make a little overtime! It was a case of the better time you made the further you had to go and the harder you had to work—there was no justice! Of course, if both sides played the waiting game with equal success, they both arrived at St. Clear's—late, and a few awkward questions might have to be answered. It was a game which required an intuitive knowledge of what the other crew were up to, and it always reminded me of a game of poker, with each player calling the other's bluff. And, like poker, it took a great deal of skill to play well.

The 8 a.m. Passengers from Neyland to Swansea was also a double-home turn, arriving at Swansea at 11.30 and booking off until 2 a.m. the following morning. We worked a Castle back with the Down Parcel train, arriving home at 7 a.m. The Castle was then coaled and fired at Neyland and worked the 4.45 Parcels to Paddington with a new crew.

This was a good double-home turn for doing shopping and I spent many an hour wandering round the large stores at Swansea, occasionally buying an interesting article to take home for Win or Bette. A gas iron took my fancy one day; it was being demonstrated in one of the large stores and I thought it was a most ingenious invention! How marvellous it would be for Win, not to have to wait for the flat irons to heat up over the fire, I thought, and immediately bought one.

Win was delighted with it and from then on the flat irons were relegated to keeping the doors open in summer and keeping our feet warm in bed during the winter—suitably wrapped in newspaper, of course. The smell of scorching newsprint in the bedroom was unusual if nothing else! We scorned the easy soft-living provided by rubber hot water bottles. We were a hardy race!

The 3 p.m. Parcels to Swansea was another regular double-home shift. We left Swansea at eight the following morning and arrived back at Neyland at 3 p.m. Our double-home lodgings were ruled over by our respective landladies, who provided the comforts of home, to a greater or lesser degree, according to their respective ages, personalities and inclinations.

None of the double-home turns, however, matched up to the double-homes on the Fish Trains to either Severn Tunnel or Gloucester, at least as far as I was concerned. For, to me, the Fish Trains offered more scope for initiative and enterprise!

It was a typical West Wales summer's day—grey skies, a cool breeze and the threat of rain in the air! Win and Bette were spending a week with relations in Porthcawl and I was preparing my box for the 3.45 Gloucester Fish turn. The Porthcawl relations were considered to be the wealthy branch of the family as Uncle John was self-employed, owning the Sker Sand and Gravel, and a sleek Dodge car with trays which folded down from the backs of the front seats. Auntie Florrie, his wife, possessed a telephone, a dinner gong, a permanently reserved front seat at the Porthcawl Concert Hall, three charming daughters, a flair for flowery hats and the personal attention and interest of the local medium. They were definitely the wealthy branch of the family.

My double-home box was finally packed. Cheese and brawn sandwiches to eat on the way, a cold roast rabbit leg for supper at my lodgings, a loaf of bread and a jar of butter to cut my own sandwiches for the return run and two thick rashers of salty fat bacon and an egg for my landlady to cook for my breakfast the following morning. The square ex-whisky bottle was ready filled with cold tea (no milk) and I slipped a raw onion in my pocket just in case I fancied it. My preparations were complete, except for rolling the bundle of old newspapers which I had been saving especially for the Fish Run. With these finally tucked under my arm, my tea bottle in my pocket and my box firmly grasped in my left hand, I locked up the bungalow and set off across the windswept Prom, passing the small two-roomed cottage where old Joe Jenkins had used to live and I smiled to myself as I recollected what a character he'd been when Freddie Griffiths and I had been cleaners many years before. He had been over sixty when we had first come to work on the G.W.R., and he had never taken a day off from work since he had started on the railway many years before. He had taken a tremendous pride in his work—an unswept floor or uncared for tools were an abhorrence to him and every task, however menial, was tackled with steady conscientiousness.

He had had his own personal wheelbarrow, brush and shovel, and no-one had dared to use old Joe's cleaning equipment except Joe himself. His shovel had shone with a polished, well-oiled gleam, his wheelbarrow was spotless and the bristles of his brush were regularly combed clean of dust and dirt with Joe's own specially made wooden comb.

Holidays with pay had been introduced, and we had all been delighted with an entire week off from work every year. All, that is, except Joe Jenkins who had stubbornly refused to believe that any company would give money away for nothing! 'Nobody can expect to be paid for work that is not done,' he had contended in his strong Welsh accent. 'They are trying to trick us, just you wait and see!' he had warned. Consequently when his turn for annual leave had come round he had absolutely refused to accept it, saying that he could not afford to be without a week's wages! 'And who is to say that the Company will not give my job to somebody else when I am not there,' he worried.

We had all tried to reassure him that his wages would be paid and that no-one would take his job from him, but it had taken weeks of persuading before he had reluctantly agreed to take a week off from work, and he hadn't been at all happy about it! The week before he had been booked for his holiday he had fretted about what state the Shed would be in by the time he returned, and finally the Chargeman himself had had to promise Joe that he would personally supervise the cleaning of the Shed to ensure that it would be in a satisfactory state on his return. The foreman had made out a pass for Joe and his wife to go to Paddington and had handed it to him with great ceremony with instructions to take a real holiday. Paddington had proved to be far too adventurous for Joe, however, but he finally agreed to take his wife to Swansea for a week. Arrangements had been quickly made with one of the double-home landladies at Swansea who agreed to give them full board for the week for £3 all in.

There's a send-off they had had on the Mails that Saturday night! All the Shed, foreman and chargeman included, came to wave them on their first-ever holiday—although, by the brave smile they both had tried to put on, you'd have thought they were going to a funeral rather than on a holiday! And so, with a pair of freshly slit rabbits hanging from the luggage rack (a present for their landlady), off they had both set for the first holiday of their lives.

The following Monday the labourer who had been taking Joe's place for the week had been unable to find the whereabouts of Joe's equipment. Searched everywhere he had, but no wheelbarrow, brush or shovel could he find.

'Bet old Joe's taken it on holiday with him,' a wag had remarked. 'I thought I saw something hidden up on the luggage rack,' another had added. 'He's probably cleaning up Swansea Shed for them, boy!' And so it had gone on, the witticisms growing more exaggerated as everyone had tried to top the last remark about poor old Joe's wheelbarrow, brush and shovel, until the entire Shed had dissolved into hoots of laughter.

'The bloody things must be by here somewhere,' the Chargeman had eventually stated in exasperation, and he'd put all the cleaners on an intensive search for the elusive kit. Inside and out we'd looked without success. We'd combed the Yard as well as the Shed (taking the opportunity of turning the search into a game of High-jinks of course) but still there had been no sign of Joe's wheelbarrow, which, after all, was not a small thing to hide.

'Perhaps he took it home with him, for safe-keeping like,' someone had suggested.

'Well, if his precious barrow is worth that to him, we'll leave it there, man,' sighed the Chargeman. 'I suppose he has got a bit of a thing about it, fair play.'

And so the week went on, with everyone assuming that Joe had taken his lovingly polished shovel and barrow and his carefully combed brush home for safe-keeping.

The following Monday Joe had turned up for work a quarter of an hour before he was due to book on, as he always did, but there was still no sign of his kit! Eyebrows were raised in puzzlement, but no-one had remarked about its disappearance.

We had managed to contain our perplexity and had restricted ourselves to comments about how well he had looked after his holiday and that we'd hoped his wife had enjoyed her week in Swansea, etc.

'Follow him, boys!' the Chargeman had hoarsely whispered to Freddie and me as Joe started to make his way out of the Shed. 'He must have hidden the blessed stuff by here, after all, but where it is, Heaven knows,' he had added with a puzzled shake of his head.

Freddie Griffiths and I had needed no second bidding, and we had set off stalking old Joe Jenkins with all the stealth and cunning of professional spies! Such excitement and daring we'd felt, you'd have thought he was going to reveal the whereabouts of the Crown Jewels instead of a wheelbarrow, brush and shovel! Out of the Shed he'd gone, across the Cripple sidings and up the line, with Fred and me following, using the shunting tracks and stationary empties for cover.

'He's making for the Hydraulic,' I whispered, as Joe turned away from the track.

'Well, there's nothing hidden in the Hydraulic, for sure; the Chargeman himself searched it and there was nothing there at all,' Fred had asserted adamantly.

Rising a good fifty feet from the ground, the massive stone-built Hydraulic, looking more like a defensive stronghold of an ancient castle than a High Water Tower and Pump House, had stood directly in Joe's path, and into its hollow structure he'd disappeared. At last, curiosity overcoming our caution, we followed Joe through the doorway. It had taken a few minutes for our eyes to get used to the gloom, gradually becoming aware of the steam pumps below which fed the cranes and hoists of the Fish Stage and Pontoon, and the narrow iron ladders which crawled vertically up the inside of the stone walls. But of a wheelbarrow, brush or shovel there was not a sign—nor anywhere where they could have been concealed. Fred gave me a nudge and I saw that old Joe had been fiddling with something at the bottom of one of the ladders. He had been untying a rope which had been fastened to one of the iron rungs. Suddenly he'd sensed that he was being watched and he'd wheeled round to stare accusingly at us.

'Just thought we'd come to help you, Joe,' Fred had hastily interposed, in an attempt to allay any idea that we had been spying on him. He'd grumbled something to himself and we'd seen his eyes travel upwards and ours followed. There, suspended a good fifteen feet above our heads, in mid-air, rigged up on a pulley on one of the strengthening bars, were Joe's barrow, brush and shovel! And there it had hung the entire week, in the cavernous gloom of the Hydraulic tower, like some great metal bat.

'Well I'll be damned,' I thought. 'Who the bloody hell would have thought of looking up there?' I'd asked Fred in disbelief. Fred had just stood there with his mouth hanging open, staring upwards at the gently swaying hardware far above his head!

Slowly, the barrow, brush and shovel swung back and fore and descended from their lofty hiding-place. Fred and I had steadied the load as it had neared our outstretched hands and had guided it carefully onto the floor with a gentle bump as Joe had let out the last bit of rope. Not a word had he said to us, simply turned his back and had wheeled his beloved kit out into the daylight. We'd stood there, watching him as he'd made his way back to the Shed, stubborn pride showing in the set of his shoulders and the gait of his walk. We should have been impressed by his devotion to duty and his pride in his work, but to tell the truth, being the lads we were, and the age we were, we'd thought it hilariously funny!

But Joe and his wife had long gone from the little cottage and the G.W.R. would never see men like him again.

On, past Bert Cronin's place I walked. Now there's another stalwart of the Western for you, a guard of long standing, an upholder of the British Legion and an ex-drummer boy of the Boer War. He'd stand no messing from anyone. Approaching the station, I glanced up at the now disused South Wales Hotel, its portico peeling and scarred with the initials of courting carvers and its windows dusty-glazed or boarded up. Sad the Hotel was, one of the victims of the decline in Neyland's prosperity.

I twisted and clanked my way through the two kissing gates at either end of the Hotel Gardens, having wended my way along the winding path through the overgrown shrubs, neglect and decay where once had been care and pride. Even the station had lost some of its grandeur—the imposing glass roof had long gone, leaving the travellers open to the elements in a most unbefitting manner for a Great Western terminus—but we still had equal billing with Paddington on the coaches!

I was firing with Tommy Francis that day, a character who knew every inch of the line from Neyland to Gloucester like the back of his hand. The 53 was ready prepped for us and we took her out of Neyland Yard at 2.30, making for Milford where we would pick up the fish wagons. Also waiting for me at Milford was my own specially ordered box of one and a half hundredweight of mixed fish, which I had bought for five shillings the previous day at the Fish Market, having slipped one of the porters a shilling to hand-cart it up to the station in time for the afternoon Fish train. Sure enough, there it was, on the end of the platform as we steamed in.

'A busy run we're going to have then, Bill?' asked Tom with a grin as he spotted my fish crate.

'Hope so, boy,' I replied with a wink. 'Pity the weather isn't a bit better though,' I added, with a disgusted look at the darkening sky, as I climbed down from the footplate with my newspapers under my arm. While the twenty-odd fish wagons were being loaded and coupled up, I had far more important things to do and I was determined to use the time profitably. Laying the newspapers on a convenient seat, I prised open my box of fish and surveyed its contents with satisfaction. Cod, skate, hake, whiting, sole, plaice—the mouth-watering selection slithered through my hands as I carefully proportioned the one and a half hundredweight into roughly four-pound bundles, which I wrapped securely in my saved-up newspaper, taking care, however, to throw the best of the hake, turbot, sole and plaice into a woven frail at my feet. This was my own personal basket, and a good twelve pound of top quality fish found its way into it before I had finished my task. Securing it tightly with string I stowed it in the detonator locker for safety and then replaced the remaining wrapped fish in the crate, using the help of a passing porter to lift it onto the tender, where I carefully wedged it behind the coal.

I was all set, even had time for a sit down and a quick smoke before we were given the road and Tommy Francis took us out of Milford with our loaded fish wagons behind us. It was a heavy load and the 53 coped well, even on the banks. Better than those 29s, I thought to myself as I fired relentlessly as we pulled up from Milford; we'd have been slipping like the devil by now—useless they were on our gradients, although, mind you, you'd have a job to catch them on the flat.

The weather was still pretty miserable when we pulled into Carmarthen at 4.55, the platform glistening with the scurrying rain, the squally wind blowing sodden litter and debris into corners and niches. I screwed up my eyes as we steamed in, as I tried to peer through the rain, but I need not have worried—they were all there, waiting, in spite of the weather. Porters, shedmen, shunters, booking clerks—all my faithful customers, their shillings ready in their wet hands in order to save time—and time was very valuable in Carmarthen on the Fish Train.

Quickly clambering over the tender, I fetched armfuls of damp newspaper wrapped bundles back onto the footplate, where they were quickly exchanged for a shilling apiece by my queue of fresh-fish purchasers. Not much time for social chat, just a few short pertinent remarks or requests: 'a bit more flat next time, Bill', 'two bobs' worth next time, Bill', 'not so much of the bloody cod, this time, I hope', and so on.

Tommy kept an eye on the signal, while I picked out my specially wrapped, extra-good measure bundle for the signalman who was buying by proxy. I always made sure that the signalman was kept happy, as occasionally we were given the road before I had concluded my sales, and a happy signalman would always oblige by holding the signal for a few minutes until all transactions were completed! But today they'd been a bit on the slow side uncoupling the wagons for Carmarthen, so I had plenty of time to conduct my business before the guard gave us the off. Fifteen shillings' worth I had sold and my overall pocket jingled pleasantly as I fired to Landore, where we had a twenty-minute spell while half a dozen wagons were uncoupled for the Valleys and we took on extra water. I, of course, was busy with my fish-selling; it was pleasant to be able to have a chat with my customers instead of the usual rushed-through purchases. I always enjoyed taking water at Landore—very sociable event in any weather—we even managed a bite to eat and a spot of tea before steaming off once more. Amazing it is, what can be done in twenty minutes.

Seven o'clock and we were nearing Pyle Bank. 'Slow her down a bit, Tom,' I asked, opening the detonator locker and retrieving my twelve-pound fish frail.

'The missus on holiday, then, Bill?' enquired Tom as he slackened off the regulator and reduced our speed to about twenty. I nodded in reply as I leant over the cab-side with my fish frail clutched under one arm. There, in the fading, drizzly light I spotted them. Win waving, Bette hopping about with excitement and Uncle John with arms akimbo, all at the bottom of the embankment with the Dodge parked close by on the roadside. I waved as we approached, then, with a hearty throw I flung the frail from the cab sending it bouncing down the wet, grassy embankment towards them. I watched Uncle John scramble to retrieve the delivery as we drew away from them, and gave a disappearing wave to Win and Bette as we pulled round the bend and continued on our way up to Stormy and Bridgend. There would be a delicious fried fish supper that night at Porthcawl, tasting all the better for its unusual delivery, no doubt!

A gathering of regular customers awaited my arrival at Cardiff, where we stopped for more water and the horses took off the required number of fish wagons. Funny yard, Cardiff—used horses for shunting, mind you! Eight shillings' worth of fish changed hands and off we set again, this time for Severn Tunnel where I always considered it policy to provide the signalman with free fish, as we were often a bit rushed there, and an extra few minutes made all the difference. Well, it paid off in the long run, you see, as occasionally my customers were a bit late! Only ten wagons we had left now, and a few good bundles of wrapped fish in my crate. One I left with the signalman at Oakle Street in exchange for a basket of Victoria plums and a few boxes of apples, which I arranged to pick up on the return run on the following day, one which I was saving for my landlady at Gloucester and the last few double-weight bundles I carried away with me after we had arrived at Gloucester at 9.30.

I now had a few calls to make to round off the day's business. The first was to the East End Vaults, where I was welcomed with a pint of the best, a packet of cigarettes and five shillings in exchange for my fresh Milford fish, then off to a local chip shop where I was welcomed with open arms, free chips and another five shillings while the proprietor feasted his eyes on the whiting, sole, plaice, skate and turbot which slithered from the opened bundle.

Finally, I arrived at my double-home lodgings, where I handed over my last four pound of fish to an appreciative landlady. It had been a good day. I reckoned I had made about two pounds profit, plus a couple of boxes of apples and a basket of plums, and had provided the family in Porthcawl with enough top quality fish to last them for a good few meals. It had been a busy day.

I had also fired about ten ton of coal on the Fish Train, but that was incidental! Yes, it had been a good day's work, I thought, as I dropped off to sleep in my narrow, single bed. Fair play.

12

The only drawback with the double-home fish run was that it came round only one week in every six, which left rather a long stretch of time with little opportunity for private enterprise. Of course, there were always the Parcel Trains, which, I felt sure, could be a substitute for the lucrative Fish runs—some way or another. My maxim has always been to take any opportunity which might present itself, and as one did not seem to be presenting itself on the Parcels, I decided I had better create one myself!

Granfer Charlie May, the Western guard from the next door bungalow, had an unerring instinct for setting rabbit snares in just the correct position on the run. I was pretty good myself, mind, but where my snares would be successful five times out of ten, Charlie's would reach eight and occasionally ten. Osborne's fields behind the bungalows were good rabbiting terrain and with Charlie's help I managed to stake out the fields with two dozen or more snares a few days before starting on a double-home Parcel Train turn.

Mack, now an experienced gun-dog of five years' standing, took a poor view of hunting for dead, snared rabbits, and there's a look of disgust he'd give me if I left the shot-gun behind the pantry door and took only a sack instead! But once he'd settled for second-best he enjoyed the search for the successful gins. A good bag was fifteen to twenty rabbits which were quickly slit and gutted ready for their journey up the line to my potential customers. If I managed to pot a few pigeons or partridges in Lewis's woods, all the better.

The Parcel Train left Neyland at 4.45 p.m. and we usually had a Castle, the Pendennis 4079, the Caerphilly 4073 or the Builth 4086. Each Castle had arrived in Neyland at 7.30 the same morning with the Down Parcels, and then had been coaled and fired during the day ready for us to work the Up Parcels back in the evening. We, of course, only took them as far as Landore, but the Castles themselves went right through to Paddington. But for us the journey to Landore was joy all the way. Lovely to crew were the Castles. Ever since the first Castle had been introduced back in 1923—the famous 'Caerphilly'—they had been a great success. Seventy-nine tons of invincible, massive power with forty-six tons of following laden tender and 4,000 gallons of water, they earned the admiration of every Western employee from the youngest cleaner to the most experienced driver. They were, without doubt, a magnificent feat of engineering and we had the pride and pleasure of working them at Neyland.

The Castle class was to contribute more to the aura of romance which was to grow up around Steam, than any other class of locomotive, although the Kings which followed in 1927 also caught the imagination and earned the admiration of the public. Their now legendary success had a unique beginning back in 1927, when the first of the 6000 Class, the King George V, was sent over to America to be the main attraction at the Baltimore and Ohio Centenary Exhibition. They'd even pre-sented her with a special American-type brass bell, which was hung on the front of the loco, and an inscribed medal commemorating the Centenary. Now there's a launching for you, for a new class of loco-motive. With such a glorious beginning it is small wonder that the 6000 Class had such an illustrious career.

As for me, I still have a warm spot in my heart for the old Bulldogs. They would rival any Castle or King for glamour and prestige when I first knew them, with men like Kellick, Llewellyn and Thomas as their drivers. Dull, working-class locos they appear to most now, but they were an integral part of my early years on the G.W.R., and their name conjures up a whole way of life which has gone, taking its attitudes and standards with it.

The 4.45 Parcels Train was waiting for me that afternoon as I arrived at the Shed with my laden sack of trapped rabbits over my shoulder, and climbing up onto the footplate of the Caerphilly, I stowed it at the back of the tender, its bulk feeling rewardingly heavy as I quickly estimated a good thirty shillings profit before reaching Carmarthen. At half a crown apiece, apart, that is, from the cheap shilling ones I would sell to the signalmen at Whitland, Clarbeston Road and Carmarthen, they should find plenty of buyers. Along with the gross of eggs—fresh, farm eggs of course, which I had waiting for my collection at Johnston at a shilling a dozen and which I would sell further up the line at one and ninepence, the trip should prove pleasantly profitable!

As Tommy Francis, the driver, took us out of Neyland Station and we pulled up from Westfield Mill, the low tide reminded me that the spring tides would soon be with us, with their extra low ebb, offering the rich pickings of shrimps and cockles—not to mention the occasional hen— or scallops as I think they're called by the uninitiated. Charlie May had a few large shrimping nets and an ex-army canvas haversack, which was all that was required in order to go shrimping, and cockling needed nothing more specialised than a short-handled garden rake and a bucket. Cockles and shrimps always sold well up the line, but they did make the cab smell a bit fishy—more so than the fish did! Of course there was also the extra work of cooking them first, but Win had everything well organised with galvanized buckets on the gas stove.

There was, however, one hazard which had to be contended with, when reaping the low-tide harvest—and that was the sight of an old dame (whose name we never knew, but who disappeared up into the Common Hills with her buckets), with her billowing skirts tucked into her voluminous, well-gusseted knickers, bending down to gather her cockles, displaying vast expanses of ham-like mottled bare legs, streaked with caked mud, and firmly entrenched in an enormous pair of men's boots. This rear view has been known to bring a shudder to many a strong man and has even put a few weaker mortals off cockles for life! Fair play, it took some stomaching when one leg of her knickers was minus its elastic, causing it to flap at least eight inches below the level of the other. Grey they were—very grey.

But Charlie May and I were made of stouter stuff and it would take more than a holey pair of directoire knickers to put us off acquiring a good few pound of seafood, which would be bought with such alacrity up the line. I always reckoned we were living examples of the parable of the talents!

Trade was brisk that day and I only just remembered to save one rabbit for the signalman at Llandeilo Junction! I felt so elated at my quick sales and profit that I decided to donate the last rabbit free of charge in the interests of future trips. 'On the house, mate!' I shouted as I threw the furry offering towards the signal box .

'You're a crafty bugger,' laughed Tom. 'You'd better save the next free one for me or I'll be the one to cut your selling time short, mind!' I could see I was going to have trouble with Tom—he'd be putting the guard up to demanding free produce next!

The eggs always sold better as we neared the more industrial Valleys. Seven dozen carefully changed hands at Llanelly, four dozen at Landore and I took one dozen with me to my landlady at my double-home lodgings, leaving a new crew to take the Castle on her way to Paddington.

Old Mags was my landlady. All of four foot ten, her sharp, town-Welsh tongue assailed my ears as soon as I opened the door.

'There's no sense in it, Mr. Morgans, no sense, indeed,' she complained before I had time to put down my heavy double-home box in the narrow hallway. 'They should make ladies' shoes to fit small ladies with small feet, Mr. Morgans,' she went on, looking up at my collar stud from her diminutive height. 'A frit of a gel she was, insolent she was, Mr. Morgans. I said to her, "size thirteen I want and a lady's shoe, mind." And do you know what she did, Mr. Morgans? She laughed. She did. Mind you, I complained to the manager. Now look here, I said. . . .' The staccato sounds continued to assail my ears as she followed me into the tiny back kitchen where I poured some water from the can into a washing-bowl to have a quick swill over my face and neck. 'That's all I ever get, Mr. Morgans,' she finished in disgust, looking with distaste at her plain black, single-buttoned schoolgirl's shoes. 'Maid's shoes they are, maid's shoes, Mr. Morgans.' And off she trotted into the pantry clutching her dozen eggs to her flat bosom, reverting to Welsh mutterings as she reappeared and put on the coal-blackened kettle.

Her only relative was an equally tiny sister named Mary-Ann, who occasionally visited her from somewhere up the Valleys. They quarrelled vociferously the entire duration of any visit I had ever witnessed, reminding me of two bantam hens as I sat in the old Windsor chair listening to them verbally pecking at each other.

'There's good she is, Mr. Morgans,' would be the change of tone as soon as Mary-Ann's visit was over. 'Never once comes to see me without a piece of market material, Mr. Morgans.' I winced inwardly at the invariably added 's' to my name. I had long ago given up trying to convince Old Mags that there was no 's' on the end of Morgan, but without success. Now, I tried to grin and bear it but it would have proved easier to ignore if only she had not pronounced it with such fervour, making it sound more like Morganzzzzzzzzzzzzzz, revealing a seemingly inordinately large number of very false teeth in the process!

At least no-one could accuse me of taking free eggs to my double-home landlady in the hope of being repaid. Not like old Darkie and Joe.

Darkie and Joe were both Neyland drivers who had developed a penchant for the favours of the same Llandeilo lady. She was not exactly their landlady, at least not their official one, but all Neyland Shed knew of their visits, although not a word was said in comment when either was present.

Neither Darkie nor Joe would admit to the other that he was particularly interested in Bella, but each tried a bit of surreptitious checking up on the other's visits!

'Seen Bella lately?' Joe would enquire off-handedly of Darkie.

'No, boy, haven't seen her for some time now,' would be the equally studied disinterested reply, both men quite unconscious of the winks and grins going around the cabin whenever such surreptitious checking up went on. It was a case of Joe knowing that Darkie knew that Joe knew ... but neither would admit a thing or give anything away. Cases they were!

One particular week Joe turned up at the Shed on a Monday morning with a still feathered rooster under his arm. He was double-home Llandeilo and everyone knew who the rooster was for. On the Wednesday, Darkie, on his way up the line with coal empties to Llandeilo, spotted a few ducks waddling around near Johnston Station. Quick as a flash, he was off the footplate and in a few minutes one duck had had its neck expertly wrung and was promptly tucked away in the detonator locker. Bella was going to be showered with feathered offerings that week it seemed!

On the Friday, Joe was on his double-home run once more and I think his suspicions must have been aroused by the sight of two plucked and cooked carcasses keeping company on Bella's pantry shelf! The scene was set for a confrontation at last. This was too blatant for even Joe to ignore or play down.

The cabin was full and, by now, everyone knew of Bella's feathered offerings and we all awaited the consequences with relish. Joe and Darkie sat there, Joe looking like a thundercloud, but poor old Darkie quite unaware of the atmosphere or, apparently, of the fact that his rival knew of his duck-offering.

The smoking and small chat went on desultorily as we all waited for Joe to explode.

'Seen anything of Bella lately, Darkie?' asked Joe, unable to keep quiet any longer, his voice sounding half-strangled with emotion.

'No, boy,' came the inevitable reply. 'Haven't seen her for some time now.' And Darkie casually blew a smoke ring in the air as we all held our breath. Up Joe jumped, like a thunderbolt, strode across the cabin, pushed his face close to Darkie's and snarled through clenched teeth, 'Quack, quack, you lying bugger!'

Poor old Darkie looked dumb-struck, but fair play, he quickly recovered his wits about him and to the delight of us all he smartly replied with 'And a cock-adoodle-do to you too, you bugger!' They stood there glaring at each other as the whole cabin roared with laughter. Joe turned on his heel and left, slamming the door behind him, while Darkie stood there looking sheepishly around him, until he too finally joined in the laughter, and the tears streamed down his face.

The following day, letters four feet high appeared, painted in lime, for all to see, on the side of the Iron Bridge. It read 'Bella's waiting for you tonight'. No-one knew who put it there, but both Darkie and Joe could be seen washing it off with pet-pipes from suitably placed locos under the bridge!

Yes, indeed, you had to be very careful about taking presents to double-home landladies. It could let you in for a great deal of trouble or leg-pulling. It never paid to take anything too often, no matter how unlikely looking your particular landlady might be . . . but surely no one would think that Old Mags with her size thirteen maid's shoes would . . . surely not. But I played safe all the same!

Tommy Francis and I worked the eight o'clock down from Llandeilo the following morning, and as we were idly passing the time during our two-hour wait at Carmarthen, Tom reminded me about the newspapers and magazines for Bill Llewellyn's dog. I was glad he had remembered, because I knew it meant so much to Bill and his wife, living as they did, out in the wilds, away from any decent road. Near the line between Johnston and Haverfordwest, their farm was, with the farmhouse up on the bank a few fields away. Bill Llewellyn and I had always had a pally relationship, ever since we'd derailed the loco when attempting to winch the trawler off the mud nearly twenty years earlier, and I wouldn't have liked to be the one to forget his dog's newspapers and magazines. Most of his particular friends made a point of collecting them from the empty carriages and waiting-rooms along the line, and that was how I spent a good hour during my wait at Carmarthen that day. Quite a sizeable bundle I collected from various compartments and waiting-rooms, *Picture Posts*, London *Evening News* (last night's), *Illustrateds*, a *Home Chat*, a few day-old newspapers and an advertising booklet. Not a bad haul, indeed. I'd keep my eyes open at any other station we stopped at to see if there was anything worth adding, but I didn't want too many old newspapers. One zealous fireman had collected an enormous bundle, thinking he was doing the Llewellyn's a favour by providing so much reading matter, but Bill had complained the following morning that his poor dog, finding his jaws incapable of opening wide enough to pick up the huge bundle had proceeded to rip it to pieces instead! From then on, if a particularly large collection of bulky magazines was made, we were advised by Bill to tie them into two or three separate smaller bundles which his dog could then cope with, with ease.

As Tom and I brought the North Mails down to Neyland later that afternoon, I found that at each station I discovered a great deal of rather good reading matter, which was really too good a bargain to leave behind, consequently I had to tie Bill Llewellyn's newspapers and magazines into three bundles before I judged them small enough for his dog's jaws.

As we left Haverfordwest I placed them conveniently on the seat, ready for distribution. Round the bend we came and through the cutting, where I blew the necessary crow to inform Bill's dog that there was a delivery coming up. Sure enough, when we emerged from the cutting there he was, Bill's mongrel-cum-sheepdog, hurtling down the hill from the farm, wriggling under the gate and bounding towards the line. Using my best fish-frail throwing technique, I flung the three bundles into the neighbouring field, more or less at the panting dog's feet.

As we drew away on the straight, I looked back with interest to see how he would tackle the three bundles instead of the usual one. He seemed to be working on a complicated form of relay. Eagerly pouncing on the first parcel, ears flopping up and down, he carried it roughly fifteen yards up the field where he dropped it and bounded back for the second which he carried only about ten yards before returning for the third! This, he dropped by the second parcel which he picked up and carried as far as the first, which he exchanged with the second. A rare old time he was having, racing, wheeling, turning, galloping back and forth, and the last I saw of him he was carrying the third (or was it the second?) bundle on its second stage of the relay, tossing it into the air as he skidded to a stop and raced back down the hill for the first (or was it the second?) package. It was all very complicated, the intricacies known only to the dog himself who would, I felt sure, unfailingly manage to deliver the three bundles to the farmhouse some time within the next three hours! As it was just starting to drizzle, I imagined that the reading matter would prove to be a trifle damp by the time it had survived the wet grass, the dog's salivary glands and the rain!

So keen was I to collect magazines for Bill Llewellyn, I had clean forgotten to keep any for myself to take home. Now there's *twp* for you!

* * *

It was a beautiful day for the races. A drying wind had firmed up the turf and the going would be good. The Lydstep Point-to-Point was a meeting not to be missed and this year I had managed to work my shifts so that I had the day off. Not so for poor old Georgie. He was a keen punter like myself, cross doubles and sixpence each way was music to our ears. I had started to wager a shilling a week on the football pools when they had started back in 1921, but I had never won anything on them. Besides, the pools were nothing compared to the thrill of attending a Point-to-Point where you could actually see your money being won—or lost, as the case may be! We won quite often, however, stubbornly believing in 'Lucky Streaks', and Georgie was firmly convinced he would have a 'Lucky Streak' at Lydstep, if only he could get there. He was booked to take the train through from Pembroke Dock to Whitland at 3 o'clock on the day of the meeting, and as Lydstep

154

was actually on his route, it opened up endless possibilities to try, before giving up the idea of attending the races.

'I'll make it somehow, Bill,' were his parting words on the previous day. 'I'll see you on the course, boy, by hook or by crook,' he promised.

'Right-O, then,' I replied, fully confident of his ability to work something out. 'I'll look out for you boy.'

The tweeds, the brogues and the shooting-sticks were well in evidence as I trampled over the hummocky grass towards the bookies' boards. The 'County' turned out in style for a Point-to-Point. Bristling Harris-tweed hacking jackets flapped over expensive cream-coloured breeches, rich, mahogany-brown leather leggings, gleaming with polish, enclosed their calves, heavy, far-reaching binoculars hung around their necks and a leather-strapped Bentley grazed in the neighbouring meadow. The 'County' had arrived.

It was a clear case of 'us' and 'them', I thought as I espied one of 'us' hurrying towards me from the far side of the course. It was Georgie, complete with G.W.R. overalls and his day-box. It made the gulf seem even wider. But it didn't prevent us from enjoying ourselves, no indeed. 'We' simply ignored 'them' and 'they' completely ignored 'us'! I pushed my trilby to the back of my head and began to study the odds —at least they were the same for everybody!

I had just handed over my shilling on a ten to one outsider when Georgie reached my side.

'There's a pal for you, my mate,' he panted in my ear. 'Booking on for me, he is, at the Dock at 2.30 and bringing the Train up as far as here. I'll only have to miss the last race, see, then I can take it on to Whitland. He'll go back to the Dock on the cushions. There's a pal for you,' he repeated, his eyes scanning the bookie's board for a quick, profitable bet.

'What you got there, then?' he queried, peering inquisitively at my betting slip. 'A bob straight win—you're sure of yourself, aren't you? Know this bookie do you, then? What's his name? Owen Davies? Never heard of him,' he concluded with a disdainful sniff, and off he wandered to find a bookie whose name he recognised. We had had trouble with strange bookies at the Scoveston Point-to-Point, earlier in the year. Two of them had disappeared before the end of the meeting with a good bag of unpaid winnings. A rowing boat they had had waiting for them at Llanstadwell beach, mind, and they'd made a quick getaway across the harbour to Pwll Crochan. Crafty they were, so I couldn't blame old Georgie for looking for a familiar name. Even if the odds might not be so good.

The afternoon slipped by all too quickly. The first race had brought my outsider in, winning by a nose, and a crisp ten shilling note was soon in my pocket. It heralded well for the remainder of the afternoon. It was definitely a 'Lucky Streak' I was on, I could feel it in my bones. Georgie, who was having varied luck, envied my big win of the first race, and spent most of his time between races drifting from one bookie's board to another, looking for high odds on a good outsider in order to make up on his losses. There were quite a few unknown bookies there that day, all complete with boards and clerks, and eventually they were as well patronised as the well-established firms. As race followed race, the punters no longer looked to see who the bookie was, they merely looked at the odds he was offering.

'Damn and blast,' cursed Georgie, 'that bloody train'll be here soon. I'll have to get down to the station, Bill.' He looked irritably at his pocket watch. 'Old Hitchins is going to put my last bet on for me,' he added, and off he went with a wave and a thumbs-up, heading down over the meadow to the railway below.

It suddenly occurred to me how convenient it would be if I, too, could catch the early train to Tenby, where I could meet Win and Bette who were spending the day there. I'd miss the excitement of the last race, though, and that made me hesitate, but finally I decided that I had had a good day, so off I ran, across the field towards the little station, where Georgie was leaning out of the cab of the loco, looking longingly back at the track he had left so reluctantly.

Quickly climbing into a compartment, I slammed the door and dropped the window, just as we started to pull out of the station. Suddenly, two other early leavers appeared racing across the field, waving and gesticulating for the train to wait for them. Georgie had obviously seen them, for he slackened our speed and came to a halt, just managing to leave the last coach still at the platform. The two grateful passengers shouted their thanks at Georgie and climbed aboard as, with a toot, we started off once more.

It wasn't until Georgie met an irate Hitchins later that he realised that the two gentlemen he had so considerately held up his train for were two absconding bookies. And, of course, they just had to be the ones that his winning bet had been placed with! It took Georgie a long time to get over that. For weeks he would suddenly interrupt a conversation with 'And I even held up the bloody train for them. . . .' Poor old Georgie.

* * *

Our gambling interests were not solely confined to horse-racing, however. Whippets and greyhounds also held a certain fascination for us. Not really to compete with the horses, mind you, but just for an occasional flutter. That is, until Teddy Johnson (the bookie), Frankie John, Billie Sutton and I (who were all on the Western), decided to buy our own greyhound. Well, we didn't actually buy it, we sort of borrowed it.

It all started on one of my ferreting expeditions with Dai Mordecai (which we pronounced Mortikee). Dai was a farmer on the Burton side of Barnlake and he owned the best pair of ferrets in Pembrokeshire, I reckoned. Ruthless he was with any strangers he caught rabbiting on his land, but, because in his youth he had been a cleaner on the G.W.R. for a short while, I knew him well and we got along just fine.

Dai would stand one side of the hedge with his ferrets and his favourite farm dog—a three-year-old lean, lithe greyhound, while I stood on the other side with my double-barrel. The rabbits didn't stand a chance, man. If they avoided the shooting side they were brought down by Dai's greyhound before they had covered quarter the length of the field. Very gentle he was with them, mind, brought them back to Dai without a single puncture in the skin. All they needed was a sharp clip on the back of the neck and it was all over.

'You've got a damn fine dog there, Dai,' I remarked one day as we were returning to the farm with our bag of ten rabbits strung by their feet over my shoulder and the ferrets ravenously gnawing at the liver of a gutted one in their tough canvas sack, which bounced up and down on Dai's back. 'Ever thought of racing him?' I queried, speculatively eyeing the greyhound's muscular flanks.

'Haven't got the time, man,' he answered. 'Never thought of it anyway.'

'Mind if I have a go with him then?' I tentatively suggested.

And so it came about that the next time Billie Sutton, Frankie John and I rowed up to the Jolly Sailor at Burton for a drink, we paid a call on old Mordecai to make arrangements about training his dog. A bit doubtful he was about it on second thoughts, until we mentioned that Teddy Johnson the bookie was also going to take a personal interest in the training sessions. Of course, Teddy wanted to have a preview of the dog's capabilities before actually committing himself, and the following evening we all met at Dai's farm for a few demonstration runs.

Off we set with Dai's ferrets and nets and we soon had a dozen rabbits trapped ready for racing. Teddy Johnson, resplendent in his customary smart outfit, watched shrewdly from the side of the field. Dai held his quivering dog as Teddy gave the signal and I released one of the netted rabbits. We gave him a twenty-yard start before Dai set the dog free. Marvellous to watch, he was, lovely action he had, and within seconds the rabbit was delivered to Dai who gently released him from the dog's jaws and sharply broke its neck with the usual swift clip. We weren't cruel, you see, only let a rabbit be chased once, after all.

Again and again we tested our future canine prospect, each time allowing the rabbit a longer run before releasing the greyhound, but he never failed to catch his prey and Teddy Johnson was visibly impressed.

'Waterston track we'll train him on, boys,' he announced as we made our way back to the farm, where we bedded down the dog and then proceeded to the Jolly Sailor to christen our new venture with a few drinks, before rowing home.

It was beautifully warm the following evening as we all met at the old 'Tute, Teddy having brought the dog over on Billie Darkie's boat and up over the Iron Bridge. We all set off on the two and a half mile stroll to Waterstone, Billie Sutton, Frankie John, Teddy, me and our noble greyhound—brown he was actually. Along the Prom we walked, up the Military Road, turning off to Leonardston at Mastle Bridge in order to cut off the long trek up to Scoveston Fort. Cross country we scrambled, until we reached Waterston Village Greyhound Racing Track. Well, a field it was really, with a converted bicycle for winding the hare round the roughly staked out course. Handles replaced the original pedals, and Frankie John volunteered to do the winding.

'We'll train him on the straight first, Frank!' shouted Teddy at Frankie's retreating back, while Billie Sutton and I stood viewing our greyhound with speculative eyes.

Poor old Frankie hadn't realised that he'd have to trek the bracken-stuffed rabbit skin right round the track each time before he could start winding, and he was relieved to hear that he only had to wind the rabbit half-way, to the bottom of the field.

Eventually we were all set. Teddy held the dog, I gave Frankie the signal, the stuffed rabbit started its erratic course around the track and our greyhound streaked off into the setting sun after it.

Caught the blessed thing he did before he was half way down the straight, but he shook it something wicked when he realised that for some strange reason there was no life there. Five times on the straight we raced him, with Frankie hand-pedalling like a demented organ-grinder, but at least Billie and I carted the rabbit back to the starting-point for him; well, we all had to do our bit. Teddy Johnson eventually gave his professional opinion that we were on a winner, and that we'd run him enough for one night, so back to Neyland we walked, the two and a half miles seemingly over in no time as we built castles in the air on the future prospects of our champion.

When we arrived at Waterston the following evening, however, a few of the locals were already on the field with their dogs. Our training session of the previous evening had not gone unnoticed it seemed.

'Mind if we gev your dog by there, a race, Mr. Johnson?' slyly suggested one of the lads as we made our appearance. The track was only used for flapping races, and this was a good opportunity for a bit of new blood.

After due consideration Teddy guardedly agreed, pointing out, however, that he hadn't run the full course yet.

'A good start we've been concentrating on, you see, boys,' he explained. 'But let's run him round once on his own and then we'll give you your race. Eh, boys?' he asked, turning to Billie, Frankie and me with a broad wink.

'Frankie—the wheel, boy,' he ordered and off went Frankie, cursing the mad moment he had volunteered to do the winding! Spectators appeared miraculously from nowhere, it seemed, and we soon had quite a gathering round the track. Why, there must have been a good thirty people there. We were certainly the centre of attraction that evening in Waterston Village.

We had no intention of letting our champion catch his prey this time and Teddy crouched, holding the animal's shoulders waiting for the 'hare' to get well ahead. The warm air hung still as we waited for the off. The bicycle started to creak, the 'hare' erratically started off on its plotted course, quickly gaining momentum as Frankie wound his heart out. Then, with a surge of muscle power, Dai Mordecai's greyhound leapt forward. Like a streak of lightning he raced along the chicken-wire fenced track, round the U-bend at the bottom of the field and back up the other side to the hectic cheering of the crowd. He was fast all right, bloody fast, all the way too. The four of us smiled smugly at each other.

'Give us half an hour then, lads,' insisted Teddy. 'Then we'll give you a race,' he added, soothingly stroking the quivering animal at his knees.

Well pleased with our first full-run, we stood back to watch a few of the other locals who were waiting to train their dogs.

Five there were, racing against each other, so of course we couldn't resist a few small bets on the side. But we had reckoned without Jacky Comber's little white sealyham.

Right across the track he nipped, directly in front of the streaking greyhounds, who immediately sprawled and tripped all over each other in utter confusion. Ruined the race was and by the secret grin I caught a glimpse of on Jacky's face, it looked as if it was not entirely unplanned either! The lads were tamping mad, mind, but when the little white ball of fluff repeated its well-timed intrusion on the second attempt as well, their rage was beyond bounds. Damn we laughed—after all, our dog wasn't racing, was he?

So all bets were cancelled and we each had our money back while Jacky Comber beat a hasty retreat from the field with his little white sealyham tucked well under his arm, under dire threats of extinction if ever he set foot in the track field again—but we all knew he would just the same!

By the time all the confusion had died down it was time for the serious race of the evening to begin. A few spectators who had nipped off to the local for a quick drink had all returned and Teddy crouched, all serious now, holding our dog at the starting-line with four others. Everyone took a last look round to make sure that there was no sign of Comber and his sealyham, and Billie, Frankie and I prayed that Dai Mordecai's dog would run just as well with other greyhounds as he did on his own. After all, it was the first time he'd ever actually raced another of his kind.

The wheel started to turn, the 'hare' quickly gained speed, a hand-kerchief was dropped and they were off.

Past the chicken wire they sped and on down the straight. Bunched they were, but good old Mordecai's dog was definitely beginning to lead. The excitement was intense.

Then disaster struck. The four of us watched with disbelief and dismay as our champion suddenly left the track, jumped the wire, cut across the centre of the field and caught the 'hare' as it came up on the return leg! Our dog was no fool; he had been trained all his life to catch rabbits, not merely chase the damned things, and having once un-successfully followed his prey right round the U-bend and back, his intelligence told him that the obvious thing to do was to cut across the centre of the field and catch his prey. Which he did!

There's an uproar there was. Hooting and laughing, jeering and shouting, yelping and barking, moaning and groaning and a gnashing of teeth, and Jacky Comber's white sealyham madly yapping around everyone's heels.

We never broke him of it. Try as we would. Every blessed time he raced he took his short cut across the centre. We even tried lining the spectators shoulder to shoulder along the inside of the track, but the cunning dog got through just the same. It was useless, and so, with all our hopes of making a fortune gone, we sadly returned our protégé to Dai Mordecai and Burton Farm, where he continued to spend the rest of his days catching rabbits to his heart's content, chasing them in any direction which took his fancy.

Lucky, wily old dog.

L

13

'Disqualified!' hollered Doctor Douglas in exasperation. 'The lot of you'll be disqualified before you even reach the quarter finals. Bandaging a fractured collarbone and splinting a broken femur you're supposed to be, not embalming an Egyptian Mummy!' And he ripped off the bandages, slings and splints which adorned the 'patient', who, on this particular evening, was Archie Crawley. Poor old Arch had already suffered multiple contusions to face and body, collapsed from a coronary, survived an attack of cramp whilst swimming, inhaled toxic fumes, sustained a compound fracture of the tibula, severed an artery in his leg, and all in the space of one hour. He was beginning to feel just a little fed up! Ben John, Dai Thomas, Bertie Davidge, Teddy Morgan, myself and a few others stood gazing down at the luckless Arch, who was spread-eagled on a Red Cross blanket on the dusty floor of the Ladies' Waiting Room on Neyland platform, half-hidden under the tangled mass of bandages, splints and slings, with the irate form of Doctor Douglas astride him.

The Annual St. John's Ambulance G.W.R. competition was but three months away, and Neyland was entering three teams, all keenly trained by Hecky Williams, a local driver, and supervised twice a week by Doc Douglas. Personally, I thought I'd made a first-class job of splinting Archie's femur—I prided myself on my knowledge of First Aid and my ability to diagnose and treat the various sneaky test cases

162

Doc Douglas often set us, but he was a hard task master. Still, I consoled myself as I viewed my strewn handiwork, it was because Doc Douglas was so particular, that we managed to enter such first-class teams each year, and often with good results too.

The Great Western was divided into various regions for the Ambulance Competition, and Neyland was in the West Wales division which included all stations west of Neath. Competition was extremely keen as the prizes were really worth winning. Canteens of cutlery, clocks, barometers, etc., awaited the lucky finalists in Paddington. Inter-station competitions took place before the inter-region meetings and the finalists went to Paddington each year where the Top St. John's Ambulance Team for the year was judged. Considering its size, Neyland was a station which was regarded with healthy respect by all entrants. We won inter-station and inter-region competitions regularly, and once, one of our teams actually won the championship at Paddington. But it didn't look as if we would be finalists this year, I thought ruefully, as I surveyed my rejected handiwork once more!

'Aaaah!' drawled Doc with a change of heart. 'It wasn't too bad, on the whole, boys. You'll stand a good chance at Swansea if you keep your wits about you.' His Irish accent fell strangely on our ears as we started to re-roll the bandages for the umpteenth time that evening. 'They're setting trickier situations every year, remember,' he warned, 'and I'll tell you now that I'm going to set you a real test case next week, so stay alert!' And with that parting shot Doc Douglas left us to chew over the post mortems of each case we had tackled that evening, with Hecky Williams our instructor.

The following week found us practising in the Old Chapel, listening to Hecky reading out the test case which Doc had set.

' "The patient is found, unconscious, lying on a pavement, having fallen down a steep flight of steps. Treat! Two bystanders are present," ' read Hecky aloud, holding the paper up to the hissing gas lamp for easier viewing.

'Well, the patient is bloody well not going to be me tonight,' hastily interposed Archie Crawley. 'Somebody else can take a turn.'

Fortunately another member of our team was willing to volunteer to be our patient and he prostrated himself on the Red Cross blanket at our feet.

'I wonder if I was drunk?' he murmured.

'Shut up you, you're supposed to be unconscious,' interrupted Bertie, as Archie and I volunteered to be the bystanders.

'We'll have ourselves an easy number for once, Bill,' uttered Arch, in a low voice, offering me one of his Goldflake with an apology that it wasn't his usual Woodbine.

Dai Thomas, Ben John, Bertie Davidge and Teddy Morgan started to treat the patient, one holding the head steady, one holding his feet, while the other two felt for broken bones. Any injuries were established by referring to Hecky who had a list of possible things which they could find wrong with the patient.

'Any fracture of the arm?' queried Teddy, gently exploring the humerus, while Ben was asking the same question regarding the femur and tibia. When it was eventually established that there was a compound fracture of the left femur and right tibia, treatment commenced. Suddenly, the door burst open and in rushed Doc Douglas shouting incoherently. He grabbed the startled Ben by the shoulder, dragged him up off his knees, spun him round and gave him a resounding thump which sent him reeling against the wall. Dai was up off his knees like a shot, grabbed hold of Doc's coat collar and pulled him off poor old Ben and punched him on the nose. The tumult continued as Arch and I watched in amazement, our Goldflakes half poised to our open mouths. Teddy joined in the fracas. Doc, with his shirt ripped and dirty, was grappling on the floor with Dai while the now deserted 'patient' jumped up and immediately fell over again as his half-splinted legs and trailing bandages tripped him over. The utter confusion inside twenty seconds was unbelievable. As to what had got into Doc Douglas we could not imagine. Realisation gradually dawned on us as Doc, clothes torn and dirty and panting hard, suddenly waved his arms back and forth in front of his face and shouted that oft heard word . . . 'Disqualified!'

We all stared unbelievingly round at each other. What a bedraggled crew they looked too! Who the hell would have thought that Doc Douglas would go in for such realism, I thought to myself, as I viewed the stricken room. What a bloody mess! Suddenly Doc's parting words of the previous week came back into my mind. 'I'm going to set you a real test case next week,' he'd warned us. 'So stay alert.'

'This,' panted Doc, 'is a typical situation you might be called upon to deal with in one of the tests this year,' and he dabbed at his sore nose. 'You should never, I repeat, never, allow yourself to be distracted from attending a patient.' He glared accusingly at poor old Dai who was regretting his hasty punch on Doc's nose. 'In such a case you call on the assistance of any bystanders . . .' and he glared at Arch and me, 'to help in the control of any interfering nuisances, such as I was representing.'

We all looked suitably sheepish as we started to restore the room to its usual order, and Dai endeavoured to apologise for causing Doc's sore nose.

'It was just instinct, see, Doc. I've been a bit of a boxer in my time and well . . .'

'And he won the Croix de Guerre in France,' interrupted Bertie, as if that would account for Dai's hasty action! Doc shrugged his shoulders; after all there was no answer to that, now was there?

'You chaps must realise,' he continued after a few moments when we all had simmered down a bit, 'that you are not merely being tested on your efficiency at treatment or your skill at diagnosis, but also on your ability to deal with emergency situations, no matter how bizarre they may seem . . . your patient must be your first concern at all times and nothing should stand in your way of administering treatment.' He was right, mind you. After all, we were all first-class ambulance men who knew the St. John's First Aid Book from silver starred cover to cover. We could treat any patient in theory or in the calm of a practice, but it was the emergency situation where we might be needed in reality. And I must admit that after his dramatic manner in proving his point, none of us ever forgot it.

A few weeks later, our team in the Fishguard Eisteddfod Ambulance Competition found themselves sitting in the ante-room waiting for the call to enter the Examination Chamber. Other teams had already gone through the portals, their failure or success unknown to us, as each team exited through another door so that no hint could be dropped to the waiting competitors about what type of test it was—a straightforward oral examination on the St. John's Ambulance Manual (although this was comparatively rare as all competitors knew the book backwards and inside out, as I previously remarked, and were all extremely competent First Aid men—in spite of the humorous aspects of some of the practices!), or a 'situation' requiring quick thinking and split-second action and decisions in order to gain valuable points. Some towns entered two or three teams, so security was essential. It came the turn for the Neyland Team to compete. I was not actually participating as it was my turn to be available if the Team required a 'patient'. We clipped our cigarettes, straightened our ties, pulled down our waist-coats and boldly entered.

The room was large, brightly lit in the centre merging to dim shadows at the sides. There, in the middle of the floor, lying face down, was what appeared to be the body of a blonde young lady, partially lying on, and mostly covered by, a travelling rug. Standing silently in the shadows at the edge of the room were three doctors, notebooks in hand, observing the Team's every move. The team were allowed to ask pertinent questions as to the supposed condition of the patient, although, sometimes, this was replaced by the relevant information being printed on a card.

Ben, Dai, Teddy and Bertie slowly approached the patient. Clearing his throat noisily Dai asked, 'Is the patient conscious?'

'No,' came the reply from the shadows. Silence descended once more on the room, then, as if reluctant to furnish them with more information, the voice continued, 'The unknown person is found on a beach.'

'Is the patient breathing?' asked Ben quickly.

'Yes,' came the brief reply. No need for artificial respiration then, I thought from my unobserved position by the door. There was obviously no further information forthcoming from the shadows, so they arranged themselves around the patient, who was so unhelpfully entangled in her travelling rug.

'Here, help me turn her over, Ben,' asked Teddy. They gently rolled their patient over, the rug falling away as they did so.

'*Arglwydd Mawr!*' gasped Dai, reverting to the few expressions of Welsh he used in cases of extreme provocation or amazement. The patient lay there before them, clad in the briefest of two-piece swim suits, and there's lovely she was too, I can tell you. We all did our fair share of gulping and blinking, as it was far more revealing than any-thing we had ever seen outside the bedroom! After all, it was the one-piece-clad 'thirties we were in, not the bikini-conditioned 'seventies! Bertie looked at Ben and swallowed hard, Ben coughed nervously and Teddy pulled the knot of his tie a little higher. They knelt around their lovely patient trying to pull themselves together as they considered her condition. A well-simulated ugly bruise marred her forehead and a trickle of 'blood' streaked the top of her thigh, its source very obviously hidden beneath her swimsuit. She lay, unmoving, breathing very gently, her eyes closed. The Team held a brief, muttered consultation on their knees at her side, while Ben took her pulse for something to do. The bruise they could treat with ease, it was the cause of the bleeding on her thigh which was proving difficult to ascertain! And precious seconds were ticking away.

'There's only one thing for it, boys,' whispered Dai, taking a deep breath, and he leant over the lovely body, caught hold of the top of the lower half of her swim suit with both hands, and with one swift, firm tear, he ripped it apart! I waited for the outraged roar of 'Disqualified!' from the shadows, but the only sound in the tense room was the sudden release of air as the four of them started to breathe again as they realised with relief (or was it disappointment) that their lovely patient was wearing an even briefer garment beneath her swimsuit, which revealed an ugly 'wound' in her groin with a small, sharp piece of driftwood still deeply embedded. Very realistic it was, indeed, so they told me. Quickly they pulled themselves together, whispering congratulations to Dai on his bravery as they lost no time in giving expert treatment. This was described to the silent watchers by Ben who stood back while the other three got on with the treatment—removal of driftwood, pressure point firmly held, constant check on pulse and breathing, clean sterilised pad on the wound from Ben's First Aid Box, treatment of bruise on forehead, bandages all correctly applied, final check to make sure that they had not missed anything—and it was all over. They stood to attention.

'Well done, Neyland!' came the suddenly friendly voice from the shadows. 'Time was of the essence, and you wasted not a moment. Thank you, gentlemen.'

Other teams, we learnt later, had attempted to treat the groin wound without removing any garment or had spent too long plucking up enough courage in deciding to do so! They obviously had not had to deal with Doctor Douglas in one of his 'realistic' training situations!

Neyland had won! They had actually won! There's great we all felt, thanks to Intrepid Dai rushing in where even St. John himself would have feared to tread! Well, after all, Dai did have the Croix de Guerre, and the French don't give that away for nothing!

By hedges, that story went round the Shed a few times during the following week. We wondered who she was, the lovely patient—some lucky doctor's wife no doubt. Ah well. . . .

Our good fortune did not last long enough, however, to take us through the Inter-region competitions that year. The glory of the Paddington Finals with the canteens of cutlery and barometers was not to be ours. And all through a silly omission.

Our luck and skill ran out when we had to admit ourselves completely baffled by a 'patient' found unconscious on the floor of a compartment of a train at the Neath All-line Competition.

Old Winter was our spokesman and captain, but there was nothing he could really give a commentary on as all our investigations drew a blank. No bleeding, no fractures, no temperature, heart normal. We spent so long trying to find out what on earth could be wrong with the blasted man that the judge announced that our patient had ceased to breathe! Our attempts to resuscitate him were ineffective, we were told, and a few seconds later the judge pronounced our patient 'Dead', and ourselves well and truly disqualified!

We had omitted one of the simple procedures in a case of inexplicable collapse—we had failed to search the patient's pockets. Our rival team had found the bottle of poison in the first two minutes and had applied treatment which resulted in the patient's recovery and their winning the competition! Slipped up we did there. Doc Douglas was heartily ashamed of us I can tell you!

* * *

Mack thumped his tail on the kitchen floor in greetings, as he heard the tinkle of a watch-chain as I carefully lifted my waistcoat from the back of a chair. It would be a good two hours before dawn, and by that time I would be well on my way with the coal empties to Duffryn Yard.

'Back to sleep, my beauty,' I whispered, giving a stroke to the smooth, sleek head under the table. A nose, still warm from curled sleep, pushed itself into my palm, then, deciding that this was not to be an early hunting expedition, Mack settled himself back to his dreams of catching rabbits, chasing swans across the mud, and other favourite pastimes which, no doubt, floated through his canine reveries.

My box was ready packed, and wedging the bottle of cold tea into my coat pocket, I let myself out into the cool pre-dawn night, leaving

Win and Bette sound asleep behind me. The moon was setting and the Plough shone startlingly clearly overhead. Only the sound of my boots broke the silence, even the wavelets were barely audible, so small they were with the lack of wind.

I suddenly became aware, however, of the slow splash of oars. I stopped and leaned on the railings, peering curiously across the water, racking my brains who would be setting off so early on a fishing trip. Around the point appeared the dark outline of a small rowing-boat with a hunched figure quietly pulling on the oars. I walked on slowly until the boat and I drew level, when my hailing whistle was rewarded with an answering wave from the silhouetted figure, but without an answering call. I was still trying to figure out who it could be when I realised that whoever it was was towing something behind him. I was becoming increasingly intrigued by this nocturnal aquatic exercise being carried out before me, and once more I strained my eyes, this time trying to see what it was which was being towed so surreptitiously and with almost splash-free oarsmanship! But for the life of me I could not think what the two large, but completely flat objects were. The unknown oarsman continued on his way leaving me completely baffled. As I rounded the bend at the end of the Prom I took a last look back across the beach and was surprised to see the boat being pulled up on the pebbles, and though I would dearly have loved to have nipped quickly back to find out what was going on, I regretfully continued on my way to the Shed, mindful of the passing time.

There's a dreary place Duffryn Yard was. Coal, coal and still more coal. Those Welsh valley towns with their towering, malignant tips, their fiery red dust clouds from the steelworks and their huddled smoke-blackened houses, always made me feel grateful that I would soon be on my way back to the rich green, dust-free lands of Pembroke-shire, where the grass grew unstunted by sulphur and slag and where there was plenty of space for everyone.

Duffryn Yard was a double-home turn, and I passed the time away that evening in catching up with latest news in the G.W.R. Magazine, the current edition of which I had tucked inside the lid of my double-homer.

The Great Western Railway Magazine, price twopence, came out every month, containing, on average, forty to forty-five pages of interesting topics ranging from the millions of tonnage dealt with by

the G.W.R. to the retirement presentation of a clock and a case of pipes
to a clerk in the coal shipping section at Barry.

Fetching the magazine from my box in the narrow passage of my
lodgings, I settled myself down for a good read under the gas, first
adjusting the chain down to eliminate the unnecessary hiss of extra gas
which gave no extra light but which merely offended my ears.

I had to admit it was a good twopennyworth, fair play. It was just
trying to find the time to read one of the blessed things before another
came out! That was the only trouble, but double-home evenings, with
the landlady out at a whist drive, was just the time to catch up on the
news. I had had a short nap during the afternoon and was just marking
time until I was due to book on for the return working to Neyland,
just before midnight, when I would be taking the coal trucks down
with coal for the Milford trawlers. It was just after two in the morning
when I eventually booked off at Neyland Shed, and I must admit I was
feeling a bit weary after firing the 53 with its loaded wagons behind.
No joke it was in the early hours of the morning.

' 'Night, Georgie,' I mumbled as I passed by Georgie Lewis the
fireman on my way out from the Shed.

'Hey, Morgy,' he called. 'Heard about the Railway Gas House
doors?'

'Gas House doors?' I queried back at him, stopping in my tracks.
'What about the Gas House doors then?'

'Somebody's gaffed 'em, boy,' he answered with a grin. Now the
G.W.R. Gas House was situated near the Shed on the side of the
tracks, and the railway had made its own gas there until a few days
previous, when the job was taken over by the Neyland Council and our
independent Gas House was no longer required.

'Why aye, man,' he went on. 'They've both gone—screws, hinges
and all,' he added with what sounded suspiciously like admiration!

'Get out!' I exclaimed in disbelief. 'How the bloody hell could anybody manage to carry two great doors past the Shed without anybody
seeing them, then?' I asked wonderingly.

'Blowed if I know, Bill,' answered Georgie with a shake of his head.
'But they've bloody well gone just the same!'

Suddenly a mental picture of two large, strangely flat objects floating
quietly down the harbour behind a small rowing-boat came to me. I
chuckled to myself at somebody's craftiness—but whose? I said

nothing to Georgie, but gave a farewell wave and crunched my way between the tracks to the station and made my way towards the Prom.

They looked beautiful in the pale moonlight. A perfect fit for a double-side entry. They certainly hadn't been there when I had passed by the previous day on my way to work, but they couldn't be the G.W.R. Gas House doors, now could they? After all the Gas House doors were a bright red and these looked a dark colour. No they couldn't be the Gas House doors, could they, I thought, as I tip-toed up the path and gave one a slight touch of the finger. Not even if the paint was ever so slightly wet? I asked myself with a smile.

Of course they couldn't be. . . .

'You'll never guess where the Western Gas House doors are, Win,' I whispered as I climbed into the warm bed. But she was too sleepy to care and I never mentioned them again after that!

14

I was working in Carmarthen Shed with Driver Simpson that 3rd September, 1939. The talk was of nothing but War. Black-outs had been hastily put up and every engine was checked that it was carrying a canvas sheeting—a long time it was since they'd been called Zeppelin Sails, and I had a feeling that they would be a lot more necessary than they had been a quarter of a century before. Men reacted differently—some were exhilarated, others depressed, some couldn't wait to join the forces, others dreaded the idea of receiving their calling-up papers. Me? Just wait and see what comes boy, whatever it is, I'll make the best of it.

My first job on returning to Neyland was to arrange with the Chief Ganger for a dozen good sleepers to be delivered to the bungalow. Ted Harkett, a driver on one of the G.W.R. lorries, offered to drop them off for me on one of his runs, and sure enough, within a few days, my front path was full of heavy, splinter-bristling sleepers. While Win stocked up the attic with tinned food and soaked net curtains in glue to stick on the windows, I determinedly started to build my own air raid shelter at the top of the garden, digging into the bank and strengthening the inside with my sleepers, reinforced with concrete on both sides. I finally covered the entire fortifications with earth and sods and installed two small benches and an old chair in its dark interior. The old chair had been a sort of second-hand wedding present from 'Granny' Journeaux, but it wasn't until many years later that we were to discover that it was a 'Country Chippendale'! There's polishing it had then, with Win marvelling that the years it had spent in our damp air raid shelter had done it no harm! But in 1939 it was just an old wooden chair —just right for turfing out to the shelter. A formidable blast wall protected the entrance, but dismally failed to keep out the chickens, ducks, the occasional hedgehog and, on one damp occasion, a foot of water! The feeling of security and reassurance it was supposed to give was not exactly enhanced by three little crosses mounted on the top where my daughter Bette had buried the remains of a canary, a budgie and an evil-smelling dead crab, their final resting places suitably marked! Empty fish paste jars filled with daisies, celandines and buttercups decorated the graves which were regularly despoiled by Mack who seemed to find the roof of the shelter an excellent place for burying his bones! Whatever the pair of them did before I built the blessed thing I cannot think!

Coastal Command had long realised the importance of our Cleddau Harbour and had proceeded to establish a flying-boat base at Pembroke Dock. The silver Sunderlands gleamed as they swung rhythmically with the tide at their moorings, the ferry-boat now having to weave its way between their anchoring chains. The harbour, which had grown quieter since the closure of the Dockyard in 1926, suddenly became alive again with the bustling R.A.F. launches darting back and forth ferrying crews to and from their heavy-bellied flying-boats. Each day, as the War progressed, we counted the number at their moorings, noting how many flew out on their Atlantic convoy escort duties and how many returned—or failed to return. They took off, leaving a trail of spray behind them as they rose into the air, flying low over the bungalow, the crew waving to us as we shielded our eyes from the sun and watched them disappear over the brow of the hill. Only lads they were.

The passenger trains were packed now with soldiers and airmen. The outside world was coming to Neyland again, although it had taken a war to make it realise that we were still there. The look of dismay on the faces of the alighting servicemen as they surveyed the long, desolate platform, devoid of the trappings of larger stations, was almost laughable. 'But it looks as big as Paddington on the name boards!' was the usual cry of disillusionment!

Further down the harbour towards Milford Haven, Canadian and British warships, frigates and destroyers came for shelter and refuelling, while across the estuary an ominous number of large oil-tanks stood on the brow of Pembroke Hill, their squat, circular outline defying camouflage.

The formidable strength of Germany had been brought home to us by the sinking of the Aircraft Carrier *Courageous* and the Battleship *Royal Oak,* and by the evacuation of our troops at Dunkirk. By hedges, we were going to have a tough fight on our hands this time.

It was a beautiful summer afternoon in 1940 when Ted Rees the driver and I were berthing coal wagons in the shunting yard at Neyland. A warm, drowsy afternoon it was, when even the bees seemed too lazy to collect their nectar from the seapinks growing alongside the disused fish stage. The air around the engines shimmered with heat and the footplate became unbearably stifling every time we drew to a halt. Shunting was no job for a hot afternoon such as this, the cab was like a bloody oven. We were due to take the Parcels out at 4.45 and at about 3.30 we steamed our Castle into the Goods sidings near the pontoon, and coupled up to the parcel wagons in readiness for off.

Ted and I climbed thankfully down from the footplate for a breath of fresh air, when our attention was attracted by the faint ringing of the Time Bell.

'Yellow alert, by the sound of it, Bill,' remarked Ted, the Time Bell being the means of warning staff that a yellow or red air raid alert had been received from up the line. We were used to working for hours on end on yellow alert, so we didn't take much notice until we heard the penetrating, anvil-like clamour of one of the men, wielding a large spanner, banging the buffers of a tankie near the Shed.

'Must have been a red one, then,' Ted added in a surprised tone, for who would expect a raid on such a lovely afternoon with such clear blue skies? We stared apprehensively up.

'By Christ, Bill, there they are!' exclaimed Ted, pointing down the harbour at a group of slow moving dots in the sky. We stood there in the sidings, fascinated as we watched the dots change to the heavy menacing shape of enemy bombers.

'They're after the tanks, boy,' I commented apprehensively to Ted, 'and by the looks of it there's nothing to stop them.' The higgledy-piggledy pattern of falling bombs dropped with seeming slowness onto their target, followed by deafening explosions, sheets of flame and curling black clouds of dense smoke. The ground beneath our feet shook and shuddered as the droning planes continued to destroy the oil tanks with sickening efficiency.

Firefighting teams and equipment were rushed from every possible town from as far away as Swansea in an attempt to get the blaze under control, but it continued to burn for weeks, the firemen themselves being machine-gunned by returning aircraft, as they fought the billowing sheets of flame. The black smuts from the burning oil ruined everyone's clothes for miles around and the leaking oil, running into the harbour, coated every seagull, swan and johnny dipper with its filthy deadly tar. The beaches were black with oil, the sky dark with the rolling clouds of smoke and still the tanks blazed on, week after week after week, a beacon to guide future night bombers to the Milford Haven. The War had brought the world to us again all right, and no mistake.

The station was already on yellow alert when Freddie Eynon and I booked on one bleak afternoon a few months later. Instead of the usual Castle awaiting us there was a 53 class loco. The Castles arrived at Neyland in the morning with the Down Parcels and were prepped ready for the return run with the Up Parcels later in the afternoon, but war-time emergencies and shortage of men caused many irregularities and so we found ourselves with a 53.

Daylight faded fast and we fixed the sails early. With a yellow alert on it paid to cover the glare from the fire-box, even when it was merely dusk. I hooked the rear of the sail to the metal uprights attached to the front of each tender for that purpose, while Fred threw back the side flaps onto the top as we avoided fastening them down until absolutely necessary, as the footplate quickly became stiflingly hot when entirely closed in by sails. After carrying out all the necessary checks I stood and looked, with some misgivings, at our centre and sidelights which denoted we were a Parcel Train. Two penetrating beams of light they threw before us—too bloody penetrating by half when you thought of the possiblility of their being spotted by enemy aircraft. Like a search-light announcing our presence they seemed to be—especially if we had an ammunition train behind us with a red alert on! It seemed ludicrous to us to take such stringent precautions over the blacking out of stations —and then to advertise the actual trains with the full blaze of our headlights.

Each of these lamps had a powerful bulls-eye reflector which concentrated the light into a far-reaching beam. A slit was positioned behind the front plate of glass where red or green slides could be fitted in order to change the role of the light, and many firemen and drivers started to place a slip of white paper into this slit which had the comforting effect of reducing the strength of the bulls-eye and of diffusing the light. But as soon as this practice was discovered, a ruling was issued that it was illegal and disciplinary action would follow any discovery of lights so tampered with. So back we were with our blazing lights, cutting through the blacked-out countryside like beacons. We tried turning down the wicks in order to reduce the strength, but the damn things promptly went out altogether as soon as there was a bit of rough track and we would find ourselves signalled to a halt by the signal-man who noticed the absence of lights. We also tried turning the wicks up too high, hoping that they would burn too fiercely and blacken the glass, but that didn't work either, so we were stuck with our gallus bulls-eyes. But whenever I found myself pulling an ammunition train loaded with bombs and mines from the Milford Mining Depot, I decided that if a slip of white paper might save my life, then a slip of white paper I would use. After all, you can recover from disciplinary action . . .!

But on this particular run with the 53, having only innocuous parcels behind us, I reckoned we had better abide by the rules and Fred agreed with me. So off we set into the dusk with our two headlamps blazing their way through the cuttings and countryside and our side sails firmly secured down round the cab. Bloody ridiculous it seemed to me as I grew hotter and sweatier by the minute, as I shovelled the coal into the fire-box.

We had travelled about fifteen miles when Fred gave a growl.

'There's a blasted leaky valve on this bloody engine!' he snarled as a huge drop of condensation landed with unerring accuracy on the back of his neck. Using complete sails was bad enough. Even without a leaky valve, condensation eventually started to form on the insides of the sail and the heat and humidity was barely tolerable, but, with a leak, it became more like a steaming, dripping jungle with the humidity draining you of all energy. Bloody miserable it was, I can tell you.

With Fred's curses ringing in my ears and the sweat pouring off me, I closed the fire-box door to prevent any glare and opened the side-sails to dry out the air and blow some clean fresh air into our lungs. Clean, fresh air it might have been, but the sudden drop in temperature was like a physical assault. From the steamy swamps of Africa to the ice plateau of The Pole in two seconds flat! I didn't fancy either very much, but there was no happy medium, so we continued our run to Llandeilo Junction with that blessed top valve of the pet-pipe hissing away in spite of all our attempts to bandage the thing up with waste and twine. We were back in the jungle in no time at all, with the condensation relentlessly dripping all over us, and to cap it all, by the time we reached Llandeilo Junction the yellow alert had changed to red.

'Looks as if Swansea is going to cop it tonight, Fred,' I remarked resignedly, 'and it looks as if we're going to run right into it too,' I added without relish. The pair of us were standing alongside the track, drinking a lovely cup of tea when we first became aware of the drone of high aircraft. We strained our eyes up into the dark night sky and then we spotted, low in the sky, the white outlines of parachutes, slowly descending carrying burning flares.

'Hold this a minute, Fred,' I said, handing him my half drunk tea, 'I've had enough of this, boy,' pointing to the searchlight beams gleaming from our headlamps. 'Look the other way and you needn't know anything about it, see,' I added with a wink as I climbed onto the footplate and fetched my two emergency pieces of white paper from the lid of my double-home box. I felt a lot safer when they were securely inserted into the lamps, and I gave them a defiant pat as I returned to finish off my cup of tea. Well, ridiculous it was, with us heading straight into trouble—fair play.

As we steamed away from Llandeilo Junction the flares continued to light up the sky ahead and the ominous sounds of exploding bombs began to reach our ears. Our sails were well down as we rattled and swayed along, no longer conscious of the build-up of heat and humidity, but only of the menace in the skies above us.

We approached Llandarcy Tunnel with some degree of thankfulness, at least we would be unseen and comparatively safe for a few minutes. Our speed was restricted through the tunnel as there was a signal just on the other side, it was always off, but there's always a first time—and this was it.

'The signal's on, Fred!' I exclaimed in surprise as we neared the end of the tunnel. Fred quickly slowed us down just outside the tunnel, the signal was about seventy-five yards ahead—the first time I had ever ever seen it on.

'No sense in us waiting out by here, Bill, we might as well get back into the tunnel until we have the road,' and without more ado Fred took us back the few yards into the welcoming shelter of the tunnel. Like a tortoise's head our loco was, just tucked into its shell. Our view was restricted on both sides by the steep sides of the cutting, but there was no mistaking the sight and sounds which lay directly before us. The horizon was aglow with orange fire, brilliant flares still fell by parachute, although their original purpose was out-done by the numerous fires which lit up the area with uncomfortable brilliance.

The loco shuddered beneath our feet as explosion followed explosion. 'That one was bloody close,' muttered Fred as a particularly deafening, earth-shaking bomb exploded nearby.

'We'll be lucky if we have any signal left at all if this goes on,' I remarked with a grim smile, and we just stood there watching the destruction going on before our eyes with a blank calm. After having waited the Regulation Three Minutes we should have abided by Rule 55 and one of us should have approached the signal-box to discover the reason for our delay and to check that we were properly guarded.

'Well, we know what the reason for the bloody delay is, don't we?' announced Fred after about five minutes.

'We do that, boy,' I agreed, as the barrage of guns and bombs continued outside. 'I'll take a run up to the box when this little lot dies down a bit,' I suggested, instinctively ducking as a screaming whistle heralded yet another descending bomb near us. The thunderous explosion was quickly followed by the sharp crash of breaking glass— lots of it.

'That sounds like the signal-box,' I said to Fred with dismay, 'I'll go and check,' I added, climbing down from the footplate and making my way to the entrance of the tunnel. Cautiously I made my way past the boiler of the 53 and peered out into the hellish night. Searchlights swept in wide arcs across the sky, anti-aircraft guns thudded their shells into the air and the whining of the descending bombs made me wince with the expectation of each one landing. And over it all, like a blanket, was the continuous drone of aircraft above. Crouching low, with my arms instinctively over my head I started to run along the track—past the signal, still standing and still on, until a particularly brilliant flash gave me a few seconds proof that the signal-box, which was a good hundred yards further on down the line, was still actually there. I hurried on until I reached the base of the steps, the blank, dark, eyeless signal-box looming over me with not one pane of glass left and no sign of life. Rushing up the steps two at a time, I pushed open the ricked door with my shoulder and entered the draughty, silent, deserted box, my feet crunching on the broken glass as I picked my way through the debris.

'Anybody there?' I shouted, although it was obvious that there was no-one. I couldn't understand it. Then in the orange glare of a nearby fire I spotted the tall metal box standing in the corner. It was approximately six feet high and three feet square, with a narrow letter-box type slit on the sides. Of course, I thought to myself in exasperation at having forgotten about it—the signal-man's shelter. Quickly I made my way over to it and heaved the door. A startled face looked up at me—for all the world looking as if he was sitting on a lavatory! He held a torch in one hand and a book in the other.

'Iesu Grist! There's a fright you gave me,' he exclaimed in annoyance.

'A fright I gave you,' I retorted. 'What about this little lot then? Are you all right man?' I demanded in exasperation as it looked as if he was about to return to his reading matter without further conversation!

'Yes, yes, man,' he replied testily. 'Never you mind about me, you're supposed to be back in that tunnel, I haven't given you the road yet—no communications see? So just you go back there and sit and wait like me, boy,' and he pulled his metal door closed and left me standing there amongst the broken glass and splintered wood, while all hell was let loose around the fragile little box. I couldn't make up my mind whether he was the bravest man I had known—or the daftest! But it must have been a hell of a good book, I thought as I hastily retraced my steps back to the safety of the tunnel where Fred was anxiously awaiting my return, bursting with curiosity and concern as to what was going on at the box.

We waited for nearly two hours while that interminable raid of destruction spent itself. Gradually the explosions became fewer, although the glare on the horizon was fiercer than ever. We discovered later that it was not Swansea which had suffered most that night, but Llandarcy which had borne the brunt of the attack—Llandarcy with its oil tanks.

'It's off!' shouted our guard from his look-out post at the entrance of the tunnel. I had gone back to his van to let him know what was happening and he had come down to the engine to wait. Back he hurried to his van now, as Fred and I prepared to move.

'Take her slow, mind,' I warned, as we steamed out into the open.

'What did you think I was going to do then?' Fred retorted irritably. We were all edgy. The signal-man could be seen ahead, waving a red light back and forth and Fred drew to a halt alongside the shattered box.

'Take her steady, driver,' he warned us unnecessarily. 'I think the line's intact, but keep a look-out for debris on the track. Still no communication so Proceed On Caution,' he ended formally. We left him climbing back up into his draughty signal-box, giving a wave to our guard as the tail-end of our late Parcels passed by.

We eventually arrived at Briton Ferry after a slow journey at five miles an hour. Surprisingly we had met no obstruction on the line, although there were dark, shadowy craters in the fields alongside. Just luck it was.

We found we could go no further than Briton Ferry with our Parcels and we were told to leave the 53 there and go to the cabin where jugs of hot tea were waiting for us. There were eight of us altogether in the cabin, all waiting to reach Landore, where we spent our double-home on this run, so it was decided to give us a light engine and we could all get on the footplate and take ourselves down. There's crowded that footplate was, but nobody complained, although the journey seemed endless because of the speed restrictions. As we approached Landore an increasing number of fires could be seen all round us, ambulance bells were ringing and spasmodic explosions told their story of more oil tanks catching alight and of gas mains broken.

The driver of our light engine taxi brought us to a halt just before the iron bridge outside Landore. He was a local man from Swansea and knew every inch of the track.

'One of you walk over and check that damn bridge before I take this engine across, now,' he ordered. One of the others quickly jumped down, watched keenly by the remainder of us as he walked slowly over the bridge, examining the track and hanging over the side to check the supports.

'Looks all right,' he announced on his return, 'a job to see really, but we may as well risk it.' Which we did—at walking pace. I don't think anyone spoke a word or moved a muscle until we reached the other side.

By the time we reached Landore another wave of bombers were coming over and Fred and I hurried apprehensively through the deserted streets and up the hill to old Mags. We tried the door, which surprisingly for one o'clock in the morning, was open. We entered the inky blackness of the tiny passage, calling, 'It's all right, it's only us, Bill Morgan and Fred Eynon.'

'Is that you Mr. Morganzzzzzz?' came the querulous little Welsh voice from the pantry under the stairs. Old Mags and her sister were sitting hunched beneath the undersides of the stair-treads, clutching their gas masks in their laps. The rather strong smell of gas from the gas meter did not exactly suggest that this was the safest place in the house to be in the middle of an air raid, but as the smell was always there I suppose they took no notice of it!

'There's glad we are to see you now, safe and sound isn't it, safe and sound,' repeated Mags, patting her gas mask reassuringly. We declined their offer to crouch under the stairs with them, and instead spent the remainder of the night sitting in the back room chatting, smoking and drinking mug after mug of good strong tea, as the raid resounded around us.

We left at six o'clock that morning after the All Clear had sounded, and took a light engine to Swansea Station, but the entire area was in such a state of upheaval and disorganisation that our eight o'clock Passengers simply didn't run that day and we gratefully came home to Neyland on the cushions of the 10.15 Mails—sleeping most of the way, needless to say.

Win had heard of the raid on South Wales. She was glad to see me walking up the path.

* * *

'There's someone on the track, Bill!' Ted's words stopped me in mid-shovel as he pulled off the regulator and slammed on the brakes. I looked over the side of the cab, and there, less than fifty yards ahead of us was a lone figure of what I took to be a man, waving his hands back and fore above his head.

'Bloody fool,' muttered Ted, 'could have killed the stupid bugger!'

We soon discovered our assumptions to be wrong, however, as we drew to a halt, not alongside a man, as we had both thought, but a woman! She wore Company uniform—including, much to our amazement—trousers! We had gradually become accustomed to the sight of women working on the platforms, since the war had created a shortage of men, but they always wore skirts. Never before had we seen one in trousers—big, heavy serge ones they were, which stood circular around her legs like stiff black rolls, in fact, the entire uniform looked at least two sizes too big for her!

'Can you give me a lift, fellers?' she asked, looking up at us from the trackside. 'I've got to light the signal lamps see,' she continued, holding up her can of paraffin as proof, 'and they're such a bloody long way apart from each other, it'll take me all day to walk.'

We could realise now, why she had been given a special uniform—with trousers. The Company obviously had thought that the sight of a female Signal Lamp Lighter, climbing up to the top of the ladder in a skirt, might well prove something of a distraction to Company Men!

She was grateful for our agreeing to give her a lift along the line, and I hauled her up onto the footplate where she perched on my tip-up seat, clutching her paraffin-can.

'I thought you were supposed to carry lit replacement lamps with you, then?' I remarked as we got up speed once more.

'Why aye, man, I'm supposed to, but they're too bloody heavy,' she answered with a shrug, 'I just refill and light the ones that are already there. Just as good, isn't it?'

I looked at Ted and he looked at me. Women, we thought . . .

We slowed down for her to jump off as we neared the first signal. Her beat covered the next mile or so of track, and we left her with a wave and a warning not to flag down an engine from the centre of the track next time!

We were on local Pilot Work between Haverfordwest and Johnston that day and about two hours later we were steaming back along the same track when Ted exclaimed, 'Well, I'm damned, that gallus woman's still there!' I leaned over the cab side and espied her sitting forlornly at the side of the track, leaning against the bottom of the signal, her oversized serge uniform almost covering her completely. We slowed to a halt.

'What's the matter then, love?' I asked with a grin. 'Can't you climb the ladder or something?'

She looked up morosely at us and stated flatly,

'I forgot the bloody matches!'
Women lamp lighters indeed!

* * *

The clatter and clangour of the unloading milk churns echoed around Clynderwyn platform. A miserable night it was, pelting rain and gusty wind chilling you to the marrow. It was at least a quarter of an hour's stop at Clynderwyn on the Down Parcels as there were over two hundred empty milk churns and about a hundred rabbit boxes to be unloaded. It was one of the turns I was acting driver and I took a glance out of the cab back along the darkened platform to try to see how Charlie May the guard was getting on with his unloading. Usually, at this time of night, he was lucky if there was one porter to help him and it was a tiring, irksome job.

The blustery wind blew the driving rain into my face as I peered through the gloom of the ill-lit war-time platform. I could make out no distinct forms, but the metallic clatter of the churns was still continuing so I pulled my head back inside the cab and sat down with my young fireman to wait for a few more minutes. I kept an ear cocked for the sound of Charlie's whistle, but with the wind and rain it would be sheer luck if I heard it.

Another peer out down the platform. By the lack of noise, the milk churns had obviously been unloaded, but there was still something going on—must be the rabbit boxes, I thought, so back for a few more minutes wait and a few final drags at my rather damp cigarette.

'Charlie ought to be finished by now,' I remarked, peering once more down the platform, and sure enough, there was the green light. I couldn't hear the whistle, but that was understandable in that weather.

'Right-O, mate, we're off,' I announced flicking my damp butt out of the cab side. I opened up the regulator and off we steamed to Clarbeston Road, about eight miles down line, passing the Up Goods about half-way.

'What the hell's up here, then?' I muttered to myself as we drew near Clarbeston Road signal-box. The signal was on and old Cockles the signal-man was swinging a red lamp out of his window. Anthony his name was, but everyone called him Cockles because he came from Kidwelly—lovely big cockles there were at Kidwelly. I shut off the regulator and brought the loco to a halt right under him. Before I could query the reason for the red light, however, Cockles leaned his two elbows on the ledge and shouted through the rain,

'What's the game, then? What d'you think you're playing at?'

'What's up then, Cockles?' I shouted back, completely puzzled by his remarks.

'You've only left your Guard behind at Clynderwyn that's all, man,' he replied. 'Just shot off and left him, you did. Still unloading he was, mind!'

'Never!' I called. 'He gave me the green light, man, plain as day.'

'Ah well, whatever happened, you haven't got a guard with you now, anyway. They phoned through to tell me, so I'll put you in the loop until he can catch you up. He's following with the Mails—be here in half an hour,' and with that he withdrew his head and shut his window. The loop signal came off and, still puzzling how on earth Charlie May could have been left behind at Clynderwyn, I steamed slowly into the siding. It just didn't make sense. What on earth would possess Charlie to give me the Right-O if he hadn't finished unloading? I couldn't fathom it out at all, so there was nothing to do but wait until the Mails brought him along and then perhaps we could sort it out.

The rain continued to throw itself down as my fireman and I drank a quick cup of tea while waiting in the loop. Eventually, a good three-quarter's of an hour later, Charlie's wet face appeared at the cab side. He climbed up onto the footplate, shaking the rain off his cap.

'You trying to get rid of me or something Bill?' he asked, half-joking —a good natured sort was Charlie May. I explained that I had been given the green light so off I'd gone.

'Something funny, here,' suggested Charlie with a puzzled shake of his head. 'I definitely didn't give you any green light. Not me, boy. Why no, I was still busy unloading those damned rabbit boxes and off you shot!'

I believed him, and he believed that I had seen the green light, but further than that we could not go! The mystery was still unsolved.

The following night on the same trip, I was sitting in the cab of the loco once more, listening to the clatter of the milk churns on Clynderwyn Station, and still trying to fathom out where that green light had come from. I leant over the cab side, staring back down the dark platform as I had done the previous night. It was still wet, unpleasant weather and the gloom was as impenetrable as before. Into

Loco leaving Neyland Shed to work the stopping passenger train to Carmarthen.
The hydraulic pumping house towers to the skyline on the right.

Neyland Shed in all its glory, photographed from Railway Terrace.
A lone cleaner leans against his tiny cabin whilst an exalted driver, complete with
double-home box, stands outside the drivers' cabin.

Driver Bill Morgan at Gloucester Shed, May 1952. The big wheels of his Saint Class 2951 would not have suited the gradients of South Wales!

Relief crews at Severn Tunnel Junction, waiting to travel 'on the cushions' back to Gloucester.
Bill Morgan is sitting second from the left and Doug fourth from the left.

Driver Bill Morgan with Fireman Ivor Smith on the stopping passengers at Newport.

Driver Bill Morgan with Fireman Ivor Smith in the cab of their loco at Gloucester Shed, waiting to work the 2.15 to Hereford.

Express Driver—Bill Morgan in his retirement.
'By, hedges, it was a grand life!'

my mind suddenly came the recollection of the Up Train which had passed us a few miles out of Clynderwyn on our way to Clarbeston Road the previous night, and an idea began to form in my head.

'Hey, kid,' I called to my young fireman, 'take a stroll down to the signal-box and ask whoever's there to take off the Up Starter Signal for a second, will you?' He looked at me in surprise. 'Just tell him, for a second will do. The Up Starter. There's something I want to check.' So off he went, disappearing into the wet darkness while I kept my eyes fixed down platform.

I waited expectantly for five or six minutes, then, suddenly, as I had expected, a green light appeared out of the gloom for a few seconds and then disappeared again. 'Well, I'm blowed,' I said aloud to myself. The mystery was solved. The Starter Signal was normally obscured from my view by the buildings on the station, but when the signal dropped to 'Off' it just became visible under the overhanging platform canopy. The green light.

'Well, I'm glad to hear it,' smiled Charlie when I went back along the platform to give him the solution to the mystery. 'I was beginning to be afraid to move a step away from my van door, in case you took it into your head to repeat last night's little episode! I didn't fancy another walk in the rain. And while you're here, give us a hand with these damned rabbit boxes!'

* * *

I shaded my eyes from the glare of the sun as I tried to make out what Win was waving in her hand. She was standing on top of the air raid shelter calling to me at the top of Osborne's field, where young Dai and I were ferreting for rabbits.

'I bet it's a call paper,' I grumbled, giving an answering wave. Dai was the proud owner of a good pair of ferrets, and I had enlisted his services that afternoon to chase out a few rabbits. We had nets set carefully at all the burrows along the hedge. The ferrets had disappeared a good five minutes earlier, Mack lay crouched, nose to the ground, every muscle quivering—and then that blasted call paper had to arrive.

It must be a special, I thought, as I ran back to the garden to find out the details. I was correct in my assumption. Special, Landore Relief, 5 p.m. I read, noticing that the call paper was made out for Dai as well

—somebody must have known where he was with his ferrets that afternoon! Five o'clock, I thought with exasperation, it was gone four already and we had two valuable ferrets down a rabbit hole! An emergency indeed!

I raced back up the field to Dai and told him the situation.

'What about my ferrets, then?' he asked in a worried tone.

'Well, is there any sign of movement yet?' I enquired anxiously.

'Why no, not a blessed thing, man. Damned Specials,' he muttered angrily.

'Well we can't just leave them, they'll have a bloody great feast and that'll be the last you see of them.' I looked at my watch. We had to decide on something quickly. 'I'll fetch a couple of spades, and we'll block 'em in,' I suggested. It took nearly twenty minutes to button down that hedge, watched by a very confused dog!

'I've got no time to go home and change,' remarked Dai as we climbed over the hedge and jumped down from the air raid shelter. I looked at him. He was wearing a seaman's blue sweater and blue overalls tucked into thick white socks and seaman's boots.

'You'll do, boy,' I answered. 'Nobody'll notice what you're wearing and Win can pack a box for you.'

It was a Special all right—an ammunition train, loaded with mines and bombs from Milford. A Manor was prepped ready for us at Neyland Shed and I took it light to Milford where we coupled up to a hellishly long line of ominously covered wagons.

'Thank God there's no alerts on red or yellow, and I hope it stays that way,' I added fervently as I let off the brake, opened up the regulator and felt my deadly load move behind me.

It was a relief to have an uneventful trip to Landore, although Dai wasn't too keen on firing in heavy rubber boots! We handed our load over to the Landore men with our very best wishes, and, as we were a Special and travelling back on the cushions, we sat on one of the benches on Swansea platform and munched our sandwiches which Win had prepared in such a hurry. Two were spam and pickles and two were of a slimy concoction which defied recognition but which smelt faintly of bananas—I made a mental note to ask Win what on earth they were, and whatever it was, not to use it again!

The pair of us sat there on the station, waiting for the Mails and semi-dozing, my box tucked under the seat, when I suddenly became aware of a little old lady standing in front of us and Welshily nattering away to Dai who was also only half awake.

'Wonderful you are,' she was saying. 'Brave isn't the word for you young sailors—out in those ships with all those old torpedoes. Torpedoed you were, was it?' she asked pushing her hand down into her voluminous handbag and bringing out a large bar of chocolate. We stared at the chocolate in disbelief and at the little old lady in confusion. What the hell was she nattering on about? There was no mistaking that blue and gold wrapper which we hadn't seen for a very long time. Chocolate—I'd almost forgotten what it tasted like.

'You deserve it more than I do, young man, wonderful you are,' she repeated and thrust the bar of chocolate onto Dai's lap and before either of us could gather our wits about us enough to try to explain the situation to her, she was gone—through the ticket barrier and out into the night!

'Well,' beamed Dai in pleasurable anticipation as he viewed the rare offering in his hands, 'we might not be sailors, but we did bring the ammunition train in, after all!' And without more ado he broke the chocolate bar in two and gave half to me.

You should have seen Bette's eyes light up when she inquisitively searched my box on my return. Chocolate! Unbelievable!

The strange concoction in our sandwiches, so I was informed by Win, had been dehydrated bananas. Two fat ferrets, with grey-furred fangs, appeared within five minutes of our unblocking the holes, but not one rabbit did we catch! What an unsuccessful day it would have been without our dear, misguided, little old lady!

*   *   *

The previous night had been a particularly stormy one even for Pembrokeshire. Bette rushed in from the fields with Mack at her heels.

'It's gone again!' she announced with some satisfaction. We both knew what she was referring to—the barrage balloon sited in the next field along The Prom. Those poor R.A.F. chaps must have had the worst record for breakaway balloons in the country. The times I had seen them sitting forlornly around the site staring at the empty mooring base. Mind you, they were a bit exposed to the Westerlies there!

The runaway balloons often caused considerable damage from their trailing steel wires, but on the other hand the skin from any balloon unfortunate enough to get itself deflated and grounded anywhere near Neyland was immediately pounced upon by the locals and carried off in pieces until hardly a trace was left! In the pre-plastic age the waterproof material of barrage balloons could be used in a variety of ways. Hay-ricks were covered as they had never been covered before, shopping bags took on a uniform silvery grey appearance which matched very nicely the new capes and sou'westers which were stitched up with alacrity on old Singers, to replace cracking yellow oil-skins. Damp chickens and shivering pigs discovered that their coops and sties were suddenly waterproof and draught-free, rowing boats sported tailored silvery-grey waterproof canopies and scrubbed kitchen tables now had beautiful wipe-over grey tops neatly tacked on. The in shade for 1940 was definitely silver-grey.

We made great friends with the lads from the balloon site. Win would make an enormous jug of coffee for them every morning and Mack was a standing joke with them, as any time he was feeling particularly bored, he would lope off to the sentry on duty and stand barking at him, running in short darts back and fore in order to encourage the stupid fellow to go rabbiting! An idle gun was beyond comprehension to Mack. I regularly exchanged eggs for tea and sugar with the R.A.F. lads there. Tea and sugar being the two commodities which were in particularly short supply—as none of the local farms grew them! Food on ration was adequate but very dull, so, of course, I decided to improve our diet by helping Jacobs or Lewis the Farm with their harvesting—and accepting bran or corn for my services. This I fed to my chickens which supplied the eggs to exchange for tea and sugar, which, in turn, could be exchanged for other goods in short supply or for clothing coupons—whichever we needed most at the time. Well, we had to use our initiative, you see.

Our potato peelings and odd scraps of food were kept for a few acquaintances who surreptitiously kept pigs. Of course, it was illegal to slaughter any beast without a permit, but many a pig or steer met a sudden end in the dark early hours of the morning, and our potato peelings would miraculously change into a side of salted bacon hidden behind the toolhouse door!

As in the days of the depression in the Twenties, I felt grateful that I did not live in a big town where life was so confining and resourcefulness was stifled before it began—and where there are too many officials!

But inspectors regularly checked farms and butchers for any tell-tale signs of surreptitious slaughtering, often turning up at the most unexpected and unusual times! It became a battle of wits and ingenuity.

One butcher drove a steer miles out into the countryside one dark night before killing it, as blood stains were the most incriminating of all evidence and the most difficult to conceal! It was not until he arrived back with the cut-up carcass lying safely on a large piece of barrage ballooning on the floor of his van, that he discovered that the rear door had fallen open and that somewhere along the way he had lost the head! It must have been a gruesome find for someone on a lonely country lane!

'Well, we've had our side of bacon this time,' were the first words Win spoke as she came into the kitchen. She had been up the town and the news was spreading like wildfire. . . . 'Caught with the knife at its throat, he was—blood everywhere, so they say, confiscated the whole pig, of course. I wonder how much they'll fine him?'

'We'll have to have a whip round to help pay it, anyway,' I replied, feeling rather despondent as I stared at the thin piece of rind which was all that was left hanging in the larder.

A week or so later, however, we were very much surprised and delighted to find our usual parcel wedged behind the toolshed door. As we sat staring at the side of bacon, unwrapped on the kitchen table, its white rind sparkling beautifully with crystals of salt, we tried to think where it could possibly have come from, as everyone knew that the pig had been confiscated.

'Well,' explained our potato-peeling collector later in the week, 'my back yard was running with blood when they took my lovely pig away, so I thought it was an ideal time to kill another one, hidden she was and could have done with a bit more fattening up, but the opportunity was too good to miss, man.' He continued, 'One's pig's blood looks the same as another's, and they wouldn't think of coming straight back now would they?' he ended with a wink.

You can't keep a good man down. The saying 'You may as well be hung for a sheep as a lamb' needed subtle changing, I remember thinking!

15

During the winter of 1940 to 1941 we listened in silence each day to the news bulletins of air raids and their dreadful toll. At first they were centred on London, but as the weeks went by other cities were attacked, Coventry, Birmingham, Manchester, Bristol, Sheffield, with an average of two hundred bombers on each night raid. The first of the intensive raids outside London to shock us was the four hundred bomber offensive of Coventry on a moonlit night in November. The Cathedral was no more and the horror and devastation we could only imagine. Every railway line out of Coventry was blocked and the station shut down, but during the following two days the breakdown gangs and engineers somehow managed to get some trains moving in and out of the city.

It was not until the New Year of that bitterly cold winter that South Wales was really hit hard. Hundreds of people were killed in Cardiff when Llandaff Cathedral was badly damaged and the docks severely hit. Swansea also knew all too well what it was like to be a target for enemy aircraft, but hitherto it had experienced nothing like the three consecutive nights of mid-February when over two hundred bombers flattened the entire centre of the town, killing hundreds of people.

Ted Rees and I were sitting in the back room of our Landore lodgings desultorily playing cards, tuning in to the wireless and listening to old Mags' lamentations on rationing, shortage of fuel, dark streets, National Margarine and Jerry's latest attacks. We were due to book on just after midnight at Landore Station where we would work our light Castle down to Swansea to couple up with the Down Parcels from Paddington.

The sirens had sounded late in the afternoon and as the evening wore on, wave after wave of enemy aircraft had flown over, some dropping flares and incendiaries while others followed up with the heavy bombing which pounded Landore and the surrounding towns relentlessly. Old Mags had come out from under the stairs just long enough to fuss over us as we filled our tea bottles. Our sandwiches had been packed a good eighteen hours before in Neyland, as there was no spare food to be bought now in the shops. The food situation on double-homes was becoming increasingly difficult.

We let ourselves out of the narrow front door, adjusting our feet to the steep angle of the pavement outside. The hilly street was deserted except for a lone, steel-helmeted Civil Defence Worker who, above the noise of the thunderous explosions of guns and bombs, shouted at us to get under cover.

'Good luck!' he yelled as a particularly brilliant flash lit up the street long enough for him to realise that we were G.W.R. men. 'The station's still there—I think,' he shouted as an after-thought. We should have had steel helmets on ourselves, we had all been issued with them and for the first few months had carried them around religiously, but gradually we started to forget the blasted things. If a raid came when you were at home, your helmet was sure to be at the Shed. If you were in the Shed, it would sure to be left on the loco. They were the most elusive things when they were needed. Like now, for example. Mine was behind the pantry door at home and Ted hadn't seen his since he left it on a Castle a few months back! We were both beginning to regret being so careless.

The Warden had been correct in thinking that the station was unscathed. Our Castle, which we had left there earlier that day, was ready prepped for us and we took her out of Landore on time, in spite of the blitz which was going on around us. We worked light engine down to Swansea, and as we drew near to the city, carefully eyeing every inch of the track before us, it seemed as if the entire town was ablaze. There was no need for sails as our little bit of fire-box glare would add nothing to the inferno which seemed to be raging all around us. Miraculously the line was clear. Ted and I wondered what we were heading into. We took it slow.

The signal was off for us to berth ourselves in our siding while we waited for our counterpart Castle and crew to bring the Parcels in from Paddington. They would pull into the buffers at Swansea and uncouple, while we coupled up to the rear and took the train the remainder of its journey to Neyland.

'I'll be glad to get the hell out of here,' I announced while we sat there like sitting ducks in Swansea Sidings. Incendiaries were falling all round us, but they did little damage, hardly even burying themselves, but causing little pockets of fire all over the tracks.

'I bet that Down Parcels will be late,' seethed Ted. 'Bound to be with this lot going on,' he added, looking round apprehensively. But just as he spoke, in she steamed, right on time. It seemed a miracle that signals, points and communications could be working so efficiently in such chaos.

'Thank God for that,' exclaimed Ted, jumping up and fingering the regulator in his impatience to get started. We watched that signal like hawks, and as soon as it came off we were away. Into the station we steamed, the platform alive with scurrying figures, their faces reflecting an uncanny orange hue from the glare of the fires raging around us. I jumped down from the footplate onto the platform before we had actually come to a standstill. I could hardly get those coupling chains fastened quick enough.

Suddenly it sounded as if all hell was let loose. The ground shook beneath us, the last remnants of the glass roof over the platform came crashing down about our heads and I flung myself down under the tender as twisted steel supports collapsed along the platform. Whistles were blowing, debris was flying, and in the uproar and confusion I suddenly noticed, with dismay, that every signal was on. Nobody and no loco was going anywhere. 'Take cover! Take cover!' the shouts rang out all over the station, as I heaved myself out from under the tender and climbed back onto the footplate to check with Ted. 'I wish I had my bloody helmet!' he shouted as I climbed back onto the footplate, and I mentally echoed his wish. The platforms were clearing rapidly as I dropped the dampers and closed the fire-box door.

'Looks as if we're stuck here for the duration, so we'd better make ourselves comfortable,' I suggested, picking up my double-homer. 'Come on, boy, under the tender with us.'

'Good idea, Bill,' he agreed, 'I don't fancy being too close to that scalding boiler, man, I can tell you.'

We clambered down from the Castle and climbed down off the platform, settling ourselves by the middle wheel of the tender, our double-home boxes making convenient seats. We stayed there, wedged between tender and platform, for the next hour while the blitz continued relentlessly above and around us. At least we had the satisfaction of knowing that nothing short of a direct hit could affect us. We were supposed to be due out at 2.45, but it was not until nearly four o'clock that there was a slight lull in the bombing and we heard that wonderful sound of a guard's whistle! At least something was on the move at last, we thought, as we climbed out of our shelter and joined the other Company men, civilians, Civil Defence Workers, W.V.S. helpers and others who all suddenly appeared from heaven knows where.

Within a few minutes we were given the signal, and getting steam up as fast as we could, we gratefully pulled out of Swansea Station, just as everyone was running for cover once more as another wave of bombers let loose their load of destruction on the town.

It was like breaking out of a blockade as we steamed through the flaming town. The tracks gleamed in the reflected light from the flashes and fires, cutting a swathe through the rubble and destruction on either side. One or two of the sidings had been hit, but our line was wonderfully straight and clear. We could hardly believe in our good fortune. We rode through it all, as if the Castle, the train and ourselves were charmed. We held our breath as we approached each signal in case it was against us, but each one came and went in our favour and gradually we left the stricken town behind us. Keeping an eagle eye on the track before us, we travelled the dozen or so miles to our first stop—Llanelly.

It was like going back into a trap again. Bells were ringing, whistles blowing, shouts, confusion and chaos greeted us as we slowed to a halt at the platform. The ominous low drone of aircraft could be heard above us and the few minutes we had to wait seemed to stretch to eternity as we stamped impatiently around the cab to ease our desire to get going once more. As soon as we had the road we steamed thankfully away from the crash of collapsing buildings and the shattering explosions of bombs.

Once on the move we became isolated from everything around us, and as we drew away from the devastated valleys and neared the comparative calm of Carmarthen, I almost felt guilty at feeling safe. The night became peaceful again instead of flaming and chaotic. Only the horizon still glowed, an orange glow which could be seen from Neyland itself, a good eighty miles away. We steamed in at 8.45 that morning, and I was never more pleased to see that dirty old Shed.

My brother-in-law, Dan, had just left Neyland for Swansea with the eight o'clock passengers—he didn't know it then, but he was to spend the entire following night lying in a gutter shielded by a piece of fallen masonry while Swansea exploded around him. 'Well, Bill, it seemed as good a place as any,' he remarked philosophically later, and it seemed that he was right!

The utter desolation and destruction which met our gaze as we returned to Llanelly and Swansea the following day was unbelievable. Landmarks were destroyed beyond all recognition, entire streets had disappeared in a mass of rubble, burnt out cars littered what few streets were left and crazily tottering buildings gaped rooflessly at the sky. We steamed slowly in under speed restriction, the tracks alive with gangers, linesmen and engineers, repairing, checking and rechecking. Craters yawned at our side, the track already shored up and strengthened by the labourers. They certainly wasted no time in getting the railway running again.

A little further away, alongside the boundaries of the line we could see the firemen, W.V.S. helpers, Civil Defence Workers and civilians trying to bring some sort of order to the confusion. Men trying to get to work, carried their bicycles on their shoulders to cross the rubble while rescue work went tirelessly on. Women and children picked their way over the ruins, the women drawn and grey, the children contrastingly excited and effervescent, salvaging pieces of furniture—a piano here, a chair there. And from our high plateau on the footplate we rode through it all, like visitors from another world. But sad it was.

* * *

The War dragged on and we in Neyland, like everywhere else, tried to make the best of it. We followed the advances and retreats on maps on living-room walls—North Africa, the fall of Tobruk, El Alamein; the Thousand Bomber raids on Cologne, the Ruhr, Hamburg and Berlin; Sicily and Italy, we traced every step and plotted every movement.

Stray bombs had landed in Llanstadwell, and two others had made a mess of my ferreting hedge behind the bungalow. Half Neyland had come to view an unexploded bomb in one of the fields and were most put out when requested to leave by the bomb disposal crew!

The air raids on Pembroke Dock and the Harbour had become so regular and heavy that we decided to abandon the bungalow and my home-made shelter each night, and sleep in the old pre-First World War Fort which was at Scoveston—about a mile and a half inland. It was built like a medieval stronghold with a moat and earthworks. Most of the rooms were below ground and looked out into the moat through narrow slit windows like a Norman Castle—and the walls were about as thick too! It was dank, dirty and full of sheep droppings when we and a few other similarly inclined families first decided to take a prospective look. But we soon had a few of the dark, stone steps and rooms cleaned up, and by the time we had installed storm lamps, one or two chairs, a few oil stoves and the necessary bedding, it began to look quite homely. My attempt, however, to make a bed out of chunks of four-by-four timber and chicken wire was not exactly a success. The two-foot-six high legs suddenly shot out sideways in the middle of the night, landing me with a resounding crash on the stone floor. I wouldn't have had such a jolt if only I had made the legs a bit shorter. I can't understand even now, why I made that damned bed so high!

Our depth underground made us oblivious of all air raid sirens, bombings, gunfire or any other sounds of battle from the outside world, and each morning we would leave our dungeons, carefully replacing the roll of barbed wire across the entrance to discourage the sheep from exploring below during our absence, and make our way to our various homes—hoping that they would still be there.

The Neyland social whirl continued in spite of the War. There were the G.W.R. Ambulance Dances, the Church Socials, the Whist Drives and the numerous Chapel Eistedfodds. Great care had to be taken when arranging the dates of performances of Choir Anthems, however, or it might be discovered with dismay that both bass performers were on a loco half-way to Carmarthen! I have myself been known to carry the tenor part alone, when the call of G.W.R. duty claimed the remainder of the St. Clement's tenors! In great demand we were, we male singers during the War.

The Sunday School treats, which had always gone for char-a-banc trips to Tenby or Broad Haven had to suffice with cucumber sandwiches in a tent and running races in Jacob's the Farmer's Top field, Lily Ted had to give up making her home-made yellow ice-cream in her wooden churn, pancakes had to be eaten without lemon juice and Harry Jones' currant buns had no currants, but, on the whole, things hadn't changed much.

The season started with sweeping the chimney (not relighting the fires regardless of the weather) and spring cleaning, to collecting armfuls and basketfuls of cowslips and primroses to decorate the churches and chapels for Easter, dressing up the children in net and woven flowers for Queen of the May, and then the Eistedfodd season, followed by blackberrying, nutting, Harvest Festivals, Hallowe'en, Guy Fawkes, and the long preparations for Christmas. There was always something being planned, regardless of the War.

All the women developed bottling fever. They bottled everything they could think of! Apples, pears, blackcurrants, redcurrants, gooseberries, raspberries, loganberries, strawberries, mountains of blackberries, plums and damsons.

And if they weren't bottling, they were jam-making. Whole families, armed with walking-sticks, marched out into the fields with enormous baskets, ready to strip every hedge of every blackberry—not even the topmost bramble escaping their crooked-handled sticks and blue-stained picking fingers. Every hazelnut was gathered and layered in salt to keep them fresh for Christmas, whilst the best apples were carefully wrapped and laid in the loft ready to be brought out and polished before the great day. Busy, everybody was, right through the year in Neyland.

Work on the line carried on very much as usual, except for one or two little events at Neyland Shed. One took place on an early evening in mid-winter. The sky was black and the steady drone of high-flying bombers on their way to unfortunate Liverpool could be heard overhead. Of course the station was on alert black-out and practically everything came to a standstill. We just sat in the darkness and waited. All lights were out and all fire-boxes closed down. Shunting was stopped and an unusual silence descended on the Yard, except for the seemingly endless drone of the aircraft overhead. There must have been hundreds of them they took so long to pass.

I was sitting on the footplate of a small Tankie with Tom the

Chargeman, quietly smoking a cupped cigarette, when we both became aware of the sound of gushing water—not in the direction of the harbour but on the opposite side of the Yard by the Hydraulic.

We both peered through the impenetrable darkness but could distinguish nothing.

'Anybody there?' Tom called, his voice striking the silence like an anvil.

'I can't shut the valve off!' came a panic-stricken answering cry from the direction of the gushing water.

'I'll go and give him a hand, Morgy,' volunteered Tom. 'It sounds like one of the young cleaners in trouble.'

The valve controlled the supply of water to the engines, and one had obviously just filled up when the cleaner discovered that he couldn't turn it off, consequently the water was gushing all over the place. It was unbelievably black in the Yard, you could hardly see a hand in front of your face, so I wasn't surprised when Tom asked me to pass him a flare lamp so that he could see where he was going and what was happening.

Carefully opening the fire-box door a fraction, very conscious of the drone from above, I lit a small flare lamp and shielded it with my hand.

'We don't want to give those bastards up there any encouragement, eh, Tom?' I asked as I carefully handed him the shielded flare. Tom held the lamp with equal caution as he heaved himself down off the footplate and started to pick his way across the tracks towards the Hydraulic. I tried to follow his progress, but the darkness soon swallowed him up before he had gone more than a few yards. I waited, taking a few more drags on my cigarette, and listened to the drone overhead and the gushing water. Tom should have reached there by now I thought, waiting for the sound of the water to stop. I peered into the darkness, straining my eyes for a sign of movement, but not a thing could I see. I was just beginning to think that I would follow Tom to see if there was anything I could do when there was an almighty roaring sound and a huge flame shot thirty feet into the air like an enormous blow-torch! I stared open-mouthed at the suddenly brilliantly illuminated scene before me. There was the cleaner running for his life down the line and Tom standing staring in utter disbelief at the gigantic torch flaming above him. I realised in a flash what had happened. The gas valve and water valve were adjacent, and somehow the wrong valve had been turned, which only needed Tom's little flare lamp to set it off like a blow-torch! Quickly grabbing two shovels I jumped off the engine and raced across the tracks to where Tom was ineffectively trying to throw handfuls of earth and ashes over the jet of flame as it was impossible to get close enough to turn it off. He grabbed a shovel from me as I raced up and we both started throwing earth over the jet as the entire Yard seemed to come alive with frantically shouting, gesticulating men, unnecessarily shouting 'Put that light out!' What the bloody hell did they think we were trying to do then, I thought madly as I shovelled away desperately, conscious of the menacing drone still overhead. Men came running up with buckets and more shovels, the Yard was lit up like a fairground.

'Well boy,' I thought to myself, 'if they don't hit us now they never will.' We eventually managed to get the man-made flame-thrower under control, somebody turned off the still gushing water valve and darkness thankfully returned to the Yard once more. We all stood still and listened for any change in the pitch of the drone, but on it went just as before, pulsating like a giant purring cat. The sighs of relief could be heard all round and none were louder or more heartfelt than my own! And after all our panic, I don't think those bombers even noticed us! Yes, work went on very much as usual on the line. . . .

There was one train, however, which no-one was keen to work on. It was the regular munition train from Milford, the one nicknamed 'The Bomber'. It consisted of mines, shells, torpedoes, bombs and anything else which could possibly be made to explode. About thirty-five wagons were sent out from the Mining Depot each night and they left Milford by rail every night at ten o'clock. Neyland men took them as far as Carmarthen if their destination was north, or on as far as Llanelly if they were on their way to the southern ports or airfields. Night air raids were still a distinct possibility, although the intense bombardment of the early part of the War had slackened off in our area. But we still did not like taking The Bomber out.

It was a hot, sticky summer's night when Fred Howells the driver and I were booked for 9.15 to take the usual coal empties from Milford to Duffryn Yard. We had a deplorable R.O.D. loco, she really was in an awful state. It was a work of art to get any steam up at all, leave alone pull fifty wagons, but we had to make the best of it as she was the only one available. Many engines were in poor shape with the shortage of men in the Sheds and we drivers and firemen had to do the best we could with them.

I spent all the time at Milford making sure we had a good head of steam up so as to give us a good start. The air around us was heavy and torpid, the intense heat from the fire-box sending the temperature on the footplate to well over 120 degrees.

'Put those damn sails up!' yelled a testy voice from the blacked-out platform. I nearly gave a mouthful of abuse back, but realised the reasonableness of the request when I glanced over to the sidings where the heavily-shrouded wagons of 'The Bomber' lay waiting for their loco to take them across the country.

'We'd better put 'em up, Fred,' I sighed, wiping my face with my waste. 'At least, until we get away from that little lot over there,' I nodded to the quiet wagons in the siding.

The boards came off and we steamed out of Milford, tackling the uphill climb to Johnston with our uncooperative loco. The old R.O.D. didn't do too badly and Fred and I gave ourselves a pat on the back for managing to coax the miserable thing along at a steady thirty. But, as we drew near Whitland, I could see the steam pressure was falling and the water in the boiler was definitely dropping. I tried to inject more water, but there just wasn't enough steam to let it through. Fred and I anxiously watched the gauge glass, it was falling fast and we had a hard climb just ahead of us between Whitland and St. Clear's. Our speed dropped, twenty, fifteen, ten, until we were heavily chugging at five miles an hour up the gradient.

'We've got to keep her going to the top, Bill,' muttered Fred, wiping, for the hundredth time since we set off, the sweat from his face and neck with his damp waste.

'Bloody article!' I snarled, giving the cab a vicious kick. 'The bloody tubes are either leaking like a collander or they're blocked nearly solid. How the deuce do they expect anybody to shift a thing in this state. Phew, it's hot!' I gasped. 'Open those bloody sails a bit Fred, I'm fed up with this little lot.' Mad I was.

There was little benefit from the sails being thrown back as we were moving so slowly. I tried the injectors again, as we both stared at the gauge glass, willing it to climb just a fraction, but to our despair it continued to drop.

'This is getting beyond a joke now, Bill,' announced Fred with the understatement of the year. 'There's scarcely a bubble in the nut, boy. Nurse her along, we must, to the top of the rise and we'll stop on the crest.'

It might seem strange that we did not intend to coast down the other side, but there was one definite reason why we could not do so. Once the engine went over the top of the rise and headed downhill, the little remaining water in the boiler would flow to the front leaving the back of the boiler, nearest the fire-box devoid of water. To prevent the boiler burning out in such circumstances, a lead safety plug was fixed at the back of the boiler near the fire-box. The lead would remain intact as long as it was covered with water, but if it became dry the intense heat melted the lead which released water straight into the fire-box completely dousing the fire. Naturally we didn't want that to happen or we would be well and truly crippled.

Well, nurse her and coax her we did, until we crawled to the top of the bank. Fred put the brake hard on and anchored us securely on the crest. And the exact crest it had to be too. A few yards still on the climb and we would never get enough steam up to start off the load, and a few yards on the down slope and we'd be out of business altogether!

'Let's get out of the furnace,' suggested Fred, taking deep lungfuls of fresh night air over the side of the cab. Although it was a humid night, at least it appeared cool in comparison to the temperature on the footplate of that R.O.D. I set both injectors on quietly before climbing down to join Fred who was sitting on the bank savouring more of the night air.

'They ought to be able to cope, Fred,' I remarked, referring to the two injectors which were gradually trickling water into the boiler now that the engine didn't have to cope with pulling fifty coal wagons uphill.

'We'll give her ten minutes, that should be enough, then we'll take her quietly down to St. Clear's,' suggested Fred, now lying spread-eagled on the grassy bank. I flung myself down beside him and breathed deeply.

'I've had the red light from the guard,' added Fred, staring up at the sky. 'He's off down the track with his detonators. Not much point though really, we won't be here that long, and the box knows where we are anyway.'

The black outline of the R.O.D. loomed over us, radiating heat into the night air, its gentle hissing mingling with the secret noises of the night countryside. A cricket rhythmically rubbed its legs near my left ear and a nightjar called in the distance. Lovely it was, lying there on the sparse grass, looking up at the stars.

Fred heaved himself up reluctantly to check the gauge glass. 'She's coming up slowly, Bill,' he acknowledged as he returned to the bank. 'There's a time we've taken on this run, mind. Still, another five minutes and we should be away. Fag Bill?' He offered his crumpled packet of cigarettes. I took one gratefully and inhaled deeply.

Silence descended once more around us as the minutes passed by, until, gradually into my subconscious, I became aware of a slight intrusion. Reality suddenly hit me as I shot bolt upright, my ears straining.

'Listen Fred,' I whispered urgently. There was no mistaking that distant sound—the heavy tugging of a loco straining every ounce of power to pull a heavy load uphill.

Fred stared at me in disbelief and horror. 'The bloody Bomber's chasing us!' he shouted, scrambling frantically down the bank to the track.

'How the hell did it get into this section before we left it?' I shouted, clambering after him onto the footplate.

'Buggered if I know, but she's here so let's get the hell out of it,' Fred replied, quickly checking the gauge glass as I shut off the two injectors.

'Perhaps it was a trick of the night air, Fred,' I suggested as he rapidly took the brake off, opened the regulator and started us on the move. 'Perhaps it isn't chasing us in this section at all—after all, things like that don't happen, man,' I argued.

'No point in taking any chances, are there boy?' replied Fred as we felt the old R.O.D. picking up speed beneath our feet, as we gathered momentum down the bank.

'How far do you think she's away then?' I asked, throwing shovelfuls of coal into the glaring fire-box.

'Four or five miles, if she is in this section—at least she's got that long pull ahead of her, but if she is there she'll gain on us on the flat boy. A good 53 she's got,' finished Fred uneasily.

'Well, there's one sure thing, we daren't stop at St. Clear's to check, in case she rams us in the rear—blown to smithereens we'll all be, and. . . .'

'Get a red lamp Bill,' interrupted Fred as we swayed and rattled along at our top speed of thirty-five miles an hour. 'I'll blow the whistle as we pass the signal-box, and you swing the lamp over the side of the cab. They'll know something's up when we go through like a scalded cat, and if The Bomber is behind us it'll give them a chance to signal her down.'

The signals were off as we approached St. Clear's, the whistle blowing full blast and me hanging over the side of the cab waving my red lamp back and forth, for all I was worth. I caught a quick glimpse of a white, startled face at the window of the signal-box and then it was gone behind us as we hurtled through the station at our breakneck speed of thirty-five miles an hour! The way that old R.O.D. was working you'd think we were doing eighty!

'It's registered, Fred,' I gasped as I pulled myself back into the cab. 'If The Bomber's there they'll stop her for sure, and if she isn't they'll be wondering what the hell it was all about!' I laughed with relief.

With the erratic turns of wartime workings, we found ourselves on a different shift the remainder of the week, and unable to check with the signal-man. And we never did get round to it. To this day I don't know whether that Bomber was actually chasing us that hot night, but I still take a deep breath at the thought of it!

16

During the latter years of the War, Neyland Yard became much less busy—especially during the night shifts. In fact with the Fish trains drastically curtailed because of the lack of trawlers bringing in the fish to Milford Haven and the general cutting back of trains, Neyland was almost imperceptibly becoming just a little 'unused'.

'There's not a bit of good keeping this station open all night any longer. Ridiculous it is.' Affie Jenkins the foreman puffed deeply on his pipe as he made his dramatic announcement. Close Neyland Station? The idea seemed unbelievable.

'From midnight to five in the morning, we might all just as well be home in our beds,' he went on. 'There's Herb Evans sitting in his box doing nothing at all—ridiculous it is,' he repeated.

And so it came about that Neyland Station and Yard closed at midnight and the signal-box shut down—with the proviso 'that there was no train in the vicinity'. It didn't seem right at all and there was a lot of head shaking going on. The whole status of the place seemed to be affected if we didn't remain open the full twenty-four hours. After all, we were a G.W.R. terminus.

During the first week of the new regime, however, Tommy Francis and I were called out one evening for a special. Light engine to Milford, take troops and armaments to Carmarthen and work light engine back. We booked on at seven o'clock, took the staff, steamed to

Johnston and onto Milford where we coupled up to our waiting coaches. It was a good run and we handed the train over to the relief crew at Carmarthen on time. We took it steady coming back light and arrived at Johnston at five minutes before midnight. We could have made it quite a bit earlier, but that did not fit in with our plans! Bill Morgan the signal-man telephoned Neyland for the staff to let us through, but no reply could he get. It was just midnight and with 'no train in the vicinity' Neyland signal-box had closed down! Everything was going according to plan. It was impossible to travel those short few miles of single track without the staff and anyway there would be no-one to operate the points in the Yard if we did get there. Tommy and I settled ourselves down smugly for a long wait. We kept the signal-man company most of the night, he had a few trains to attend to coming up from Milford, but most of the time we drunk tea, chatted and smoked. Five o'clock sharp he gave Neyland box a ring, we had the staff and off we set.

There's a lovely bit of overtime we had! Too much, it seemed, to risk its happening again and so Neyland Station returned to its former glory and henceforth kept open every night. Our little plan had succeeded!

* * *

Promotion had been slow in Neyland during the thirties, and now we 'Passed Firemen'—Freddie Griffiths, Billie Harrison, Dan James, Billie James, Jackie Benjamin, Ivor Lewis and myself, for example—were now all about the age of forty. Although we often did have the opportunity to drive, the majority of our turns were still as firemen. Both the Company and the men realised that for a man of forty to be expected to fire an engine on a long run was unreasonable. Young men's work that was. Consequently we each, in turn, according to seniority, were put up for promotion to drivers. It meant another trip to Swindon where we were examined on all the procedures for running engines, breakdowns, signals—everything in the Rule Book—and also to be given another medical.

We were all successful and returned to Neyland as 'Paper Drivers'. This meant that although there was no vacancy for a driver, we could remain there on driver's pay until a vacancy occurred or until we were posted elsewhere. Some of the men applied straightaway for posts at other stations, but most of us simply wanted to stay where we were.

Neyland Yard was part of us and we were part of the Yard. We had grown up with its temperamental turn-table, its sulphurous old wooden Shed, its rickety cabins and its own private single track which meandered unhurriedly to Johnston. We knew every inch of line as far as Carmarthen with our eyes closed, we knew every little bank where a bit of sand at just the right spot would keep even a 29 from slipping— and that was saying something—and we knew every idiosyncrasy of every foreman and chargeman we'd ever had!

We left the long runs to the younger firemen now, who crewed with the older drivers like Georgie Lewis, Albert Blackmore, Bill Llewellyn and others, and we 'Paper Drivers' took over the First Link completely while we waited for vacancies.

Well, man, it was like a club! There were five turns in the First Link, which we worked between us—early and late Haverfordwest Pilot, early and late Yard and the Carmarthen Goods. We were all passed drivers so we took it in turns to fire and drive. It was a good life with good company to work with and drivers' pay, but it was too good to last of course.

'You must apply for a driver vacancy up the line, Bill—it's regulations,' Parnell the foreman informed me. 'You can't go on for ever in Neyland Yard, waiting for a post here—there'll never be enough for you lot and there'll be ructions if you don't get an application in straight away. Mind now!' he warned.

I knew it had to come. It had been a good year, the War was coming to an end, everyone's spirits were high. Where to apply? That was the big decision. Swindon? Gloucester? Definitely not anywhere in the Valleys. Then an idea slowly started to form in my mind. . . . Weston-super-Mare—that was the place. I immediately put an application for transfer as driver to Weston-super-Mare.

'You'll not stand a chance there, man,' remarked Parnell as I handed him my form. 'Very popular place, Weston, sure to be a waiting list as long as my arm. It'll take ages to get to the top of that list.'

'You don't say now,' I replied with open-eyed amazement. 'Well, I never thought of that now! Well, that's my choice and I've put an application in as you requested. Not my fault is it, if I have to wait a while, now is it?'

Parnell looked at me sideways. 'You crafty bugger, you don't want to get there at all, do you?'

'Prove it!' I replied with a grin as I walked out of his office and strolled over to the cabin for a cup of tea.

I was fortieth on the list of applicants for Weston-super-Mare, said head office. Would I like to re-apply elsewhere? No thank you very much, I'll put up with the wait! I knew it was only a delaying tactic, before they insisted that I re-apply, but I thought it might work for a year or two and who knows what might turn up in that time?

Although the First Link turns were very congenial, we couldn't make much money as there was seldom the chance of making any overtime. We had to rely on replacing the actual Neyland drivers on their long runs in order to make a little extra money. There were three main reasons which provided us with opportunities for driving the Expresses and Mails—a driver off sick, on holiday—or, the most common one, the driver unable to take his shift because of late working which would leave him less than twelve hours off between turns. This was the one which gave us our golden opportunities for driving the Manors, Granges, Halls and Castles with the long distance Express Passengers, Mails and Fast Goods. Mind, it made us a bit impatient and dissatisfied with our First link when we had to return to its routine. Perhaps that was a good thing as our appetite for main-line driving was whetted to such an extent that we would want to apply for transfers—even at the expense of leaving Neyland.

The 5.20 Llandeilo Goods offered the best chance of a crew not returning in time to take their twelve-hour rest period. They booked on at five in the afternoon and often were unable to make the working back by five the next morning. Consequently we Paper Drivers were called in to take over, usually with an experienced Cleaner acting as fireman, while the original crew took on the Yard Piloting for the day—making, of course, no overtime. They didn't like it one bit, I can tell you.

After a few weeks, Freddie Griffiths and I suddenly realised that there was not nearly as many requests for relief crews as there had been. We were making no extra money and as there was no apparent reason for this, I decided to do a little surreptitious checking on my own.

I took a wander over to Ted Lloyd at the signal-box to pass the time of day. 'What time did the Llandeilo Goods come in this morning, then?' I queried.

'Five-twenty today, Bill,' came the reply. Right then, I thought, let's see if we get that turn this afternoon, and if we don't . . . .

We didn't.

So that's what was happening, the crafty devils—still I'd do the same myself no doubt. It obviously paid the men better to lose half an hour or so of overtime and say they had finished at five, rather than miss their shift for that afternoon. This was possible because no-one ever actually signed off—or on, for that matter—at Neyland Shed. It was just a case of putting your booking slip into the box—it was up to you what time you actually wrote on it!

I checked for a few more mornings with Ted Lloyd at the box and discovered that sometimes the train was still at Milford at five o'clock! Other occasions they would arrive at Neyland five or ten minutes over time, but not one call was there for us Paper Drivers to take relief. Something had to be done, but we didn't want any trouble—just our fair share.

I was booked for Late Yard and had made a few previous arrangements on the side with the Chargeman. The scene was set for a confrontation. Taking one of the experienced cleaners with me I took my place on the footplate of the Manor waiting to take out the Llandeilo Goods. I had nipped along to the signal-box from home that morning to check what time the shift had arrived in, and everything was arranged.

'You'll have an easy time today,' I greeted the main crew as they walked up to the Manor ready to climb aboard. They looked up at me in surprise with puzzled expressions on their faces. 'Not much doing in the Yard this evening,' I went on, 'give you a nice rest, it will.'

'What the hell are you talking about? We booked off before five this morning. You've had it for today, mate.'

'Ted Lloyd signalled you in at 5.35, mate,' I replied with equal vigour, emphasising the 'mate'. 'Did she come in by her bloody self then?'

Impasse.

They looked at each other. 'Well, we had a good run for our money, boy,' said the driver to his fireman philosophically. 'Come on, over to the Shed,' he sighed in complete capitulation.

Victory was sweet—and so was the overtime!

* * *

I had just come in with the Sunday morning parcels. I'd enjoyed driving down from Carmarthen, the work had been good. I put my booking slip through the slot and was just about to make my way home when Tommy Mount came out of the Chargeman's Office with a piece of paper in his hand.

'You've pushed 'em too far, Bill,' he said, holding out the official-looking paper before him. 'You've got your marching orders now and no mistake.' I took the proffered slip and read my orders—Transferred to Gloucester as from Monday. Blow me, that was tomorrow, I thought with a sinking heart. They must have got fed up with my continued application for Weston after all, I thought ruefully. Ah well, Gloucester it would have to be unless I was prepared to return as fireman and take a drop in salary. But, much as I loved Neyland I could not afford to do that.

It wasn't too big a shock for Win, as we had both been expecting something like this to happen for some time. My delaying tactics had run out at last. At least it wasn't the Valleys. Gloucester wasn't too bad a place after all—quite pleasant really—plenty of plums! And so, off I set the following morning, my hurriedly packed suitcase on the rack, as the eight o'clock Passengers steamed out of Neyland Station. I took long looks at the Yard, the Shed, the Hydraulic, the Iron Bridge, the Turn-table as we gathered speed on our single-tracked way to Johnston. I hadn't realised when I had brought the Parcels in the previous morning, that it would be the last time I would book off at Neyland Shed. There certainly had been no time for sentimental farewells! It was March 1945.

On my arrival at Gloucester I reported to the supervisor and was given one of the young cleaners to conduct me around the city looking for lodgings. I hadn't been in Gloucester since my pre-war fish runs as a fireman with salesman tendencies, but it hadn't changed much. The War had left it pretty well untouched and I was delighted to discover that my memories of Gloucester as a clean airy city were correct. Cities did not have to be smoky, dirty, overcrowded and depressing after all.

But by hedges, it was different from Neyland. Every face was that of a stranger. I even had a new name to get used to, as right from the first day I had reported for duty at Gloucester Shed, I had been rechristened 'Taff'.

I spent the first few weeks learning the road of the Yard, followed by a term of Pilot Driving round the Yard. By the time Win and Bette came up to Gloucester and we had bought a house, I was learning the road again, this time moving up to number Four Link which included Swindon, Birmingham, Worcester, Hereford and Cardiff. It took three months before I was booked to drive along these lines and then after another term I moved up to number Three Link and started learning the road to Moreton Cutting, Worcester via Honeybourne, Bristol and Stratford, remaining in this link for a number of years before moving up to the Second Link which was the Express Passengers to Derby. I appreciated that. Great it was, driving on those Express Passengers.

There had seemed no heart in Gloucester Shed when I had first moved there. Everything was on such a vast scale, with so many men it was difficult to imagine a common bond. But I soon realised that the Top Link drivers were as venerated and the cleaners were as cheeky and as full of practical jokes as any I had met! The hierarchy remained the same, with each level striving for the one above. We had the sober-sides and the leg-pullers, the reliable steadies and the flippants, the clever and the awkward, all contributing towards the heart of The Western in their own way. But behind them all was the backing of the hard core of stalwarts whose whole life had been dedicated towards the steam locomotive. The casuals may come and go but they went on for ever.

* * *

Doug was my fireman for most of the time I spent in the Relief Link at Gloucester, and a reliable, efficient fireman he was at that—once he'd got used to handling the pricker, that is!

It was in the early days of my crewing with Doug that we were taking loaded iron-ore wagons to Severn Tunnel with a 53.

'She's a bit sluggish, Bill,' he remarked—Doug was one of the few who didn't refer to me as Taff. I looked in the fire-box, the heat forcing my eyes to slits. There was a bluish look about the fire instead of a healthy pale orange.

'You've got a fair bit of clinker in there, Doug, better try and loosen it a bit,' I suggested. Doug was already pulling the seven-foot long pricker out of the rack and proceeded to ram it into the fire-box, loosening the choking clinker with his fierce jabs. With a bit of help from the blower we were soon rewarded with a few spots of white-hot fire.

'That's it, Bill,' he remarked with some satisfaction as he withdrew the white-hot pricker.

'Mind that bloody pricker!' I yelled as Doug whipped it round within a hair's breadth of my legs in order to replace it in the rack. Admittedly it is an unwieldy instrument to handle, especially in the limited space on a footplate, but never before had I practically had my legs scythed off by its fiercely-glowing end! The fact that my overalls weren't already in flames was solely due to the alacrity with which I had jumped back.

'Aw, sorry about that, Bill,' he apologised profusely.

'Take the bloody thing round the other way, next time man,' I shouted in exasperation. 'Over the side of the cab or you'll burn my bloody legs off. The other way now . . . don't forget. . . .' Peace descended once more on the footplate and we continued on our way to Severn Tunnel. It was a rubbishy lot of coal we were stuck with, however, and no mistake, and we hadn't travelled far before Doug was forced to use the pricker again.

Damn me, he scythed that wicked looking, white-hot iron round my legs again.

'Now, look here, Doug,' I seethed, controlling my temper with difficulty. 'Once more and I'll. . . .' Words failed me. 'Take the blasted thing the other way, man,' I repeated amidst his protestations that he would not do it again and that he would remember the next time.

Peace descended once more. We travelled a few more miles. The third time Doug withdrew the pricker from the fire-box, he remembered what I had told him. So pleased he was, with himself, as he swung the glowing pricker away from me, that he turned his head towards me, gave me a wink and said, 'There you are, Bill, told you I'd remember,' and at the same time he proceeded to use the pricker as a torch to set fire to my overcoat which was hanging from his side of the cab!

'My coat!' I yelled in dismay, as Doug continued to stare at me in bewilderment, while holding the blazing pricker at my coat behind him. Being my working coat it was generously dabbed with oil and with the advantage of the strong draught it was enveloped in flames in a matter of seconds, disappearing over the side of the cab as I frantically tried to rescue it, and the last I saw of it was a flaming bundle alongside the track! But at least I hadn't had my legs burnt off, so I suppose I had to be grateful for small mercies!

The shock of losing my coat was nothing, however, to the one my guard, Harry Wilden, sustained late the following Saturday night as we were waiting in the Relief Cabin on Gloucester Station. There was nothing much doing and we were all a bit drowsy when in burst Harry, excited as hell and waving his football coupon in the air.

'I've done it! I've done it!' he shouted jubilantly. 'I've got eight draws up!'

We all stared unbelievingly at him as he continued to display his excitement and delight. There's envious we all were, mind, as we viewed the winning line on the coupon as it was reverently passed from hand to hand. I'd never seen an actual winning line before, in all the years I had been doing The Pools, and I was really impressed.

There was no doubt about it—the eight draws matched the last line of his entry. Congratulations and speculations on the amount Harry would win were the talk of the cabin for hours.

It wasn't until I saw a forlorn Harry the following Monday that I heard the sad news. His son, trying to be helpful, had taken down the draws as they were announced on the wireless early on Saturday and had left the coupon on the sideboard for his Dad. Harry had come in later, when his son had gone to bed, and had proceeded to mark the results from the newspaper, alongside his son's line!

Poor Harry! He had a lot of sympathy in Gloucester Shed that week.

* * *

A few months later we were steaming up the long bank towards Sapperton with a full load of goods wagons behind us. The Manor was doing well, but she needed a lot of sand to stop her slipping. Fifteen to twenty miles an hour was all we were making and Doug was firing his heart out.

I spotted them in the distance, a beautiful pair of swans, gracefully flying towards the line, necks outstretched, wings beating powerfully. There was no doubt about it, we were on a collision course, they seemed to have an unswerving directness of flight path which nothing would alter. Nearer they came, blindly ignoring the noise and size of the loco and my warning whistle. I craned my neck to watch them disappear before the boiler. We must have missed them by inches, I thought as I took a quick look out of the other side of the cab. There was only one.

'We've hit her, Doug,' I shouted, looking back along both sides of the track to see if there was any sign of the huge bird, but not a trace was there, not even a feather.

'Keep her going steady, Doug,' I commanded, 'I'm going to look for her. Poor bloody thing,' I called as I climbed out of the cab and made my way carefully along the side of the boiler, holding on grimly to the handrail and trying to keep smuts and cinders from going in my eyes. I knew we were only making about twenty miles an hour, but it seemed a lot more than that once I had climbed out of the cab! If we had stopped it would have been a devil of a job to get going again on that bank and with the weight behind us, so investigation in motion was the only solution. I neared the front of the boiler and rounded the smoke-box.

There she was, white feathers fluttering in the head-on breeze, her wings broken at an angle which made me wince. But she was still alive. I held on to the smoke-box handle with one hand and tried to pick her up off the walk with the other. The ground came rushing towards me as the Manor steamed along, swaying and jolting, sending me off balance every time I bent down. I reached out once more, she was surprisingly heavy and her feathers so silky smooth, I could get no firm grip.

I couldn't just kick her off to die, so bracing my feet firmly, I let go of the smoke-box rail, balanced myself with the swaying loco and slowly bent down to pick up the poor thing with both hands. I pulled myself upright, clutching the frantic bird, caught hold of her neck, gave her head a mighty bang against the smoke-box and she was dead. Out of her misery, thank God, I thought. I was just about to throw her off when the thought suddenly occurred to me—can you eat a swan? I had never heard of anyone in Neyland ever attempting to do so, but I'm sure I'd read somewhere that Royalty did!

Since working up in Gloucester I had to admit that I missed the opportunities of potting something for dinner from the footplate with my Winchester, and I hadn't stopped an engine to pick mushrooms since I had left Neyland, so this seemed a heaven sent opportunity to take something home for dinner. Main line workings did have its disadvantages, as even I didn't imagine I could conceal a rifle aboard at Gloucester! So, tucking the bulky frame of the unfortunate swan under my arm I made my way back alongside the boiler to where an amazed Doug was waiting for me.

It took me nearly three hours to feather that damn bird and my fingers were nearly cut to shreds by the time I had finished.

'What shall I stuff it with?' Win asked in great perplexity, not having roasted a swan before. But I forget my answer! It had a huge frame which absolutely refused to fit into our oven, no matter which way we tried it, so eventually we ended up by cutting it up into pieces and roasting it with sage and onion. It smelt wonderful whilst cooking, but, somehow, when it was placed on the table, nobody wanted to be the first to try it! We had all heard so many stories about swans since I had brought it home. Nobody, it seemed, ate swans, except gypsies, and they even ate hedgehogs! We all sat round the table, we nibbled cautiously at it. Various verdicts were proclaimed—a slight fishy taste? A trifle on the tough side? Definitely unusual flavour. We tried to convince ourselves that it was a rare delicacy, but without a great deal of success, and reluctantly, nearly all of the carcass and meat ended up in the dustbin.

Poor swan, what an ignominious end.

17

It was round about this time, a few years after the War that the Great Western introduced its oil-fired steam engines, and Doug and I found ourselves on an oil-converted 28 class heavy freight loco, on the run from Gloucester to Severn Tunnel. These converted locos were mostly used on the South Wales runs, pulling coal and heavy goods trains. It took a bit of getting used to, but at least I had no fear of a white-hot pricker being waved around my legs! The tender had been converted to carrying about two thousand gallons of oil which was fed through a nozzle into the fire-box where it fed blazing jets. The only difficulty was judging exactly how much oil to allow to the burners. Too much and it would flow unburnt into the old ash-pan below, too little and you would lose steam. Coasting along the flat, even with a heavy load took only a small steady flow of oil, but as soon as an incline was encountered there was a sharp increase in the amount of oil needed. On the other hand idling in a siding was a bit tricky as very little oil was needed and the margin between the small amount of oil burnt and the burners going out altogether was critical.

It was an early morning run we were on, 3 a.m. and a hang-up at Beachley, that was all we needed—coupled with the one great drawback with oil-fired locos—we couldn't make a cup of tea!

'I'll take a stroll up to the cabin and try to get us some, Doug,' I offered. 'Try and keep her ticking over nicely and if she gets too hot let off a bit of steam,' I added.

I managed to get a can of tea from the cabin and was on my way back down to the sidings when I could hardly believe my eyes—there was my loco on fire! I broke into a run, suddenly seeing the leaping form of Doug coming flying down off the footplate. Flames were licking from beneath, curling round the wheels and boiler and shooting into the air and round the cab.

'Did you turn off the oil?' I yelled at him as he ran towards me.

'Yeah, yeah,' he answered, nodding his head violently. 'It just went up round me,' he gasped.

'Must have been oil in the ash-pan,' I suggested. 'We'll just have to let it burn itself out.' By this time a crowd had collected in the fiery glare and we all stood and watched until it did actually burn itself out. But we were crippled. The old 28 would not move another inch under her own steam that trip. We were ignominiously towed in to Severn Tunnel where we handed her over to the Shed and made out our report. But that was the only incident we experienced with those oil-fired locos. Many other trips we made with them with great success—but you did have to watch that feed. Efficient they were, but tricky.

We all thought that the Great Western Railway was going to make a big breakthrough with these locos, but it all came to nothing. And the hours of the Great Western itself were numbered. British Rail was knocking at the door, and the diesels were soon to be pushing Steam into the history books. We didn't realise just how soon.

*　*　*

I made thousands of routine trips from Gloucester during the next few years and drove tens of thousands of miles. Some on Goods and some on Express passengers, but regardless of what was behind me, watchfulness was my byword, as with all drivers on the rail. It had been instilled into us since we were cleaners, and every rule in the Rule Book made for safety on the line.

One trip which brought all the regulations regarding protection of trains sharply into focus took place one Sunday afternoon when I was taking coal empties from Gloucester to Severn Tunnel with a 28 class loco. We were technically a non-stopper unless signalled down for expresses to pass through. We approached Lydney Station at about

forty miles an hour, as we were signalled straight through. We crossed
a set of points just before we reached the platform and followed the
left-hand curve of the station. Suddenly I felt a slight tug, I looked
quickly back from my cab side, but, of course, could see nothing of the
wagons behind me as they curved away in the opposite direction

'Check our rear, Doug,' I asked, a little puzzled by the strange tug
I had felt. He leant out of his side of the cab which afforded a good
view of the entire train on the wide bend.

'We're broke away, Bill,' he shouted in alarm. 'There's no van.' I
rushed over to look out of his side and sure enough we had only about
forty wagons still on, the remainder and the guard's van nowhere in
sight. The natural reaction was to come to a grinding halt, but this could
have proved very dangerous if the breakaways had been chasing us.

'Keep a look-out, Doug, and let me know when you spot them,' I
ordered as I returned to the driver's side of the cab, easing off the
regulator as I did so, waiting for the call from Doug that he had
sighted our runaways. I was slowing her down gradually but we had
covered a good quarter of a mile before Doug eventually shouted in
exasperation, 'There's no sign of them, Bill.' We were obviously not
being chased so I applied the vacuum brake and we came to a halt about
half a mile down line. We listened, but nothing could we hear, the wide
curve of the track hid all sight of Lydney Station from us and what had
happened to our breakaways was a complete mystery.

'There's something queer going on here,' I pondered. 'Those breakaways could never have come to a halt on their own in that short space,
even with the help of the guard's brake. They must have jumped the
rails, boy, that's the only explanation.' Quickly I opened the box at the
side of the tender and brought out the sealed pack of detonators and a
red flag.

'Here, Doug, fast as you can, boy, run ahead on the Up Line and
protect.' He raced off with the flag and detonators, needing no second
bidding. We were safe enough where we were, but a train coming into
Lydney on the opposite track might find themselves running into a
derailment fouling their line. There was no way I could find out what
had happened at Lydney Station, but precautions were essential
whether the circumstances were known or not. I stayed on the footplate,
straining my ears for any clue about what had happened behind us, but
the slow hiss of my own loco was all I could hear.

I watched Doug place his detonators, one at a ¼ mile, one at ½ mile and three at ¾ mile. He came trotting back, gasping for breath by the time he reached the loco. With the detonators set we had only now to mark the place where any approaching train could, if possible, come to a halt. It wasn't as essential as the detonators, but it helped. I took the red flag from Doug's hand, crossed over to the Up Line and dug the warning flag into the ballast at the side of the track.

'Off you go, then, Doug,' I announced when I returned to the loco. 'Back to Lydney Station and find out what's going on.' He heaved himself up off the step, where he had been recovering his breath, inhaled deeply and set off at a jog-trot, leaving me to wonder what had really happened when I had sensed that slight tug behind me. We had just come over the road level-crossing on leaving the station, I recapitulated in my mind, which would mean that the rear portion of the train would have just been entering the station.

'The points,' I said aloud, there was nothing else I could think of which would cause us to break. There was no great weight in the wagons, which were all empties, so that ruled out the couplings giving way under undue strain. This would have been most unlikely anyway —almost unheard of, as a matter of fact. I awaited Doug's return with impatience.

He eventually reappeared round the wide curve of the bend, half running, half walking.

'They're right on the bloody platform!' he shouted between gasps, still a good fifty yards away from me. I could hardly believe my ears—wagons actually on the platform? It seemed incredible. I ran down the track to meet him, waited a few minutes to hear a few breathless details, then set off to see for myself what had happened, leaving instructions for Doug not to move the loco. He waved a weak hand in acknowledgement of the last order, as if to banish the thought from my head that he would voluntarily move another inch for the next few hours! Poor chap, whacked he was.

He had not exaggerated. The wagons were well and truly on the platform, five or six of them lay in incongruous mêlée amongst the wrecked buildings, equipment and seats. The next few were derailed, but the remaining wagons, including the guard's van, were miraculously still on the track.

It was the fault of the points, as I thought. A spread rail had caused one of the wagons to jump the rail causing a breakaway, and the remainder followed it. Being so close to the platform, the leading wagon had run straight up the slope of the platform's end, followed by the next five or so before the guard's hand-brake could have any effect of reducing the speed. The Up Line was not blocked, and no-one had been injured, but all signals were on Danger or Proceed on Caution as a breakdown van had to be sent for from Gloucester. The Down Line was completely closed for the day and single working was in force from Lydney to Beachley.

It was a quiet Sunday afternoon, which obviously contributed to the fact that no-one was injured, as very few railway personnel had been on duty at Lydney Station, and the prompt action of the guard in applying his brake had prevented further destruction from concertina action.

After obtaining Relief from Lydney men, Doug and I returned to Gloucester on the cushions of the next Up Passengers. It certainly had not been one of our routine trips, but fortunately incidents such as this were extremely rare.

* * *

Promotion in Gloucester was at an entirely different rate from that of Neyland and not many years after I had been in the Second Link, I was all set for the London Express Passengers in the Top Link.

Jimmy Clarke, another exile from Neyland was already one of the top men in Gloucester, and had been driving the Paddington Passenger Expresses regularly. He was a few years older than I, and I was looking forward to joining him in the Top Link.

But my career took a different route and I became Relief Supervisor instead. Had I taken further promotion and moved to Swindon, I would have continued as Full Supervisor until I retired. But the thought of uprooting myself and my family once again was too much to ask, and I declined the promotion and returned to the footplate. But by this time the diesels were coming in thick and fast, and small stations were falling equally thick and fast under Beeching's axe.

The times were changing. Golden Handshakes were pensioning off the old stalwarts who had helped to build the almost legendary history of steam rail transport, and I knew it would not be long before that Golden Hand reached out to shake my own.

Those 1960's, they were an era of the last this, the final that. Where-ever I drove on the line there were the enthusiasts with their ever-ready cameras and tape recorders, waiting to freeze that moment in time when the last steam loco left a certain Shed, or when the last train pulled out from a proud little station before it was finally closed. They froze the moment when a well-worn piece of permanent way was used for the last time before the weeds finally took over, they taped the sound of steam before the bullet-nosed, powerful diesels honked their cheer-less efficient way through the countryside. They photographed the last ticket to be sold before a station shut its booking office for the last time. The Age of Steam was drawing to a close, and so was my service to the Railway.

Neyland drivers who had started as cleaners with me back in 1916 had almost all been offered early retirement and the Golden Handshake.

'It's all over, Morgy,' they'd say, as we sat on the pontoon with our fishing tackle drifting in the strong current. 'The yard's at a standstill, boy. Look at it now, how on earth can they keep it going?'

The twenty years I had lived away from Neyland still seemed but an interlude. Win, Bette, her husband Noel and I had been constant visitors throughout the two decades, spending uncountable week-ends and holidays with Win's sister Margaret in Frederick Street. I kept a finger on the pulse of Neyland Yard and now it was weakening fast. The last steam train to have pulled out from Neyland had been in October 1963 when Driver George Morgan had taken out the 6.20 Evening Mails, along past the Shed, where, over half a century before, Bill Llewellyn had insisted berthing his newly-cleaned Sir Lancelot 3302, because she was getting wet out in the rain, and on under the Iron Bridge, its old planks breathing in for the last time the sulphurous steam and smoke as George Morgan drove Loco 6994 on its way to Johnston.

The diesels had arrived. And so it was, that less than a year later, the last passenger train to leave Neyland before complete closure from Beeching's axe had to be a damned diesel. But at least the spirit of the old G.W.R. rode with it, Harry James (You'll never have a dirty hand, Willy boy, as long as you've got some waste), his son Hilliard drove her out and Tommy Harrison (hard work never kilt nobody, boy, only medd'em goa deaf); his son Jack was in the role of guard. Now you can't do better than that, fair play.

Their fathers would never have believed it could have happened. But happen it did on that sad Sunday of June 1964.

Neyland Station was closed.

And I retired.

It was fitting.

Postscript - 1972

Nearly sixty years have passed since I jauntily walked this Platform One with 'O.C.S.' ready on my lips. The platform is all that remains of the Great Western Railway Terminus of Neyland and now it stands bordering a rail-less expanse of flattened, denuded ground. The Loco Shed has gone and a powerful crane slowly swings massive slabs of reinforced concrete through the air, while cement silos, miles of reinforcing steel and churning concrete mixers heavily litter the Yard. Strange intruders they seem to me, as over them all, the old Iron Bridge still stands, its approach overgrown and disused, its planks slowly rotting as it leads—nowhere.

The water lies still. A water for pleasure now instead of work. Small craft from the Neyland Yachting Club try to catch a small breath of wind to send them cutting across the harbour and a few expert water-skiers trace their foam path behind speeding tows. The estuary is empty of Irish steamers, Trinity boats, fishing trawlers, cattle boats and Sunderlands. Only I see them still.

A giant box-girder bridge struggles, as yet unsuccessfully, to span the Cleddau over to Pembroke Dock, meanwhile the ferry-boat see-saws back and forth with its summer cargo of tourists exploring the Pembrokeshire National Park coastline, and I smile, inwardly, realising that I too am one of the visiting tourists. None of the holiday-clothed passers-by realise that I have an affinity with this concrete-strewn waste land. I hear echoes of wedding detonators, the gentle hiss of an idling loco, the menacing drone of enemy aircraft with the station on red alert, the banging doors of an empty mail train, the care-free whistling of young call-boys. Sounds come flooding back.

It's all gone, I thought. There's nothing left of the spirit of our old G.W.R. terminus. And yet ... I turned and walked swiftly across towards the Prom. I stopped and stared. They were still there.

But they couldn't be the G.W.R. Gas House doors, could they? Not even if the paint had been just a little bit wet? Unknowingly saved for posterity? Could they?

I hoped so. By hedges, I hoped so!